School Connections

School Connections

U.S. MEXICAN YOUTH, PEERS,

AND

SCHOOL ACHIEVEMENT

EDITED BY

Margaret A. Gibson

Patricia Gándara

Jill Peterson Koyama

foreword by   JEANNIE OAKES

TEACHERS COLLEGE PRESS

Teachers College
Columbia University
New York and London

Published by Teachers College Press, 1234 Amsterdam Avenue, New York, NY 10027

Library of Congress Cataloging-in-Publication Data

School connections : U.S. Mexican youth, peers, and school achievement / edited by
  Margaret A. Gibson, Patricia Gándara, Jill Peterson Koyama ; foreword by Jeannie Oakes.
     p. cm.
  Includes bibliographical references and index.
   ISBN 0-8077-4438-7 (alk. paper) — ISBN 0-8077-4437-9 (pbk. : alk. paper)
      1. Mexican-American youth—Education (Secondary)—Social aspects—United
States—Case studies. 2. Children of immigrants—Education (Secondary)—Social
aspects—United States—Case studies. 3. Peer pressure in adolescence—United States—
Case studies. 4. Underachievers—United States—Attitudes—Case studies.   I. Gibson,
Margaret A. II. Gándara, Patricia C. III. Koyama, Jill Peterson.

  LC2683.4.S35 2004
  373.1829'6872'073—dc22

                                                                                  2003067206

  ISBN 0-8077-4437-9 (paper)
  ISBN 0-8077-4438-7 (cloth)

Printed on acid-free paper

Manufactured in the United States of America

11   10   09   08   07   06   05   04   8   7   6   5   4   3   2   1

Contents

Foreword

Families across the nation's diverse communities understand that high quality schooling and college access are crucial to children's life chances and their contributions to our democracy. They know that living-wage jobs are scarce for high school dropouts, and that even high school graduates scramble to find meaningful work. They hear the talk of "college preparation for all" in the growing movement for high school reform.

At the same time, Latino students' prospects for high achievement, high school graduation, and college admission remain dim. Despite Latinos emergence as the nation's largest minority (and new majority of school children, in some states), significant disparities remain between Latino students and their non-Latino peers. Latinos are more likely to drop out of high school. Those who do graduate are less likely to be prepared for college. They are the least likely of all ethnic/racial groups to take the SAT I and ACT exams, and they are consistently underrepresented in four-year colleges and universities. The growing popularity of "race-neutral" admissions policies further threatens their chances at highly competitive four-year campuses.

These discouraging indicators should not surprise us. As the authors in this volume make clear, young people of Mexican descent are more likely than other students to have low aspirations; be vulnerable to gang influence; lack knowledge about college as an option; and feel as though they "do not belong" at school. They are also most likely to be taught by school staff who lack knowledge of their cultural or linguistic backgrounds. Rare is the school reform that addresses head-on these discouraging conditions. Who would expect students feeling as such to do well?

In California, a group of university faculty have come together to challenge these patterns. UC ACCORD, the University of California's All Campus Consortium on Research for Diversity, provides research as a catalyst for high-quality, equitable, and diverse schooling and college going. Put simply, UC ACCORD conducts research to make a difference in students' education trajectories. ACCORD researchers study the conditions that support high achievement and college participation for young people whose chances are now slim. We focus on creating safe school environments, and promoting college-going school cultures that include rigorous, academic curriculum, high-quality teaching, and plenty of additional academic and social support for students. We investigate the salience of college-going identities that embrace students' cultural and linguistic backgrounds, as well as their academic aspirations. We explore how families and communities develop relationships with schools and in the process make all of these conditions "normal" in schools serving low-income students of color.

It was with these research goals in mind that UC ACCORD supported Margaret Gibson, Patricia Gándara, and Jill Peterson Koyama in their bringing together a talented group of researchers around their shared interest in the effects that peers have on the hopes and disappointments of Mexican-origin young people. Gibson and her colleagues' studies, impressive in their own right, contribute to a growing and remarkably coherent body of work that addresses sorely neglected educational and social concerns. ACCORD is proud to have played a small part in bringing this book to fruition.

The studies in this volume yield important new evidence about the complex patterns and interrelationships of peers, school life, and students' school performance. With empirical richness, Gibson and her colleagues expand our understanding. We learn that peer relations and influence take many forms; that even distant peers shape students' attitudes and actions; that peers affect school performance, both positively and negatively; and, perhaps most important, that a school is neither helpless nor blameless in structuring peer relationships. Cumulatively, this work teaches us how peers become either resources or liabilities to each other and how schools can shape peer relations to either promote or discourage school success among Mexican-origin youth.

These studies push us to understand more theoretically about Mexican-origin youth who often fail to develop close connections in school except with other young people who also feel disconnected from the mainstream of school life. Such youth have little opportunity to internalize norms that promote school success or to connect with those who can guide their academic progress. Drawing on theories of social capital, Gibson and her colleagues argue that peer social capital—as well as the more familiar social capital acquired through interactions with well-connected adults—can enhance school performance. We learn that peer networks rich in social capital can provide tangible forms of support that enable low-status students to access institutional resources and funds of knowledge that help them "decode the system and participate in power sharing." That is, they help young people navigate and negotiate the policies and practices that so often limit their academic opportunities.

The nation is desperate for practical and effective ways to overcome the educational disparities that compromise our democracy. But new policies and programs must be based on trustworthy research that provides new insights into problems and suggests creative new directions for policies and programs. Margaret Gibson, Patricia Gándara, Jill Peterson Koyama and their colleagues offer just such research. In the spirit of UC ACCORD, the task ahead is to see that this fine work makes a difference.

Jeannie Oakes
Presidential Professor at UCLA and Director
University of California's All Campus
Consortium on Research for Diversity

Acknowledgments

This volume grew out of a 3-day conference held in September 2001, at which a small group of California scholars came together to explore their common research interest in how peer groups and peer relationships influence the school engagement and academic achievement of high school age youth of Mexican descent. The discussion promoted a rich exchange of ideas which continued through the drafting and rewriting of the chapters herein and which also proved essential to the evolution of this volume. Our thanks go to the University of California's All Campus Consortium on Research for Diversity (UC ACCORD) for underwriting the conference, as well as other expenses associated with the production of this volume. The preparation of this volume was also supported by a Spencer Foundation grant (MG #199900129), and by the Educational Partnership Center at the University of California, Santa Cruz, which provided office space for the project.

In addition, we extend our thanks to Nicole Hidalgo and Mina Spisak for their very able assistance with conference arrangements. We also wish to acknowledge the expert technical help provided by Cony Rolón, who on numerous occasions massaged the individual chapters into a coherent whole.

To those who have contributed chapters, we thank you for your wonderful scholarship, your colleagueship, and your constant responsiveness to our requests for further revisions. We also extend our thanks to the Teachers College Press staff members and anonymous reviewers who have supported the book's preparation from its inception to publication and whose insights along the way helped us to clarify our own understanding of a complex area of scholarship. In particular, we are grateful to Susan Liddicoat for guiding us from an initial and sometimes sketchy vision towards a cohesive volume.

Finally, we wish to thank all the young people who shared their concerns, their fears, and their aspirations with us over these many years. Without their candid remarks and observations, this book would not have been possible. We fervently hope that each one of them has found the pathway to realize his or her aspirations.

Margaret A. Gibson
Patricia Gándara
Jill Peterson Koyama

School Connections

1

The Role of Peers in the Schooling of U.S. Mexican Youth

Margaret A. Gibson, Patricia Gándara,
& Jill Peterson Koyama

The past century has seen a huge shift in the median education level needed to compete in the U.S. job market. In 1900, only 6% of America's children finished high school (Mondale & Patton, 2001), and most job seekers were able to obtain manual-labor positions that required little schooling. Today, four out of five jobs require a high school diploma, and those individuals without a high school education have limited kinds of work available to them (United States, 1996). Better paying positions generally require a college degree. In most cases, there is a direct relationship between years of formal education and one's employment opportunities. However, not all segments of our society enjoy either equal access to or equal benefits from schooling. Our specific interest in this volume centers on the academic performance and school persistence of students of Mexican origin, both U.S.- and foreign-born. We choose this focus because research shows that in the aggregate U.S. Mexican youth are completing high school and college in significantly lower numbers than young people from other major ethnic groups in this country.[1]

Latinos, some two thirds of whom nationwide are of Mexican origin, have just emerged as this country's largest minority group. They are also the youngest population group and the fastest growing. Latino children now account for 14% of the public school population in the United States and more than 25% of students in central city schools (National Center for Educational Statistics, 2000; Tienda, 2001). Over the next 20 years the overall number of Latino children is expected to double, and based on current projections one in four school children in America will be Latino by the year 2025 (White House Initiative, 1998).

SCHOOL ACHIEVEMENT PATTERNS

Because of their numbers, Latino youth, and more specifically youth of Mexican origin, are of enormous public policy interest, and their educational achievement is a matter of growing national concern. The rapid growth of the Latino population is especially pronounced in California, which is home to almost half of this country's Mexican-descent population. In California today, Latino students—80% of whom are of Mexican origin—have already surpassed non-Hispanic Whites as the largest K–12 student group, and sometime in the next 10 to 15 years they will surpass Whites in the overall population of the state (Johnson, 1999). The high school completion rate for Latinos lags behind that of other major ethnic groupings. Only 81% of U.S.-born Latinos, 70% of the foreign-born who are naturalized citizens, and 40% of the noncitizen Latinos ages 25 to 29 have a high school diploma compared with 87% of African Americans and 94% of both Asian Americans and European Americans within the same age group (United States, 2003; U.S. Census Bureau, 2000). Moreover, only 8% of Latinos ages 25 to 29 have finished 4 years of college compared with 18% of African Americans, 34% of European Americans, and 54% of Asian Americans (U.S. Census Bureau, 2000).

To explain the educational experiences of Latino youth and specifically their unequal pattern of school attainment, research has centered largely on what are thought to be the key obstacles to their academic success. The most frequently cited barrier is language, and most of the federal activity aimed at increasing the achievement of Latino youth during the 1970s and 1980s focused on English language development for students with limited English proficiency. Only recently have researchers and policy makers begun sounding the alarm that Mexican-origin youth whose home language is English may perform as poorly or even more poorly than those for whom English is a second language (Mitchell, Destino, & Karam, 1997; Rumbaut, 1996). Although improvement in educational outcomes from the first generation to the second is substantial, it is not sustained in future generations (Grogger & Trejo, 2002; Portes & Rumbaut, 2001). By the third generation progress stalls, and there is no significant wage or educational improvement. This defies the normal pattern of multigenerational immigrant mobility and points to the schools themselves as a crucial variable in changing educational outcomes for U.S. Mexican youth.

Some of the barriers to equal educational opportunity for Mexican-origin youth—such as schools with underprepared teachers, inadequate materials, and substandard facilities—can be addressed through increased resources (Rumberger & Gándara, 2000, 2001; Shields et al., 1999). However, even in well-funded institutions, teachers often have inadequate knowledge of the social, cultural, and linguistic backgrounds of their Mexican-descent students. As a result, many of these youth feel misunderstood, even marginalized in school, as though they "do not belong." The situation of not belonging is even more difficult for students who experience frequent mobility between schools (nonpromotional school changes), as such moves disrupt friendship networks and sources of institutional support (Rumberger, 1998). School transfers are especially pronounced among Mexican-origin youth and impinge on not only academic achievement but also access to peers as social resources (Ream & Castillo, 2001).

Students' aspirations for higher education also affect their educational attainment. Of all Latino groups, U.S. Mexican youth have the lowest aspirations for postsecondary education. They are less likely to believe that a 4-year college degree is within their reach (Portes & Rumbaut, 2001), and they frequently lack adequate knowledge about college as an option (Kao & Tienda, 1998). Even when these students do aspire to college, it is usually only to a 2-year institution (see Chapter 3, this volume).

These patterns of low educational aspirations and attainment must be understood with reference to the historical burdens of poverty, economic exploitation, discrimination, segregation, and the ongoing cycles of "nativist hostility" that have affected Mexican Americans throughout the past century (López & Stanton-Salazar, 2001; Portes & Rumbaut, 2001; Trueba, 1998).[2] Framing their work within this larger historical and social context, contributors to this volume center attention on the role of peers in the schooling of U.S.-born and immigrant high-school-aged youth of Mexican descent. Their analyses look to the processes that lead peers to be an impediment to school success as well as a pivotal tool in promoting academic achievement.

THE ROLE OF PEERS

Although the general condition of Latinos in U.S. schools has been well documented in recent years (Hispanic Dropout Project, 1998; United States, 1996, 2001, 2003; White House Initiative, 1998, 1999, 2000), the scarcity of research focusing on the role of peers and peer relations in shaping schooling outcomes of Mexican and other Latino youth is notable. Adolescents today, including those of Mexican origin, spend more time with their peers than they do with anyone else (Carnegie Council, 1995; Schneider & Stevenson, 1999), and it is widely recognized that peers play an important role in influencing adolescent behavior and cognitive processes. Families, of course, continue to play a central socializing role in the lives of adolescents, but as young people mature and become more independent, they usually spend more time with their age mates and less with their parents and other family members. Some studies have illuminated the intersections between adolescents' peer affiliations, their student identities, and their academic engagement (e.g., Cooper, Jackson, Azmitia, Lopez, & Dunbar, 1995; Davidson, 1996; Epstein & Karweit, 1983; Gibson, 1997; Phelan, Davidson, & Yu, 1998; Sieber & Gordon, 1981; Steinberg, Brown, Cider, Kaczmarek, & Lazzaro, 1988), but few of these focus specifically on students of Mexican descent or explicate the processes by which peers influence academic achievement. This volume addresses these lacunae in the literature.

As well, the scholars in this volume demonstrate that the terms *peer* and *peer group* are locally defined and situated through shared participation in particular types of behaviors and activities. These terms are used so frequently in daily conversation that we are inclined to believe that they have common definitions with which everyone agrees. Peers generally imply age mates, friends, acquaintances, and other individuals in close proximity and of equal status. For adolescents, one's peers may range from best friends to schoolmates with whom one rarely or never interacts. And relationships may vary from comfortable and rewarding interactions with friends ("kids like me") to more difficult, sometimes alienating or hurtful interactions with schoolmates and classmates who belong to different groups ("those other kids"). As studies in this volume will show, both close peers and those more distant can and do influence students' patterns of participation, engagement, and achievement during high school.

Peer Pressure and Peer Influence

During adolescence, day-to-day decisions are increasingly based on peer influence, and it is often within one's peer group that specific frames for perceiving oneself are developed (Adelson, 1980; Benard, 1990). Students care deeply about what their peers think, and they shape their behavior accordingly. The values of the group help fashion one's definitions of both social and academic success. Thus not being a "burnout" may be as important as one's affirmative identity as a "jock" or a "skater" (Eckert, 1989). Having friends that reinforce or support one's perception of oneself enhances a student's perceived self-worth and esteem while also providing a sense of belonging, importance, and security (Shulman, 1993).

Although parents and school personnel often fret over the impact of peers on students' social and academic behavior, research presented in this volume suggests that peer influence takes a variety of forms: peer pressure to engage in certain behaviors, and in early adolescence these are often risky behaviors that interfere with academic achievement; peer normative influence on attitudes and aspirations, including educational aspirations; and peer influence in regulating who "belongs" where within the school's hierarchy, which in turn influences the ways in which students participate in school. For most students the experience of peer pressure peaks at the beginning of high school and wanes thereafter (see Chapter 3, this volume). Peer normative influence and peer influence on belonging, on the other hand, may remain strong throughout high school.

Where research has focused on how peers influence the academic engagement of minority youth, it frequently overemphasizes school resistance and failure and gives insufficient attention to the ways in which peers support school success. This one-sided focus includes studies of Mexican-descent youth, which almost invariably portray peers as "bad influences." Certainly, in some situations peers can be a major source of "distraction" from schooling, and students recognize this themselves. However, narrowly viewing peer culture as largely oppositional to schooling can result in a failure to tap the power of peers as a resource in teaching and learning. It can also obscure the roles that schools themselves play either in contributing to the "acting out" behaviors of Mexican-descent youth or in structuring more positive classroom dynamics. The scholars in this volume offer a more multifaceted view, depicting situations in which peers serve variously as both positive and negative influences on school achievement.

Peer Relations and Peer Networks

Supportive and trusting relationships with teachers and other adults in school settings are essential to academic learning but so, too, are supportive relations with other students. Learning in school is not simply an individual matter; it occurs in interaction with others (Lave & Wenger, 1991; Rogoff, 1990). Students' sense of fitting in and being comfortable in school and their decisions about applying themselves to their studies are constructed, negotiated, and reconstructed on an ongoing basis through their relationships with peers.

Although always fluid and changing, peer relationships are indisputably important. For students from working-class and immigrant families, peers often play an even more significant role in shaping school performance patterns than do peers for youth from more advantaged circumstances. This is because their parents in many cases do not possess the educational background or have easy access to the institutional knowledge needed to help their children succeed in high school or prepare for college. In school, too, these students are frequently deprived of important social networks and sources of critical information about postsecondary opportunities. Thus, although peers in some instances can serve as a source of social capital, for example, providing access to important social networks, as well as critical value orientations (see Chapter 2, this volume), this requires that students have friends with the requisite social capital to share.

Mexican-origin students, even more than other students, tend to select their closest friends from their own ethnic group. As a result, their opportunities to come into contact with peers from other ethnic groups—particularly those who are more socially advantaged—are generally limited. Even when they attend high schools where students are drawn from a mix of ethnic backgrounds and social classes, curricular tracking reinforces already established tendencies to socialize with students like themselves. Low-income Mexican-descent youth may simply refrain from participating in those settings or activities at school where more privileged White students are the dominant group. For example, when assigned to classes where there are only two or three students of Mexican origin, Mexican-descent students often remain silent. They do their work but feel uncomfortable speaking out in front of middle-class White peers or seeking their help with homework, not wishing to appear "dumb," the only ones who don't understand. Or they may drop to an "easier" class in order to be among friends, even though they need the "tougher" class for university admission. In addition, English language learners may shy away from practicing English at school for fear of being teased by peers for their less than flawless English. Mexican-descent youth may also refrain from participating in the social life of the school, or in extracurricular school activities, when they feel they will not fit in and be accepted by their peers.

We often conceptualize peer groups as being initiated and controlled by students themselves, but they may also be institutionally organized and controlled (Brown, 1990). For example, teachers and other school staff have major influence on how peer relations are structured within classes and in other school-organized venues such as sports and clubs. We thus see that within school settings students are participants in relationships that are neither completely the product of external conditions nor individual choices. Schools themselves are coconstructors of peer relations. Through their organization and sanctioned practices, schools play a substantial and ongoing role in determining the types of peer relations that occur and where peer relations are nurtured, tolerated, or challenged.

Contributors to this volume not only describe the variety of peer relations that take place in schools but also analyze the school's role in constructing them. They posit that schools are active arenas in which students perform, interact, and create relations with one another. School climate and context play a central role in determining or forming the nature of students' relationships and expectations. Thus, although we recognize that students' academic orientations and achievement patterns are formed by many institutions apart from the school (e.g., home, neighborhood, church), as well as by larger societal forces (e.g., economic, political, historical), our central interest in this volume is the role of peer affiliations and relationships in shaping school performance patterns and the ways in which particular policies, programs, and practices within school settings serve to structure these affiliations and interactions.

OVERARCHING THEMES

This volume's contributors have all carried out recent field research that addresses our central questions:

- In what ways do peers and peer relationships influence the school performance of Mexican-origin high school youth?
- In what ways do schools collaborate in structuring these peer relationships?

Together these scholars represent a range of disciplinary perspectives on the topic and utilize a mix of research methodologies. Although individual chapters remain anchored in the disciplinary traditions and specific research interests of their authors, all contributors have sought to highlight crosscutting themes and findings. Chapters draw from multisite field studies that have taken place over a number of years, single-site studies that have followed cohorts of students throughout their high school careers, and studies that represent years of scholarship focused on the key issues of this volume. Considered together, the chapters demonstrate the ways in which peer relations and peer influence are created, maintained, challenged, and transformed across school settings and with varying results. They also seek to illuminate the ways in which school contexts shape peer and intergroup relationships.

Peer Social Capital

A major theme of the book is the role of *peer social capital* in promoting school achievement. In addition to sustained connections to adults in school and to traditional adult–youth social networks, relationships among students themselves can prove to be an influential social currency in high school, a specific form of social capital. Because social capital has been defined principally as social networks that provide access to the resources of the social elite, there has been considerable controversy regarding whether or not nonelite peers can be social capital providers. In the next chapter, Ricardo Stanton-Salazar delineates a compelling argument for recognizing the existence of peer social capital among working-class minority youth. In addition, Stanton-Salazar guides us, as researchers, educators, and policy makers, to understand peer relations within a critical network analysis of social capital that acknowledges the struggle for power and resources between dominant and subordinate groups. As he makes clear, many low-status students, including many youth of Mexican descent, are continually subjected to competing forces regarding whose system of "values, ideologies, expectations, emotions, and coping styles are most appropriate, legitimate and productive" (Chapter 2, this volume).

Following Stanton-Salazar, we define peer social capital as adolescents' connections to peers and peer networks that can provide access to tangible forms of support that facilitate the accomplishment of academic goals. By *support* we mean institutional resources and funds of knowledge that enable low-status students to decode the system and participate in power sharing (Delpit, 1995; Stanton-Salazar, 1997). Peer social networks that are rich in social capital can mediate and moderate the mainstream practices and organizational structures of schools that restrict opportunities for working-class Mexican-descent youth by providing them with alternative funds of school-related information, resources, and strategies.

In high schools, institutionalized policies and practices play critical roles in framing where, when, and how these peer relationships become possible, available, and resourceful to students (Conchas, 2001). Having access to capital-rich settings is far more probable in some schools than in others (see Chapter 6, this volume). Some schools seem loaded with various forms of social capital, including peer social capital (see Chapter 8, this volume). Other schools may have isolated stores of resources located amongst selective curricular tracks (Stanton-Salazar & Dornbusch, 1995) or in supportive school organizations and activities (Chapters 6 & 7, this volume; see also Mehan, Villanueva, Hubbard, & Lintz, 1996).

As cases presented in this volume make clear, whether or not students are able to cultivate and maintain peer social capital has direct bearing on their participation and achievement in high school. Peers, particularly in the form of close friends and cliques, can indeed provide the kind of moral support and integrating "social glue" that allow some otherwise marginalized Mexican-origin students to gain a foothold in school. For example, participation in an all-Mexican club at school can, under particular circumstances, offer students an important source of community that provides a sense of connectedness to the larger school, access to the social capital needed for academic success, and contact with other students on track for college who serve as role models (see Chapter 7, this volume). Working-class Mexican-descent youth may also acquire social capital from their more advantaged middle-class peers (see Chapter 6, this volume). We are intrigued by this exploration of peer social capital among working-class students and have attempted to mine the concept throughout the studies presented here. It should be noted, however, that the individual studies were not carried out with a social-capital framework in mind. Rather, the importance of peer social capital emerged as a key theme in the production of the volume itself. We think it provides not only significant explanatory power for within-group achievement variation but also an important policy lever for creating change in very difficult schooling circumstances. However, the kind of support offered by friends does not necessarily translate into school success, as demonstrated clearly in Chapters 3 through 6 in this volume.

Limited Pathways and the Appearance of Willful "Not Learning"

Many working-class and immigrant youth, including those of Mexican descent, lack the skills and connections needed to access the pathways that can lead them to college. For example, students may find their access to advanced placement and other honors classes limited, or they may find that the support needed to succeed in such classes is insufficient. Likewise, they may find it difficult to gain entrée into the high school's leadership clubs and classes. Yet skills and connections gained in such contexts play a critical role in the development and maintenance of academic identities and experience.

Young people's sense of themselves *as students* is often formed and confirmed by the spaces they occupy on a school campus, and these spaces may either promote or impede their educational progress. As detailed in the work of Varenne and McDermott (1998), the places in school where students spend time and the interactions they have there are likely more important than the traits they bring with them to these settings. When academic pathways are limited to only certain students—those whom the school has determined "belong" in a particular program or class—students' interactions become restricted to a much narrower range of peers. Thus those who have limited access to certain kinds of school settings—for example, students labeled "at risk," "special needs," or "limited English proficient"—are in fact at risk of coming to perform in accordance with the labels attached to them. It is, as McDermott (1997) reminds us, that those who "appear as if they are not learning [in fact] are *not* not learning."

Rather, they are "learning in relation to ongoing arrangements that . . . keep everyone learning how to remain in the same place one generation after another" (p. 120).

This appearance of *not learning* is another key theme of this volume, as highlighted in particular in Chapters 4 and 5 by Clayton Hurd and Diego Vigil, respectively. These scholars describe how some groups of working-class, Mexican-descent youth—most frequently males—are influenced by their peers to perform for one another in their classes, all the while not learning what their teachers are attempting to teach. Both authors point to a peer group solidarity—the backing up of a peer when he or she disrupts class, interrupts learning, or challenges authority—that gives the appearance of resistance but in reality may be more reflective of what Herbert Kohl (1994) has termed "willful not-learning." As Hurd cogently notes, however, Kohl describes not learning as an individual act, best understood through careful analysis of an individual student's history, but in reality not learning is often a collaborative act or a group process. Students' responses to schooling and their behavior in school are often group processes shaped by family and community forces, as John Ogbu (1974, 1991) has long noted, including group theories about the value of schooling. These theories, in turn, are shaped by societal and school forces related to how opportunities are distributed in society (and school) and to pressures placed on students to abandon their home and community cultures.

Drawing on his analysis of an English language development (ELD) classroom, Hurd in Chapter 4 suggests that the boys' "not-learning practices" are a type of performance that allows them to show solidarity with their friends. We see, too, that these gendered peer relations occur within a particular school setting and context, one that isolates Mexican-descent youth in slow-paced classes with a curriculum they find boring and unchallenging and with a teacher who, though well meaning, has inadequate understanding of the students' backgrounds and what motivates them to behave as they do. When students believe that their identities are being devalued or misunderstood, they are more likely to resist school authority and misbehave in class (Fordham & Ogbu, 1986; Gibson, 1982; Solomon, 1992; Waters, 1996).

In similar fashion, Vigil focuses in Chapter 5 on the nature of peer relations that exist among street-socialized and gang-influenced youth. Like Hurd, he argues that school structures, contexts, and practices themselves further socialize students, in this case gang-affiliated youth, to perform in certain ways that in effect sabotage their chances for academic success. Vigil's framework is one of "multiple marginality," where the boys feel alienated at home, in their communities, and at school. Most have weak academic skills and few or no supportive relationships apart from those with fellow gang members, and in school they lack access to much needed institutional support. As Vigil suggests, the boys' (mis)behavior in school may not be so much a reflection of resistance to mainstream culture and schooling, or even willful not learning, as it is a reflection of all the gaps in their lives and a lack of knowledge of what they need to do in order to be successful in the school setting (see also Flores-González, 2002, for her discussion of "street kids"). Although Vigil's analysis focuses solely on boys, Hurd explores as well the impact that peer-mediated interpersonal politics has on girls.

Belonging and the Need for Community Membership

Belonging and not belonging in school is another theme running through several of the chapters. Mexican-origin students in general, and perhaps females in particular (see Chapter 3, this volume), are more likely than other students to report they do not feel they belong in the schools in which they are a minority. This is a critical finding because the literature suggests a strong relationship between feeling connected to school or belonging to a school community, on the one hand, and academic motivation, participation, and achievement on the other (Osterman, 2000). Students who experience a sense of belonging and peer acceptance in school are more likely to enjoy school, to be engaged academically, to participate in school activities, and to persist toward graduation and college. Conversely, students who feel excluded or estranged are far more likely to disengage academically and to act out in class. They are also at much higher risk of dropping out of school altogether (Osterman, 2000).

For students of Mexican descent—especially those who feel they are constrained, marginalized, or limited in access to the full range of school settings—appropriation of particular physical school spaces and contexts, such as an ELD classroom, becomes significant. Some students, like the youth in Vigil's study of gang-influenced males or the disruptive males described by Hurd, make classrooms "their own" by unsettling them. Other students find safe and familiar places of belonging, places in school where peer relations feel like family. In their ethnographic examination of a migrant student club, Margaret Gibson and associates (see Chapter 7, this volume) found that students' sense of belonging in school is strongly influenced by their relationships with peers. Club members identified being part of a supportive community as critical to their sense of belonging in school and their overall academic engagement. Moreover, membership in this group gave them access to a network of schoolmates and teachers who could facilitate their academic progress. Both club members and their advisors described their relations with one another as being "like family." Similarly, Jason Raley (see Chapter 8, this volume) describes a small, privately funded multiethnic high school where the entire school community, students and staff together, functions like a family. Raley shows us how "peer-relations-like-family" are central to students' sense of school as a "safe space," an environment where expansive, transformative learning is possible, and where students from traditionally underrepresented groups are able to confront the personal and social risks involved in "becoming college students" (see Fine, Weis, & Powell, 1997, for their discussion of the importance of safe spaces). Peer relations of this sort do not just happen by chance; they are, as Raley states, an achievement brought about by the social structure and practices of the particular school and by the "kids" themselves.

However, when appropriate and welcoming spaces are not created for marginalized students, they will create alternative spaces of belonging, as Hurd and Vigil show us in Chapters 4 and 5. These spaces may involve the creation of a subculture within the school (the ELD peer group) or outside the school (the gang). In these contexts peer support comes at the expense of schooling. It need not be so. Safe spaces and spaces of belonging can be created that support schooling objectives while affirming the identity and value of Mexican-origin youth. Lewis-Charp and her colleagues (Chapter 6, this volume) compare two different schooling contexts—one in which intergroup differences are both acknowledged and celebrated, the other in which they are ignored and viewed as unimportant. They conclude not only that a supportive school environment for Mexican-origin youth should promote opportunities for "border crossing" or interaction across ethnic and social class groupings but also that border-crossing skills can and should be explicitly taught by schools. These researchers, who are not alone in this belief (see, e.g., Gándara, 1995; Gibson, 1998; Phelan, Davidson, & Yu, 1998), also hypothesize that the ability to move seamlessly among groups of students who are different from oneself with respect to social class, ethnicity, gender, and academic skills is linked to greater engagement in learning and long-term social and academic success.

The chapters to follow move from descriptions and explanations of peer influence to examinations of the ways in which teachers and other school staff mediate this influence. Taken together, they portray the complexities of the ways in which peers both help and hinder school achievement among students of Mexican descent. They also detail a variety of ways in which school contexts themselves directly influence the nature of peer and intergroup relationships. In the final chapter of the volume, the editors link the prior analyses with recommendations for policy and practice, indicating where findings may be applied to the critical issue of raising the school achievement of a significantly underachieving portion of the American youth population.

NOTES

1. We use the terms *Mexican origin, Mexican descent,* and *U.S. Mexican* interchangeably to refer to persons of Mexican ancestry who reside in the United States. In cases where national data are not disaggregated by subgroup, but exist only for "Latinos," we also employ the term *Latino* to refer to the larger group of Hispanic origin.

2. For further discussion of these barriers, see De la Rosa and Maw, 1990; Gándara, 1995; Garcia, 2001; Ginorio and Huston, 2000; Gutierrez, Baquendano-Lopez, and Alvarez, 2000; Ruiz-de-Velasco and Fix, 2000; Vernez and Abrahamse, 1996.

REFERENCES

Adelson, J. (1980). *The handbook of adolescent psychology.* New York: Wiley.

Benard, B. (1990). *The case for peers.* Portland, OR: Northwest Regional Educational Laboratory, U.S. Department of Education, Office of Educational Research and Improvement.

Brown, B. B. (1990). Peer groups and peer cultures. In S. Feldman & G. Elliott (Eds.), *At the threshold: The developing adolescent* (pp. 171–196). Cambridge, MA: Harvard University Press.

Carnegie Council on Adolescent Development. (1995). *Great transitions, preparing adolescents for a new century.* New York: Carnegie Corporation.

Conchas, G. Q. (2001). Structuring failure and success: Understanding the variability in Latino School Engagement. *Harvard Educational Review, 71* (3), 475–504.

Cooper, C. R., Jackson, J. F., Azmitia, M., Lopez, E., & Dunbar, N. (1995). Bridging students' multiple worlds: African American and Latino youth in outreach programs. In R. F. Macias & R. G. Garcia Ramos (Eds.), *Changing schools for changing students* (pp. 245–268). Santa Barbara, CA: University of California Linguistic Minority Research Institute.

Davidson, A. L. (1996). *Making and molding identity in schools: Student narratives on race, gender, and academic engagement.* Albany: State University of New York Press.

De la Rosa, D., & Maw, C. (1990). *Hispanic education: A statistical portrait.* Washington, DC: National Council of La Raza.

Delpit, L. (1995). *Other people's children: Cultural conflict in the classroom.* New York: New Press.

Eckert, P. (1989). *Jocks and burnouts: Social categories and identity in the high school.* New York: Teachers College Press.

Epstein, J., & Karweit, N. (Eds.). (1983). *Friends in school: Patterns of selection and influence in secondary schools.* New York: Academic Press.

Fine, M., Weis, L., & Powell, L. C. (1997). Communities of difference: A critical look at desegregated spaces created for and by youth. *Harvard Educational Review, 67*(2), 247–284.

Flores-González, N. (2002). *School kids/street kids: Identity development in Latino students.* New York: Teachers College Press.

Fordham, S., & Ogbu, J. (1986). Black students' school success: Coping with the burden of "acting White." *Urban Review, 18*(3), 176–206.

Gándara, P. (1995). *Over the ivy walls: The educational mobility of low income Chicanos.* Albany: State University of New York.

Garcia, E. (2001). *Hispanic education in the United States.* Lanham, MD: Rowman & Littlefield.

Gibson, M. A. (1982). Reputation and respectability: How competing cultural systems affect students' performance in school. *Anthropology and Education Quarterly, 13*(1), 3–27.

Gibson, M. A. (1997). Complicating the immigrant/involuntary minority typology. In M. A. Gibson (Ed.), Ethnicity and school performance: Complicating the immigrant/involuntary typology [Theme issue]. *Anthropology and Education Quarterly, 28*(3), 431–454.

Gibson, M. A. (1998). Promoting academic success among minority students: Is acculturation the issue? *Educational Policy, 12*(6), 615–633.

Ginorio, A., & Huston, M. (2000). *¡Sí, se puede! Yes, we can: Latinas in school.* Washington, DC: American Association of University Women.

Grogger, J., & Trejo, S. (2002). *Falling behind or moving up? The intergenerational progress of Mexican Americans.* San Francisco: The Public Policy Institute of California.

Gutierrez, K., Baquendano-Lopez, P., & Alvarez, H. H. (2000). The crisis in Latino education. In C. Tejeda, C. Martinez, & Z. Leonardo (Eds.), *Charting new terrains of Chicana(o)/Latina(o) education* (pp. 213–232). Cresskill, NJ: Hampton Press.

Hispanic Dropout Project (U.S.). (1998). *No more excuses: Final report of the Hispanic dropout project.* Washington, DC: U.S. Department of Education, Office of Bilingual Education and Minority Languages Affairs.

Johnson, H. P. (1999, October). How many Californians? A review of population projections for the state. *California Counts: Population Trends and Profiles 1*(1).

Kao, G., & Tienda, M. (1998). Educational aspirations of minority youth. *American Journal of Education, 106,* 349–384.

Kohl, H. (1994). *I won't learn from you and other thoughts on creative maladjustment.* New York: New Press.

Lave, J., & Wenger, E. (1991). *Situated learning: Legitimate peripheral participation.* New York: Cambridge University Press.

López, D., & Stanton-Salazar, R. D. (2001). Mexican-Americans: A second generation at risk. In R. Rumbaut & A. Portes (Eds.), *Ethnicities: Children of immigrants in America* (pp. 57–90). Berkeley: University of California Press.

McDermott, R. P. (1997). Achieving school failure, 1972–1997. In G. D. Spindler (Ed.), *Education and cultural process: Anthropological approaches* (3rd ed.), pp. 110–131. Prospect Heights, IL: Waveland Press.

Mehan, H., Villanueva, I., Hubbard, L., & Lintz, A. (1996). *Constructing school suc-*

cess: The consequences of untracking low-achieving students. New York: Cambridge University Press.

Mitchell, D., Destino, T., & Karam, R. (1997). *Evaluation of English language development programs in the Santa Ana Unified School District.* University of California Riverside, California Educational Research Cooperative.

Mondale, S., & Patton, S. (Eds.). (2001). *School, the story of American public education.* Boston: Beacon Press.

National Center for Education Statistics. (2000). *Racial and ethnic distribution of elementary and secondary students.* Washington, DC: U.S. Department of Education, Office of Educational Research and Improvement: Series title: Indicator of the month.

Ogbu, J. U. (1974). *The next generation.* New York: Academic Press.

Ogbu, J. U. (1991). Immigrant and involuntary minorities in comparative perspective. In M. A. Gibson & J. U. Ogbu (Eds.), *Minority status and schooling: A comparative study of immigrant and involuntary minorities* (pp. 3–33). New York: Garland.

Osterman, K. F. (2000). Students' need for belonging in the school community. *Review of Educational Research, 70*(3), 323–367.

Phelan, P., Davidson, A., & Yu, H. C. (1998). *Adolescents' worlds: Negotiating family, peers, and schools.* New York: Teachers College Press.

Portes, A., & Rumbaut, R. (2001). *Legacies: The story of the immigrant second generation.* Berkeley: University of California Press.

Ream, R., & Castillo, S. (2001, September). *Does peer social capital moderate the impact of student mobility on the mathematics achievement of Mexican Americans across immigrant generations?* Paper presented at UC ACCORD invitational conference: Peer influences on the school performance of Mexican-descent adolescents, San Jose, CA.

Rogoff, B. (1990). *Apprenticeship in thinking: Cognitive development in social context.* New York: Oxford University.

Ruiz-de-Velasco, J., & Fix, M. (2000). *Overlooked and underserved: Immigrant students in U.S. secondary schools.* Washington, DC: The Urban Institute.

Rumbaut, R. (1996). The crucible within: Ethnic identity, self esteem, and segmented assimilation among children of immigrants. In A. Portes (Ed.), *The new second generation.* New York: The Russell Sage Foundation.

Rumberger, R. (1998). *The hazards of changing schools for Latino adolescents.* Berkeley: California Policy Seminar.

Rumberger, R., & Gándara, P. (2000). The schooling of English learners. In E. Burr, G. Hayward, B. Fuller, & M. Kirst (Eds.), *Crucial issues in California education.* University of California and Stanford University: Policy Analysis for California Education

Rumberger, R., & Gándara, P. (2001). The conditions of schooling for English learners. Santa Barbara: University of California Linguistic Minority Research Institute. Available: www.lmri.ucsb.edu

Schneider, B., & Stevenson, D. (1999). *The ambitious generation: America's teenagers, motivated but directionless.* New Haven, CT: Yale University Press.

Shields, P., Esch, C., Humphrey, D., Young, V., Gaston, M., & Hunt, H. (1999). *The sta-*

tus of the teaching profession: Research findings and policy recommendations. Santa Cruz, CA: The Center for the Future of Teaching and Learning.

Shulman, S. (1993). Close relationships and coping behavior in adolescents. *Journal of Adolescence, 16,* 267–283.

Sieber, T., & Gordon, A. (Eds.). (1981). *Children and their organizations: Investigations in American culture.* Boston: G. K. Hall.

Solomon, P. (1992). *Black resistance in a high school: Forging a separatist culture.* Albany: State University of New York Press.

Stanton-Salazar, R. D. (1997). A social capital framework for understanding the socialization of racial minority children and youth. *Harvard Educational Review, 67*(1), 1–40.

Stanton-Salazar, R. D., & Dornbusch, S. M. (1995). Social capital and the social reproduction of inequality: The formation of informational networks among Mexican-origin high school students. *Sociology of Education, 68*(2), 116–135.

Steinberg, L., Brown, B. B., Cider, M., Kaczmarek, N., & Lazzaro, C. (1988). *Noninstructional influence on high school achievement: The contributions of parents, peers, extracurricular activities and part-time work.* Madison, WI: National Center on Effective Secondary Schools.

Tienda, M. (2001). College admissions policies and the educational pipeline: Implications for medical and health professions. In B. Smedley, A. Stith, L. Colburn, & C. Evans (Eds.), *The right thing to do, the smart thing to do: Enhancing diversity in the health professions.* Washington, DC: The National Academy of Sciences.

Trueba, E. T. (1998). The education of Mexican immigrant children. In M. M. Suarez-Orozco (Ed.), *Crossings: Mexican immigration in interdisciplinary perspectives* (pp. 253–275). Cambridge, MA: David Rockefeller Center for Latin American Studies, Harvard University.

United States. President's Advisory Commission on Educational Excellence for Hispanic Americans. (1996). *Our nation on the fault line: Hispanic American education.* Washington, DC: Author.

United States. President's Advisory Commission on Educational Excellence for Hispanic Americans. (2001). *Creating the will: A report to the President of the United States, the Secretary of Education, and the nation.* [On-line.] Retrieved February 13, 2002, from http://www.ed.gov/offices/OIIA/Hispanic/new/reportv2.pdf

United States. President's Advisory Commission on Educational Excellence for Hispanic Americans. (2003). *From risk to opportunity: Fulfilling the educational needs of Hispanic Americans in the 21st century. Final report.* [On-line.] Retrieved May 19, 2003, from http://www.yesican.gov/paceea/finalreport.pdf

U.S. Census Bureau. (2000, March). *Educational Attainment in the United States.* Detailed Tables. Available: http://www.census.gov/population/socdemo/education/p20-536/tab01a.txt

Varenne, H., & McDermott, R. (1998). *Successful failure: The school America builds.* Boulder, CO: Westview Press.

Vernez, G., & Abrahamse, A. (1996). *How immigrants fare in U.S. education.* Santa Monica, CA: RAND Center for Research on Immigration Policy.

Waters, M. (1996). The intersections of gender, race and ethnicity in identity development of Caribbean American teens. In B. Leadbeater & N. Way (Eds.), *Urban girls: Resisting stereotypes, creating identities* (pp. 65–81). New York: New York University.

White House Initiative on Educational Excellence for Hispanic Americans. (1998). *Latinos in education: Early childhood, elementary, secondary, undergraduate, graduate*. Washington, DC: U.S. Department of Education.

White House Initiative on Educational Excellence for Hispanic Americans. (1999). *What works for Latino youth* (1st ed.). Washington, DC: U.S. Department of Education.

White House Initiative on Educational Excellence for Hispanic Americans. (2000). *What works for Latino youth* (2nd ed.). Washington, DC: U.S. Department of Education.

2

Social Capital Among Working-Class Minority Students

Ricardo D. Stanton-Salazar

If academic success in school were mainly contingent upon individual ability and effort, then there would be no need to entertain theories that focus
our attention on the complexities that underlie social relations in organizational life and in society. If, on the other hand, as the case studies in this volume demonstrate, academic success is contingent upon engagement with
agents who control access to institutional resources vital to educational
achievement (as indicated by grades, test scores, etc.) and attainment (graduation, college enrollment), then our paradigm for understanding success
and failure in school has to be a relational one. And herein lies the utility of
social capital frameworks, which treat success in institutional life through
a relational/network paradigm.

Social capital—understood roughly as those "connections" to individuals and to networks that can provide access to resources and forms of
support that facilitate the accomplishment of goals—has informed the
study of family dynamics, the social organization of business enclaves, immigrant settlement experiences, public health, career advancement among
middle-class men, youth intervention, democracy and governance—and
increasingly, schooling and education. For analytical purposes, social
capital theory has the conceptual capacity to bring together, coherently,
"much of what has been studied under concepts such as informal organization, trust, culture, social support, social exchange, social resources, embeddedness, relational contracts, social networks, and interfirm networks"
(Adler & Kwon, 2001, p. 3). It also has the potential utility to explain how

educational achievement and attainment are closely associated with access to supportive relationships and networks.

Social capital—as captured through a wide variety of measures—has been shown to influence academic achievement (e.g., Carbonaro, 1998; Furstenberg & Hughes, 1995; Israel, Beaulieu, & Hartless, 2001; Morgan & Sorensen, 1999; Valenzuela & Dornbusch, 1994).[1] Overall, social capital in familial domains has been particularly prominent in studies of academic achievement, with the focus on family structure, parent-child discussions, and parent-school involvement (e.g., Bianchi & Robinson, 1997; Hao & Bonstead-Bruns, 1998; López, 1996; Teachman, Paasch, & Carver, 1996). Social capital has been shown to reduce the probability of dropping out of high school (e.g., Carbonaro, 1998; Croninger & Lee, 1999; McNeil, 1999; Teachman et al., 1996), and increase the probability of more years of schooling (Hofferth, Boisjoly, & Duncan, 1998; Kalmijn & Kraaykamp, 1996). It has also been associated with those behaviors and cognitive processes seen as underlying academic achievement, including effort engagement and homework completion (e.g., Bankston & Zhou, 1995; Muller & Ellison, 2001), extracurricular involvement (Fritch, 1999), and school commitment (Wright, Cullen, & Miller, 2001). Social capital, as an *outcome* variable, has also been shown to be associated with high school grades, educational attainment, occupations, and high levels of bilingualism (Stanton-Salazar & Dornbusch, 1995).

As the above-mentioned studies make clear, social capital theories and their practical applications offer a powerful lens through which to view the educational experiences and trajectories of working-class minority youth, including Latinos. As indicated by the studies in this volume, educational researchers can consider the social capital perspective to better investigate peer group processes in school and relate them to their theoretical correlates among adults. However, before its productivity can be realized more broadly in educational research, more precise understanding must be developed of how social capital frameworks illuminate fundamental processes underlying the ways people achieve "success" in society. Further understanding is needed of how individuals and groups in society mobilize their social relationships to attain their goals and solve their problems, how they experience "opportunity" and "privilege," and how they organize and coalesce to achieve collective ends.

The necessity of such an exploration is great considering that all too often in educational research, "powerhouse" concepts such as social capital (and cultural capital) are taken from their home discipline without sufficient attention to their theoretical roots and to the complexities entailed in their proper application. In the particular case of social capital, the concept has come to mean "many things to many people" (Narayan & Pritchett, 1977, p. 2), and to more critical observers, the rapid and widespread interest among scholars in different fields has taken on something of "a circustent quality" (De Souza Briggs, 1997, p. 111; both quotations from Adler & Kwon, 2001).

Research has typically suggested that working-class students most often gain social capital from middle-class peers and adult agents in institutional contexts rich in social and cultural capital (e.g., advanced placement classes, extracurricular activities). For example, Stanton-Salazar and Dornbusch (1995) examined a number of variables hypothesized to be predictive of social capital among working-class Mexican-origin students who attended predominantly White and middle-class high schools. Included was a measure of *peer social capital*, using the "proportion of a student's friendship network composed of peers who were not of Mexican-origin"(p. 122). The proportion of non-Mexican-origin was, in fact, statistically associated with having friends whose parents were engaged in white-collar professional occupations. Of significance was the finding that, relative to the others in the sample, English-proficient students and those with high educational expectations had the highest likelihood of reporting ties to non-Mexican peers. Similarly, studies examining school desegregation and the placement of working-class students of color in middle-class schools provide further evidence for the beneficial effects derived by low-status students when embedded in middle-class peer networks—and provide a justifiable basis for attributing "peer social capital" to "resource"-ful relations with their middle-class peers (Mehan, Villanueva, Hubbard, & Lintz, 1996; McPartland, Dawkins, Braddock, Crain, & Strauss, 1985).

In contrast, the idea that peer relations among working-class students might also constitute "social capital" seems less accepted. Of particular interest to this volume is whether adolescent working-class peer networks can reasonably constitute social capital. This interest parallels current questions in educational circles: Can working-class youth function as authentic "social capital" for each other? If so, in what contexts do they function as such? And, additionally, in what ways does such peer social capital relate/resemble/mirror/intersect with social capital mobilized in adult social networks?

This chapter tries to provide some resolution to these questions in two ways: (a) by bringing to the forefront the two major theoretical ways in which social capital has been conceived and highlighting how each focuses on different ways adolescent peers can potentially be supportive; and (b) by emphasizing the fact that working-class students, although sharing common socioeconomic conditions in their homes and nuclear families, and quite often, a common exposure to racializing and segregating forces in the community, do in fact regularly disaggregate themselves in very important ways. Some students find themselves in resourceful community-based organizations (Maeroff, 1998), others in residences and schools situated in middle-class neighborhoods (Rosenbaum, 2000), others in highly selective curricular tracks or programs (Stanton-Salazar & Dornbusch, 1995), and still others in supportive school organizations (Chapter 7, this volume; Mehan et al., 1996). Each context enables or promotes experiences that mitigate the effects of family socioeconomic status and often promote academic achievement. Despite the typically debilitating effects of their class origins, many working-class individuals do find themselves embedded in social networks where they enjoy privileged access to supportive contexts and to institutional agents and resources.

The question then becomes whether, by virtue of such privileged status, they now assume the function of vital "conduits" for the transmission of those institutional resources typically associated with academic success—either for their similarly privileged working-class peers and/or for their less privileged peers situated in networks outside the realm of privilege? I address this proposition and make a case for how we can carefully delineate those special conditions where working-class adolescents can, in fact, function as *social capital* for each other. Until this case can be made fully, it might very well be helpful to use the term *social resources* to speak to how peer relationships among working-class students can promote pro-academic subjectivities, behaviors, and performance in school.

ENGAGING SOCIAL CAPITAL THEORY

Delineating the basic features of social capital theory that can be strategically applied to the study of peer support among low-status youth is necessary to address the themes of this volume. I do this by describing the principal ways social capital has been elaborated within distinctive intellectual traditions in the social sciences. I begin with the tradition that has emphasized "social integration," then follow with the tradition widely recognized as the "Wisconsin model of status attainment." I then contrast these two traditions with a framework that highlights those features of social capital that make explicit the issue of differential power and privilege as well as the link between individual and group interactional processes *and* society's principal hierarchies of class, race, and gender. Exploring and contrasting these distinct perspectives (or dimensions of social capital) serves to alert us to the major ways in which peer relations generate forms of support that facilitate academic achievement and educational attainment.

In describing the more conventional use of "social capital" in educa-

tional research, I have selected the term *normative framework* for conven-
ience. According to the tradition focused on integrative processes, which
continues to dominate educational research, "academic learning, intellectual development, and persistence to degree completion are dependent
upon a student's level of personal engagement or social integration into the
social and intellectual fabric of the school" (Stanton-Salazar, 2001, p. 13).
Close relations or "connections" with parents, school personnel, and peers
each play a potentially key role through socialization processes that help
shape a proacademic identity and that facilitate adherence to the educational system's moral order and ideological foundations (Dreeban, 1968;
Parsons, 1959; Sewell & Hauser, 1980). Connections to "significant others"
is also understood in terms of socialization processes that inculcate those
cultural codes and competencies deemed necessary for literacy development and scholastic success; in sum, the writing on social capital guided by
normative frameworks typically emphasizes the inculcation of values and
cognitive dispositions and the effective enforcement of norms.

In any scenario presented via this framework, *peer social resources*
would be conceived in terms of reciprocal and supportive relations between the student and her peers and between student and school personnel; it is through these supportive relations that the individual becomes
"attached, committed, involved and has belief in the norms, activities and
people of an institution" (Wehlage, Rutter, Smith, Lesko, & Fernandez,
1989, p. 117). I summarized this view of supportive relations as follows:

> When such bonding between agent and student becomes a defining charac-
> teristic of the school community as whole, students experience a certain "we-
> ness," a collective identity that is highly consonant with increased effort en-
> gagement and academic achievement. In sum: school personnel treat students
> in a caring manner, creating the conditions for "bonding"; in turn, students
> come to identify with, and conform to, the established order; now integrated,
> students experience a heightened degree of motivation and make the neces-
> sary efforts to meet academic demands. (Stanton-Salazar, 2001, p. 13)

Peer groups are seen as vital to this integration process. This proacademic
"we-ness" is very much sustained by the peer group. Attachment to peer
groups properly "integrated" not only provides ready access to the emotional and psychological resources derived from friendship and group
membership but also provides for the accommodation to norms necessary
for school achievement. Simultaneously, the proper accommodation to proacademic norms, outside of school, facilitates "connections" to peer networks already integrated in the school.

The normative framework above shares much in common with the theoretical contributions of James Coleman (1988, 1990), who has done much to elaborate and popularize the concept of social capital, along with others such as Bourdieu and Putnam. Coleman emphasized the ability of some communities to establish interlocking ties that lay the groundwork for trust and the accumulation of experiences of mutual benefit, which in time leads to the formation of norms and sanctions that encourage people to work for the common good. In the framework above, these "norms and sanctions" are the tacit rules that guide social life and that create forms of power and influence in community social interactions. These "norms and sanctions" are treated as "social capital" of certain communities and organizations whose members are able to come together to activate or enforce these norms and sanctions for the purpose of motivating certain other members of the community (e.g., students) to engage in certain desired behaviors (e.g., the necessary effort to accomplish academic tasks).

Contrastingly, a body of literature conventionally referred to as the "Wisconsin model of status attainment" (see Sewell & Hauser, 1980) suggests that the process of social stratification is enabled greatly by key socialization processes in the family and that during adolescence peer groups become increasingly important. In this model, adolescents, as social beings, are viewed as deeply influenced by the attitudes and evaluations of their peers toward the self, and that in the course of time such appraisals are internalized and thus become reflected in the adolescents' view of themselves (Rosenberg, 1979). Specific attention to peer influences on educational attainment into adulthood focuses on the modeling of proacademic behaviors and on the influencing of educational aspirations.

In this particular tradition, different peer groups set different "standards" for what is appropriate behavior within the realm of scholastics, with such standards often lodged within the class and racialized cultures of their families and communities. These standards become the basis of the peer group "social structure" (basic rules or schemas) that drives social interaction and support. More experienced (and more firmly embedded) members of the peer community "model" and encourage appropriate or antischolastic standards of behavior and forms of consciousness while influencing and reinforcing the educational aspirations of others in the peer network (Coleman, 1961; Haller & Woefel, 1972; Picou & Carter, 1976). Aspirations drive individual effort engagement and degree of investment in school, which in turn largely determine educational attainment. Interpreted through this tradition, peer relations, as social resources, would be defined in terms of "connections" to peer groups that model and promulgate standards of academic/school behavior that promote academic effort engagement and academic success.

The normative framework represented by the two traditions above emphasizes one major way in which "connections" between people operate to facilitate purposeful actions and to accomplish desired ends—in this case, to bring individuals into a social system for the purpose of inculcating and reinforcing specific goals, cultural values, norms, aspirations, and identities seen as instrumental to academic achievement and educational attainment. Peer groups manifest their potential for acting as social resources when they are oriented toward assisting this integration process, or, in different terms, when they fulfill their capacity for reinforcing the dominant moral order through routine social relations.[2]

However, both the "social integration" and the Wisconsin traditions fail to fully address other key aspects of social structure that coexist in all forms of social relations in society. Both perspectives exist in a sociopolitical vacuum and fail to give adequate attention to those institutionalized structures and hierarchies that determine the quality of schools in different communities or that translate into blocked opportunities in the job market due to class, racial, or gender discrimination (see Kerckhoff, 1976). Thus, although communities sharing common interests may come together to pool their resources for the purpose of collective goals, it must be recognized (and addressed) that they do so while having to contend with those hierarchical divisions that organize their own community, and while contending with (or exploiting) their own location (and solidarities) in the principal hierarchies that organize society.

In contrast to the normative framework, represented by the two traditions above, a critical network-analytic view of social capital strives toward a comprehensive understanding of society, particularly as modeled in the work of Pierre Bourdieu. Bourdieu's elaboration of both social and cultural capital is situated within social reproduction theory, which seeks to explain how societal institutions perpetuate (or reproduce) the social relationships and attitudes needed to sustain class relations in a capitalist society (MacLeod, 1987). Key to this latter articulation of social capital, then, is its placement within a political-economic framework. Social capital is fundamentally an economic concept; accordingly, the concept of *capital* cannot be understood apart from the larger economic relations that dictate the control of society's principal material resources, the conversion of such resources into forms of wealth, power, authority, and social influence, and, ultimately, the unequal allocation of such "capital" to particular groups and individuals.[3] Indeed, capital—whether in its monetary, cultural, or social form—is not a thing at all but a *social relation*, which appears in the form of a thing (Bottomore, Harris, Kiernan, & Millband, 1983).

Whatever its form, capital within a particular social system and institutional context embodies a particular intergroup relation between those who have *it* and those who don't; it also embodies a particular process oriented toward continually protecting and reproducing such unequal relations. Such a process is guided by socially constructed yet tacit rules for legitimating economic relations (the distribution and regulation of wealth, power, and authority) and for constructing "borders" that regulate forms of solidarity and insidership necessary for the exclusive sharing or exchange of scarce and valued resources (Barth, 1969; Stanton-Salazar, 1997).

Situated within this political-economic framework and informed by various scholarly contributions to social capital theory, including Lin's (2001) important synthesis, I set forth the following conceptualization: Social capital can be represented as a storehouse of different types of resources, embedded in social relations, that can be mobilized when an individual or group wishes to increase the likelihood of success in a purposeful action. Access to this storehouse of resources and support (e.g., expert knowledge about scholarship opportunities) begins with personal "connections" to an individual or to an integrated network of individuals. In the literature on organizations and corporate firms, the colloquial term, "ol' boys' network" is recognizable; however, as we shall see in this volume, such "connections" can also include peers of the same social status. These social connections are mobilized on behalf of the individual or a group, either directly providing the needed resources and support or connecting the individual or group to other key figures, groups, or networks that ultimately facilitate goal accomplishment. Again, the mobilization of social relations for instrumental purposes always occurs within the context of structural relations of power, and within an economy that unequally distributes socially valued resources, as well as forms of solidarity that permit ready access to such resources through proximal ties and networks.

Our attention centers on these "connections" as the *relational* resources that are mobilized by the individual or group to secure goods and forms of support that facilitate the accomplishment of goals—within a particular institutional context organized by hierarchical relations of power and privilege and normalized by the dominant culture. Thus misinterpreting academic success as primarily contingent upon the internalization of "appropriate" values, norms, and identities by individual students is incongruent with a critical social capital theory (see my more expanded critique in Stanton-Salazar, 2001, pp. 12–16). Moral integration (i.e., conformity)—particularly for low-status students—in the absence of tangible forms of academic support, such as tutoring, is not sufficient to master the academic curriculum or decode the hidden curriculum—that tacit system of unspoken rules and regulations that organizes life in school, that determines how "ability" and "talent" are socially constructed (Simpson & Rosenholtz, 1986), that distributes pedagogical resources and opportunities, and that creates "deviants" and outcasts (see Fine, 1991; Rist, 1977). Thus, in a framework that articulates social resources as social capital, key forms of support are vital to effective participation within mainstream institutional spheres.

UNPACKING SOCIAL STRUCTURE

Recognizing social capital as "connections" to agents—who stand at the doorway of a storehouse of resources—is but the first crucial step toward understanding how individuals and groups mobilize their social relationships to attain their goals and experience "opportunities" in society. "Connections" are social capital not only because particular agents possess resources or because they have the capacity to provide key forms of institutional support; rather, such connections are "capital" because they embody key "social structural properties" that, when activated or exploited by actors, set in motion social psychological processes, deeply ingrained cultural rules, and social interactions that lead one through the door, into the storehouse, and eventually to those goods, resources, and supportive interactions that facilitate the accomplishment of goals. "Social structure" is the motor that propels all relationships, whether between individuals or between groups in society; it's what makes them *resource*-ful and, thus, enduring.

Social structures have two simultaneous and interactive dynamics that are mutually reinforcing. On the one hand, structure is composed of cultural schemas or procedures that guide social life and that create forms of power and influence in social interaction (Giddens, 1979, 1984; Sewell, 1992). For instance, relative to those who speak English with a heavy Spanish accent, Chicano students who speak without a Spanish accent, in a vernacular closely approximating standard English, are deemed to have "higher academic potential"—a cultural schema. On the other hand, forms of power and influence (i.e., resources) create and sustain the cultural schemas that guide social relations. The mutually reinforcing *schemas* and *resources* (or forms of power) operate in ways that produce what we see as the recurrent and enduring social practices that make up social life in families, schools, school systems, governmental bodies, the workplace, and the economy.

These fundamental structural properties—resources and schemas—can be translated in ways to illuminate the relation between social capital and familiar forms of social organization. Cultural schemas or procedures that value and encourage cooperative activity and reciprocal exchange, shared meaning-making, and continual assessments of common interests motivate members of large and small communities, nationally and locally. Among Latino student communities, cultural schemas underlying instances of solidarity may be linked to any number of statuses rooted in community life (e.g., generational status, length of residence, neighborhood affiliation, previous school membership, language proficiencies, mutual affiliation in school organizations, and, of course, academic track or curricular program) (see Matute-Bianchi, 1986; Valenzuela, 1999). Such schemas are mobilized as the basis for the further building of trust and for the accumulation of experiences of mutual benefit within the realm of school. On the basis of these "schemas," actors establish relationships or connections that serve as the basis for the further building of trust and for the accumulation of experiences of mutual benefit that, in time, become a form of protected and growing investment (Lin, 2001; Portes, 1998). When needed, such investments are activated into forms of social support that facilitate the accomplishment of goals. Eventual reciprocity keeps the investment, and the productive potential of these relations, growing.

However, society, with its imposition of multiple social hierarchies, is exceedingly more complex than this. A key structural property underlying social capital has to do with how connected actors and agents are themselves both linked to larger forms of social organization in society that tacitly specify the schemas or procedures for how people are to be arranged hierarchically and for how resources and privileges are to be distributed—primarily by class, gender, and race (Bourdieu, 1977; Bourdieu & Passeron, 1977; Giddens, 1984; Sewell, 1992; see also Lamont & Lareau, 1988). Such schemas or procedures, and their associated resources and privileges, are precisely those basic structural properties that can be activated or exploited for personal or collective gain (e.g., men activate their gender identity in order to secure a host of privileges in family life, in the workplace, and in public contexts; high school students who are officers or regular participants of the student government activate their organizational identity to secure support from each other and especially from school personnel).

The rules of hierarchy facilitate forms of solidarity and instant membership in "community" among those who occupy similar locations in the hierarchy. Thus actors are able to immediately "connect" with resource-ful others by activating social structure (i.e., by accelerating "the motor"), by adhering to the rules of hierarchy, by identifying their location in the larger social organization and establishing legitimate insidership. On the basis of this social structure, actors are then able to advance the investment process on a more personal level and to sooner or later turn this investment into forms of support (and forms of exclusion) that facilitate the accomplishment of personal or collective goals (e.g., admission into the university).

The rules of hierarchy, embodied in all social relations operative in society, also establish the means by which subordinate or low-status members in the hierarchy (e.g., children, women, working-class folk, minorities) are able to "connect" with their superiors (adults, men, middle-class folk, gatekeepers), make relational investments, and, it is hoped, gain access to the storehouse—particularly to forms of "institutional support" (e.g., key funds of knowledge, advocacy). However, being able to build upon those "structures" that establish immediate solidarity and access to resources and opportunities usually requires successfully negotiating institutional conditions and structural properties oriented toward exclusion from the storehouse and blocked access to forms of institutional support necessary for success within the institution (e.g., "tracking" in the school system; the "glass ceiling" in the corporate workplace) (see Portes & Landolt, 1996; Stanton-Salazar, 1997).

"SOCIAL CAPITAL" IN WORKING-CLASS ADOLESCENT PEER RELATIONSHIPS

key issue

At this point, let's return to the key issue: Can peer relations among working-class minority youth constitute adultlike "social capital?" More specifically and salient to our exploration of social capital theory: In what ways might peer relations among these youth constitute such social capital in light of both theoretical frameworks delineated herein? The research, framed by either the Coleman or the Wisconsin perspective, on the role of peers in the schooling process attends to the internalization of norms, aspirations, and identities. In these models, "peer social capital" is merely an extension of social capital in family spheres, and conceivably articulated as "connections" to peer groups that encourage standards of scholastic behavior and forms of consciousness that foster academic effort engagement, academic success, and educational attainment. Thus, although many working-class status and minority youth come from families and communities that experience difficulty in providing the proper class-specific socialization deemed necessary for school success, alternative sites within the school and community do provide compensatory opportunities for many low-status youth to receive the proper support, socialization, and integration. And within these contexts, peer relations with similar others play an important mediating role.

The potential for working-class youth to experience high levels of motivation, increased effort engagement, and academic achievement exists when working-class peer relations are situated within a supportive school context founded by interlocking ties between the school, the community, and the student community that lay the groundwork for the accumulation of experiences of mutual benefit, which in time leads to embracing norms that encourage them to work for the common good (Coleman & Hoffer, 1987; Wehlage et al., 1989). Peer networks, indeed, play a very important mediating role for the larger relationship between the school and community. Following this logic, it would also seem that other working-class students previously not participating in such supportive school contexts, but newly introduced and progressively embedded in these integrated peer networks, would soon derive substantial "benefit" from these peer relations—particularly in the form of socialization messages that assigned *value* and status to proacademic identities and behaviors.

In contrast, a critical network-analytic approach to supportive peer relations among working-class students addresses whether peers can reasonably act as agents for, and sources of, those institutional resources and forms of "capital" structurally associated with power, privilege, and insidership. In both frameworks, peer-group social structure, when oriented toward achievement in school, is defined by cultural schemas that value and encourage cooperative activity and reciprocal exchange, shared meaning-making, and continual assessments of common interests (for examples of this see Conchas, 2001; Valenzuela, 1999)—and these schemas are activated for the purpose of gaining access to forms of support that facilitate achievement in school. Both social capital frameworks described here have more or less the same capacity to articulate the role of these structural properties in the schooling process. The critical difference is that in this latter framework, three interrelated aspects are given prominence:

1. Although the normative framework highlights the role of universalistic norms, values, and identities, the more critical Bourdieuian framework highlights forms of "institutional support" that are not easily accessible throughout society.
2. Those privileged by class, race, and gender use such "support" to secure and reproduce their position in the stratified social order.
3. The concept of "social capital" highlights the common practice of discrimination and exclusion (Portes & Landolt, 1996)—a particular relation between those who have *power, capital,* and *privilege* and those who don't.

As stated earlier, the latter social capital framework often embodies a particular process that continually protects and reproduces such unequal relations, making it difficult to use in describing supportive and empowering relations among working-class youth.

And yet, in the sphere of the adult working-class community, individuals, groups, networks, and enclaves do find institutional channels that make it possible for them to accumulate economic capital, political influence, institutional resources, and connections to middle-class institutional agents and gate-keepers. In doing so, they manifest their new capacity to function as social capital to "significant others," both to similarly privileged "others" in their working-class networks and to disadvantaged "others" in their extended networks who claim solidarity and comembership (e.g., kinship) and who successfully assert their right to enter into reciprocal exchange relations. Although such pockets of working-class social capital may have little overall effect on the position of the working class as a whole in the larger political economy, they do afford significant individual social mobility and certain concessions on the part of the dominant group (Willis, 1977).

Similarly, some working-class students do find institutional channels such as resourceful community-based organizations, residential relocation programs, highly selective curricular tracks or programs (see Chapter 6, this volume), and supportive school organizations (see Chapter 7, this volume) that enable them to gain access to supportive middle-class agents and to forms of institutional support. As do their adult counterparts, they too manifest their new capacity to function as social capital for "significant others," particularly for those of similar class and ethnic backgrounds. Likewise, although such pockets of "peer social capital" within a school may have little overall effect on the position of working-class students at the school or in their community, they do often enable a good number of students to successfully complete high school and to continue on to college. And although it might be irksome to hear, our most championed reform efforts, at best, have positive effects on creating access and opportunity for a numerical minority, while leaving the structural circumstances of the majority intact (e.g., school funding, qualified teachers; see Berliner & Biddle, 1995). For middle-class students, peer social capital embodies a particular group relation among the *haves*—relative to the *have nots;* for working-class students, peer social capital embodies instances of individual mobility, of overcoming the odds, of becoming exceptions to the rule—yet with the rules and schemas still firmly in place and continually reproduced.

WORKING-CLASS ADOLESCENT PEER NETWORKS AS BOTH MEDIATORS AND MODERATORS

The unique position of peer networks might be understood in terms of their middle position between the adolescent and the larger overlapping and interacting adult networks of which he or she is a part. Seen in this way, peer networks can be said to embody the potential to take on two alternative functions. First, peer networks can *mediate* (i.e., be in an intermediate position, acting as a medium for bringing about) the proscholastic normative influences and resources generated in the larger adult network. Alternatively, peer networks can *moderate* the proscholastic normative influences and resources generated in the larger adult network, serving to restrain these influences, for example, by sustaining an oppositional peer subculture that renders them unreceptive to the forms of social support generated by adult institutional agents (see Brake, 1985; Stanton-Salazar, 2001; Chapters 4 and 5, this volume).

The mediating potential of peer networks helps explain how working-class peer networks can potentially function as authentic social capital. A specific relationship or network may not, in and of itself, function as the actual source of valuable institutional resources (e.g., insider information about college scholarships), but because this relationship, or network, functions as a genuine pathway or mediating link to such resources, it qualifies as a social form of "capital." Precisely because such capital can be converted into relations of real value in the marketplace or hierarchy, it facilitates access to agents and to networks that do, in fact, possess those resources and control forms of support and influence typically necessary for attaining difficult institutional goals (e.g., receiving a college scholarship).

Thus the issue here is not so much whether homogeneous working-class student networks generate and distribute the more obvious forms of institutional support, such as middle-class funds of knowledge pertaining to higher education and to "networking." For that matter, middle-class student networks, although they often engage in the exchange of valuable funds of knowledge and of other key forms of support, embody social capital mainly because of their plentiful connections to, and embeddedness in, adult networks situated within powerful institutional sites within the middle and upper classes. Middle-class peer groups mediate the power and influence, norms, and identities, as well as knowledge funds and cultural capital, generated in the adult communities that routinely participate in power (Ianni, 1998). Although proscholastic working-class peer groups are not, by definition, socially embedded within the middle class, they too can be embedded within institutional sites that generate plentiful resources and proacademic norms. And when such peer networks manifest their *mediating* capacity, they can and do function as social capital for those whose success in school depends on having as many open pathways as possible to vital forms of institutional support and to structures that reinforce proacademic norms and identities.

In some school contexts, socialization into norms and the sharing of institutional support occur simultaneously. For example, in a program called AVID ("Advancement Via Individual Determination," a misnomer considering that achievement of working-class minority high school students is governed largely by strong collectivist practices), peer networks both mediate and moderate in an integrative manner, demonstrating how adult and peer social-capital accumulation function as the basis for both individual and collective academic success (Mehan et al., 1996; Stanton-Salazar, 2001).

In my study of one particular AVID program (Stanton-Salazar, 2001), I found that through supportive relations between the student and the AVID teacher, and between students, AVID participants became attached, committed, and involved in academic endeavors; in a very real sense, AVID participants both activated and mediated the benefits inherent in the program's design. As a collective, AVID students reaffirmed for each other a belief that success was possible for them within a racialized and segregated school system. The AVID teacher treated students in a highly caring and personalized manner, creating the conditions for an unusual level of "bonding"; in turn, students were willing to subscribe to the high scholastic standards she set for the cohort. These normative standards became the basis of the "social structure" that governed peer relations in the group, including norms or "procedures" for mutual support based on communitarian principles. AVID students "modeled" and reinforced for each other appropriate standards of behavior, cooperative activity, and forms of consciousness that inevitably led to increased effort engagement.

However, a more tenable explanation is that AVID "worked," at least at this school, because "support" came in the form of proacademic norms and identities and, simultaneously, in the form of "institutional support" (see Stanton-Salazar, 1997). Guided by strong sociological intuitions, this particular AVID teacher made the "hidden curriculum" of the school system a key part of the explicit AVID curriculum. The tacit system of unspoken schemas that organized success and failure in the school system were unpacked, spoken, and codified in this AVID classroom. AVID students came to understand that rational decision making within the school and academic realm necessitated regular and continued access to networks, institutional agents, and funds of knowledge that often were not easily accessible for working-class minority students. Not only did the AVID teacher become a primary source or conduit for such funds of knowledge (see Stanton-Salazar, 2001), but she also instructed students how to act as conduits for each other. Thus peer relations in the AVID program functioned not only as sources of socialization and for the promulgation of proacademic norms but also as connections or pathways to a storehouse of different types of institutional support: to different funds of knowledge, to peer tutoring on academic subject matter, to individual classmates who acted as a *bridge* to resources outside the AVID classroom, and to peer counseling that focused on rational approaches to personal problems that affected progress in school.

CLOSING THOUGHTS

As I have argued in previous works, although both dimensions of social capital appear to be important in accounting for differential school achievement, at this time, these two dimensions are not equal in their capacity to illuminate fundamental sociological processes underlying how people do or do not achieve "success" in our society. Network-analytic accounts of social capital—those specifically that draw from social reproduction theory—are distinguishable by their recognition of the struggle for power and resources between the dominant and subordinate classes—in short, by their recognition of cultural, social, and economic forms of domination. In contrast, most normative accounts of social capital do not recognize this sociopolitical context. Again, the solution is not to adopt reproductionist frameworks to the exclusion of social integrationist processes but rather to depict social capital at least as a two-dimensional phenomenon that operates in a myriad of inherently politicized institutional contexts (Bourdieu's "fields"). In doing so, we not only see that "school success" is engineered institutionally largely according to the dictates of the dominant group's culture and political interests, but also that important political concessions have been made throughout our history (e.g., desegregation, bilingual education, multicultural curricula, and college preparatory programs for minority students). Perhaps more importantly for researchers, a social capital framework founded on a recognition of power dynamics and societal inequality sensitizes us to the kinds of ecological contexts in which many minority and low-status youth grow up. These contexts have regularly been described with the metaphor of ideological "battleground," where youth are subjected to contradictory forces competing over which system of values, ideologies, expectations, emotions, and coping styles are most appropriate, legitimate, and productive in key institutional sites (school, family, peer network, streets). Contemporary research on the cultural strategies of students from racialized communities alerts us to the challenges entailed in students' participation in multiple and often conflictive cultural worlds (Phelan, Davidson, & Yu, 1998; Valenzuela, 1999), and particularly to the difficulties they face when institutional practices are put in place in the school and community that function too often to generate distrust and contempt between students and institutional agents (Fine, 1991; Stanton-Salazar, 2001). The point here is that for low-status students, peer relations in school and peer support are deeply embedded in this terrain of struggle and contradiction. Thus, for such relations to manifest their capacity for social capital and proacademic support, such conflict and contradiction must be effectively addressed by those adults, policymakers, and educators who govern social life in the schools. The immediate challenge, then, for the researcher and for the educator is to find ways of neutralizing or minimizing this conflict within the school, and to assist the individual, the peer group, and/or the larger peer community in developing empowering ways to participate in their multiple and culturally disparate worlds—not only for the purpose of individual educational success, but also as a means for preparing to become an effective and determined *agent of social change* and *social justice*. For researchers and educators, this challenge includes learning much more about how this transformative process can and has happen for low-status students and for different school communities throughout the country.

ACKNOWLEDGMENTS

My thanks to the editors, and to Jill Koyama in particular, for their useful feedback and special assistance on earlier versions of this chapter.

NOTES

1. For a recent critical synthesis of published literature on social capital in the education field (including both theoretical and empirical works), see Dika and Singh (2002). Their review focuses on studies that link social capital with educational outcomes and covers works published throughout the 1990s. The authors also trace the intellectual history of the concept and its rapid adoption by educational researchers. Particularly helpful is their discussion of the gaps in the conceptualization, measurement, and analysis of social capital in educational research.

2. Many people mistakenly confuse cultural capital and social capital. Although both concepts are linked to Bourdieu's theory of social and cultural reproduction, many people link "cultural capital" to Bourdieu while linking "social capital" to James Coleman. The concepts, in Bourdieu's framework, are related but need to be seen as distinct phenomena. *Cultural capital* can be most easily associated with sociolinguistic standards and cultural behaviors, whereas *social capital* refers to social relationships and networks. Bourdieu (1977) used "cultural capital" to highlight a form of ubiquitous and hidden "power" wielded by the dominant group to ensure their survival at the top of the societal class hierarchy. Ultimately the upper middle class and the upper class in society have the power to control the school system and its curriculum—for the most part. They are able to do this by assigning value (i.e., capital) to the cultural practices of the dominant group and by designing curricula that make it necessary for students to already have these practices down in order to succeed scholastically. It is as if some children were to come to school with U.S. dollars and the others with the equivalence of Mexican pesos. Both groups may have equal currency in a technical and objective sense, but the school only officially honors dollars. The ability to do this is about the consolidation of *power* and about the domination by one group over everyone else. This is the

crux of Bourdieu's contribution. So it doesn't matter what the truth is: That is, minority students come to school with lots of cultural currency or resources, or "funds of knowledge" (see Moll, Amanti, Neff, & Gonzalez, 1992), but the school is not committed to "valuing" and sanctioning these cultural resources. Current school policies around bilingual instruction confirm this (California's Proposition 227).

3. "Pierre Bourdieu (1986) has argued that the laws governing the exchange of economic capital are applicable to human social relations in all their various forms. Thus, social capital is (1) cumulative, (2) possesses the capacity to produce profits or benefits in the social world, (3), is convertible into tangible resources or other forms of capital and (4) possesses the capacity to reproduce itself in identical or in expanded form. Just as a twenty-dollar bill represents a form of capital that can be converted into a desired service or product, a social relationship, or a network of relationships, also represent forms of capital that can be converted into socially valued resources and opportunities (e.g., emotional support, legitimated institutional roles and identities, privileged information, access to opportunities for mobility). Simply stated, social ties and networks carry the potential to generate valued resources" (Stanton-Salazar, 1997, p. 8).

REFERENCES

Adler, P. S., & Kwon, S. (2001). *Social capital: The good, the bad, and the ugly.* Modified version of a paper presented at the 1999 Academy of Management Meeting, Chicago, IL.

Bankston C. L., & Zhou, M. (1995). Effects of minority-language literacy on the academic achievement of Vietnamese youths in New Orleans. *Sociology of Education, 68,* 1–17.

Barth, F. (1969). *Ethnic groups and boundaries: The social organization of cultural difference.* London: Allen & Unwin.

Berliner, D. C., & Biddle, B. J. (1995). *The manufactured crisis: Myths, frauds, and the attack on America's public schools.* Reading, MA: Addison-Wesley.

Bianchi, S. M., & Robinson, J. (1997). What did you do today? Children's use of time, family composition, and the acquisition of social capital. *Journal of Marriage and the Family, 59,* 332–344.

Bourdieu, P. (1977). Cultural reproduction and social reproduction. In J. Karabel & A. H. Halsey (Eds.), *Power and ideology in education* (pp. 487–511). New York: Oxford University Press.

Bourdieu, P. (1986). The forms of capital. In J. G. Richardson (Ed.), *Handbook of theory and research for the sociology of education.* New York: Greenwood Press.

Bourdieu, P., & Passeron, J. (1977). *Reproduction in education, society, and culture.* London: Sage.

Bottomore, T., Harris, L., Kiernan, V. G., & Millband, R. (Eds.). (1983). *A dictionary of Marxist thought.* Cambridge, MA: Harvard University Press.

Brake, M. (1985). *Comparative youth culture: The sociology of youth culture and youth subcultures in America, Britain, and Canada.* London and New York: Routledge.

Carbonaro, W. (1998). A little help from my friend's parents: Intergenerational closure and educational outcomes. *Sociology of Education, 71,* 295–313.

Coleman, J. S. (1961). *The adolescent society.* New York: Free Press of Glencoe.

Coleman, J. S. (1988). Social capital in the creation of human capital. *American Journal of Sociology, 94,* S95–S120.

Coleman, J. S. (1990). *Foundations of social theory.* Cambridge, MA: The Belknap
Press of Harvard University Press.

Coleman, J. S., & Hoffer, T. (1987). *Public and private high schools: The impact of communities.* New York: Basic Books.

Conchas, G. Q. (2001). Structuring failure and success: Understanding the variability in Latino students' engagement. *Harvard Educational Review, 71*(3), 475–504.

Croninger, R. G., & Lee, V. (1999). *Social capital and dropping out of school: Benefits to
at-risk students of teachers' support and guidance.* Unpublished manuscript.

De Souza Briggs, X. (1997). Social capital and the cities: Advice to change agents.
National Civic Review, 86(2), 111–117.

Dika, S. L., & Singh, K. (2002, Spring). Applications of social capital in educational
literature: A critical synthesis. *Review of Educational Research, 72*(1), 31–60.

Dreeban, R. (1968). *On what is learned in school.* Reading, MA: Addison-Wesley.

Fine, M. (1991). *Framing dropouts: Notes on the politics of an urban public high school.* Albany: State University of New York Press.

Fritch, W. S. (1999). *An overlooked role of high school athletics: The formation of social capital through parental involvement.* Paper presented at the American Educational
Research Association, Montreal, Canada.

Furstenberg, F., & Hughes M. (1995). Social capital and successful development
among at-risk youth. *Journal of Marriage and the Family, 57,* 580–592.

Giddens, A. (1979). *Central problems in social theory: Action, structure, and contradiction in social analysis.* Berkeley and Los Angeles: University of California Press.

Giddens, A. (1984). *The constitution of society: Outline of the theory of structuration.*
Berkeley and Los Angeles: University of California Press.

Haller, A. O., & Woefel, J. (1972). Significant others and their expectations: Concepts and instruments to measure interpersonal influence on status aspirations. *Rural Sociology, 37*(4), 591–622.

Hao, L., & Bonstead-Bruns, M. (1998). Parent-child differences in educational expectations and the academic achievement of immigrant and native students.
Sociology of Education, 71, 175–198.

Hofferth, S., Boisjoly, J., & Duncan, G. (1998). Parents' extrafamilial resources and
children's school attainment. *Sociology of Education, 71,* 246–268.

Ianni, F. (1998). *The search for structure: American youth today.* New York: The Free Press.

Israel, G. D., Beaulieu, L. J., & Hartless, G. (2001). The influence of family and community social capital on educational achievement. *Rural Sociology, 66*(1), 43–68.

Kalmijn, M., & Kraaykamp, G. (1996). Race, cultural capital, and schooling: An
analysis of trends in the United States. *Sociology of Education, 69,* 22–34.

Kerckhoff, A. (1976). The status attainment process: Socialization or allocation? *Social Forces, 55*(22), 368–381.

Lamont, M., & Lareau, A. (1988). Cultural capital: Allusions, gaps, and glissandos
in recent theoretical developments. *Sociological theory, 6,* 153–168.

Lin, N. (2001). *Social capital: A theory of social structure and action.* New York: Cambridge University Press.

López, E. (1996). *Social capital and the educational performance of Latino and non-Latino youth.* San Luis Obispo, CA: Julian Samora Research Institute.

MacLeod, J. (1987). *Ain't no makin' it: Aspirations and attainment in a low-income neighborhood.* Boulder, CO: Westview Press.

Maeroff, G. I. (1998). *Altered destinies: Making life better for schoolchildren in need.* New York: St. Martin's Press.

Matute-Bianchi, M. E. (1986). Ethnic identities and patterns of school success and failure among Mexican-descent and Japanese-American students in a California school. *American Journal of Education, 95,* 233–255.

McNeil, R. (1999). Parental involvement as social capital: Differential effectiveness on science achievement, truancy, and dropping out. *Social Forces, 78*(1), 117–144.

McPartland, J. M., Dawkins, R. L., Braddock, J., Crain, R. L., & Strauss, J. (1985). Three reports: Effects of employer job placement decisions, and school desegregation on minority and female hiring and occupational attainment (Report 359, Center for Social Organization of Schools). Baltimore: Johns Hopkins University.

Mehan, H., Villanueva, I., Hubbard, L., & Lintz, A. (1996). *Constructing school success: The consequences of untracking low-achieving students.* New York: Cambridge University Press.

Moll, L. C., Amanti, C., Neff, D., & Gonzalez, N. (1992). Funds of knowledge for teaching: Using a qualitative approach to connect homes and classrooms. *Theory Into Practice, 31*(2), 132–141.

Morgan, S., & Sorensen, A. (1999). Parental networks, social closure, and mathematics learning: A test of Coleman's social capital explanation of school effects. *American Sociological Review, 64,* 661–681.

Muller, C., & Ellison, C. G. (2001). Religious involvement, social capital, and adolescents' academic progress: Evidence from the National Educational Longitudinal Study of 1988. *Sociological Focus, 34*(2), 155–183.

Narayan, D., & Pritchett, L. (1977). *Cents and sociability: Household income and social capital in rural Tanzania.* Washington, DC: World Bank, Social Development and Development Research Group, Poverty and Human Resources.

Parsons, T. (1959). The school class as a social system: Some of its functions in American society. *Harvard Educational Review, 29*(4).

Phelan, P., Davidson, A. L., & Yu, H. C. (1998). *Adolescents' worlds: Negotiating family, peers, and school.* New York: Teachers College Press.

Picou, J. S., & Carter, T. M. (1976). Significant-other influence and aspirations. *Sociology of Education, 49,* 12–22.

Portes, A. (1998). Social capital: Its origins and applications in modern sociology. *Annual Review of Sociology, 24*(1), 1–24.

Portes, A., & Landolt, P. (1996). The downside of social capital. *American Prospect, 26,* 18–22.

Rist, R. (1977). On understanding the processes of schooling: The contributions of labeling theory. In J. Karabel & A. H. Halsey (Eds.), *Power and ideology in education* (pp. 292–305). New York: Oxford University Press.

Rosenbaum, J. (2000). Housing programs can do more than provide shelter: They can radically improve lives. *Boston Review, 25*(3), 16–17.

Rosenberg, M. (1979). *Conceiving the self.* New York: Basic Books.

Sewell, W. H., Jr. (1992). A theory of structure: Duality, agency, and transformation. *American Journal of Sociology, 98*(1), 1–29.

Sewell, W. H., & Hauser, R. M. (1980). The Wisconsin longitudinal study of social and psychological factors in aspirations and achievements. *Research in Sociology of Education and Socialization, 1,* 59–99.

Simpson, C. H., & Rosenholtz, S. J. (1986). In J. G. Richardson (Ed.), *Handbook of theory and research for the sociology of education* (pp. 113–138). New York: Greenwork Press.

Stanton-Salazar, R. D. (1997). A social capital framework for understanding the socialization of racial minority children and youth. *Harvard Educational Review, 67*(1), 1–40.

Stanton-Salazar, R. D. (2001). *Manufacturing hope and despair: The school and kin support networks of U.S.-Mexican youth.* New York: Teachers College Press.

Stanton-Salazar, R. D., & Dornbusch, S. M. (1995). Social capital and the social reproduction of inequality: The formation of informational networks among Mexican-origin high school students. *Sociology of Education, 68*(2), 116–135.

Teachman, J., Paasch, K., & Carver, K. (1996). Social capital and dropping out of school early. *Journal of Marriage and the Family, 58,* 773–783.

Valenzuela, A. (1999). *Subtractive schooling: U.S.-Mexican youth and the politics of caring.* Albany: State University of New York Press.

Valenzuela, A., & Dornbusch, S. (1994). Familism and social capital in the academic achievement of Mexican-origin and Anglo-adolescents. *Social Science Quarterly, 75,* 18–36.

Wehlage, G. G., Rutter, R. A., Smith, G. A., Lesko, N., & Fernandez, R. R. (1989). *Reducing the risk: Schools as communities of support.* Philadelphia: Falmer Press.

Willis, P. (1977). *Learning to labor: How working class kids get working class jobs.* New York: Columbia University Press.

Wright, J. P., Cullen, F. T., & Miller, J. T. (2001). Family social capital and delinquent involvement. *Journal of Criminal Justice, 29,* 1–9.

3

The Changing Shape of Aspirations: Peer Influence on Achievement Behavior

Patricia Gándara, Susan O'Hara, & Dianna Gutiérrez

There is a saying that the apple doesn't fall far from the tree, meaning that children tend to resemble their parents in behaviors, beliefs, and customs, and also in social status. Likewise, the aspirations of most young people will reflect those of the people in their immediate environment. This tends to be painfully true for most low-income youth. However, this is not always the case, and particularly for some immigrant groups, there may be vast differences between the social status of the parents and that of their off-spring. Some immigrants, for example, have been especially successful at propelling their progeny into much higher status positions in society than the ones they themselves hold (Rumbaut & Cornelius, 1995; Steinberg, 1996). But this is much less common for Mexican immigrants or for students from Mexican-origin families than for some other ethnic groups. Speculation abounds as to why such differences exist (see, e.g., Gibson & Ogbu, 1991; Ogbu, 1978; Trueba, 1988), and some researchers point to culturally embedded differences in the way that families value school. Clearly, sociohistorical factors, as well as real differences in the social and economic strength of particular ethnic communities, affect the ways and degree to which parents are able to support their children's schooling. But students do not grow and develop in a vacuum, and the home is not the sole influence on students' behaviors. Thus such explanations fall short of providing an understanding of the different roles of families, peers, and schools in shaping students' aspirations. Nonetheless, one thing is certain: There are choices that students make in high school that either place them on a path to personal and academic success or lead them in a very different direction. To what extent, and in what ways, do peers, friends, and school context influence these choices? The study reported in this chapter attempted to answer this question by looking at the experiences of diverse high school students in both an urban and a rural context, and here we focus on the findings for English-speaking Mexican-origin students compared with all other English-speaking students in their schools. Although the study reported here included Latino students who were overwhelmingly of Mexican origin, much of the literature on these students does not differentiate among Latino subgroups. Therefore in some cases we use the term *Latino* where studies have been nonspecific, and in other cases we use the term *Latino* where the composition of the group is either unclear or may include some Latino students who were not of Mexican origin.

As pointed out in Chapter 1, Mexican-origin students are at very high risk for school failure, and academic performance indicators for this group are exceptionally low. Although this poor academic performance is undoubtedly the product of many social and structural factors, including poor schools and communities, ill-prepared teachers, overworked counselors, a tracking system that forecloses opportunity, and language barriers, the relatively low academic aspirations (desire to do well in school, complete high school, and go on to college) of Mexican-origin youth cannot be fully explained by any of these circumstances or conditions. African Americans, growing up in similar circumstances, profess to have higher aspirations for going to college, and poor Asians from the same social class do, in fact, go to college at much higher rates than Mexican Americans. Researchers have pondered these findings in an attempt to better understand the attitudes and behavior of Mexican American youth, and a number of explanations have been offered for their relatively limited success in school. One of those explanations is the influence of peers.

Peers influence each other's school performance both positively and negatively. Although there are peers who encourage their friends to cut class or skip school, there are also adolescents who put pressure on their friends to stay committed to school (Brown & Theobald, 1998). Researchers have found, for example, that Asian students tend to socialize with friends who place a relatively greater emphasis on academics than do students in comparable Black and Latino friendship groups. Overall, Black and Latino students' friends earn lower grades, spend less time on their studies, and have substantially lower performance standards (Steinberg, 1996). Valverde's (1987) study of urban adolescent Latino students concluded that the impact of peers was a stronger determining factor in students' decisions to drop out or remain in school than any other factor with the exception of grades. And, of course, a student's grades have been shown to be correlated with friends' grades (Epstein & Karweit, 1983). Thus the notion that peers may affect school achievement and academic aspirations is not without substantial support in the literature.

However, most studies of peer influence and student achievement are based on "point-in-time" data that can only partially explain a phenomenon that clearly takes place over time and is shaped by the changing forces in a young person's life. Moreover, little is reported in the literature about the circumstances under which students support or undermine each other's achievement. The study we report on here followed the high school class of 2001 from the time the students were freshmen in a large rural and a large urban high school, and attempted to map the changing shape of their aspirations and the factors that influenced them.

THE CRITICAL IMPORTANCE OF DEVELOPMENT

Developmental psychologists view adolescence as a period in which young people seek to establish a stable identity (Erikson, 1968; Marcia, 1976; Swanson, Spencer, & Petersen, 1998). Many researchers have suggested that this is a period of particular stress and turmoil (Csikszentmihalyi & Schmidt, 1998; Eccles et al., 1993), and hence of particular vulnerability to the views and judgment of others. This may be especially true for ethnic-minority students who may also have to confront personal rejection or disapproval from others if they choose to identify with their racial or ethnic group (Phinney, 1989). Erikson (1968) described the primary task of adolescence as one of "trying on" different personas in search of an integrated ego identity. Theory suggests that selection of a stable identity is influenced by the reactions of peers and others to the proposed personas. The source of potential personas is described by Markus and Nurius (1986) as a search for "possible selves" based on one's sociohistorical context and the availability of significant others in the environment who can serve as role models or prototypes. Parents, peers, and, to a lesser extent, school personnel and other members of the community may provide models of possible selves (Cooper, Jackson, Azmitia, Lopez, & Dunbar, 1995; Phelan, Davidson, & Cao, 1991). Gándara (1995) has shown that some non-Latino peers may be important role models for Latino students with high aspirations when they come into contact with each other in school. In these cases, peers may provide the social capital—information, support, and guidance—that is missing in their own environments (see discussion in Chapter 2, this volume). However, the academic segregation of most high schools impedes these opportunities for close contact among students with academically heterogeneous backgrounds (Gamoran, 1992). As such, working-class Mexican-origin youth may see many fewer possible selves available to them than do their middle-class mainstream peers.

Developmental psychologists also note that vulnerability to peer judgments may shift over time for adolescents. Coleman (1980), for example, argued that the impact of peer influence is curvilinear—increasing up to about age 14, and decreasing thereafter. Moreover, researchers have long noted that peer influence is dependent not only on the age of the student but also on the area of influence. Some have argued that long-term goals, such as post high school plans, are less vulnerable to peer influence and more related to parental influences across age groups (Kandel & Lesser, 1969; McDill & Coleman, 1965). In a meta-analysis of 10 studies, Ide, Parkerson, Haertel, and Walberg (1981) found a significant correlation between peer academic characteristics and students' educational outcomes. They also found a stronger correlation in the later years of high school. One interpretation of this, although not the only one, could be that, developmentally, students are more responsive to peer influence *on academics* in later adolescence. Socioeconomic status is almost certainly an important consideration as well, as lower income students and their families will have less social capital and consequently may be more dependent on others to help navigate educational pathways. Another important consideration, however, is that the contexts in which adolescents are developing have changed dramatically over the last few decades as young people spend much more time alone or with peers than in earlier times (Schneider & Stevenson, 1999), and peer influence may have taken on a more important role over time.

PEERS AND IDENTITY DEVELOPMENT
IN CHICANO/LATINO ADOLESCENTS

Research on adolescents is consistent in finding that peers play a critical role in development (Brown & Theobald, 1998), but it is less consistent in defining who these "peers" are. As discussed in Chapter 1, peers can be classified into a number of categories, from intimate friend to merely "other kids in this school." Most research on adolescent peer influence has been conducted in high schools with relatively homogeneous White populations (Eckert, 1989; Epstein & Karweit, 1983; Ide et al., 1981; Peshkin, 1991), so that relatively little is known about peer interactions and influence in ethnically diverse settings. What is known from the meager research on diverse schools is that in these schools peer groups are often defined primarily by ethnicity and only secondarily by other attributes (Foley, 1990; Peshkin, 1991). For all students, but particularly for ethnic-minority students, teachers' expectations of students will be influenced by the crowd the student belongs to and what the general impression is of that crowd's attitudes toward school (Eckert, 1989; Foley, 1990). Some ethnic-minority adolescents, including some Latinos, equate school with assimilation into the dominant culture and a concomitant rejection of their own language and culture. These students may actively resist this acculturation by not doing well in school. Many of these adolescents may believe they must choose between maintaining their ethnic identity and striving for high academic achievement, which to their peers may be viewed as acting superior or "acting White" (Fordham & Ogbu, 1986). Once an adolescent has identified with a particular group, the group's standards become internalized and incorporated into his or her own sense of self. Therefore, adhering to the norms and standards of the group does not feel like succumbing to peer pressure; it feels more like an expression of one's own identity (Steinberg, 1996). Inasmuch as research on adolescents' educational aspirations and expectations has found these to be generally low in Chicano/Latino students and related to social class (Gándara, Gutiérrez, & O'Hara, 2001; Kao & Tienda, 1998), having low aspirations for schooling can come to be seen as an inherent characteristic of being Mexican American. For the high-achieving Mexican American student who chooses to "hang with his homeboys" and who goes to a school in which Mexicans have been typed as low achievers, this can produce a significant dilemma. Only very popular students—star athletes, for example—seem to be able to move seamlessly across high- and low-achieving peer groups without being stigmatized (Foley, 1990).

Matute-Bianchi's (1991) research in a central valley California high school concluded that the identity that Mexican American students adopt may also signal their own achievement orientation. She found that Mexicans/Mexicanos who had strong ties to Mexico felt that what distinguished them from other "Americanized" students of Mexican descent was their Mexican heritage and their high aspirations. A second group of Mexican Americans was more oriented to the dominant American culture. These students were described as assimilated and were often called "wannabees" and ostracized by other Chicano/Latino groups who felt a stronger identity to their Mexican culture. This second group tended to hold lower aspirations than the first. A third group of Mexican-origin students—often referred to as "*Cholos*"—was held in low esteem by most other groups on campus. These students were stereotyped as not participating in school, as not carrying books, and as doing minimum work to get by. For them, doing well in school was perceived as giving in to the dominant "gringo" society and thereby denying one's cultural identity.

DESCRIPTION OF THIS STUDY

Our study took place between 1997 and 2001 in two northern California high schools, one urban and one rural. The urban school had approximately 2,000 students with relatively equal proportions of Latino, African American, Southeast Asian, and White students. The rural high school had about 1,100 students, of which approximately 60% were White and 40% of Mexican origin. Mexican-origin students in this school were divided between Spanish-speaking recent immigrants and longer-term residents who spoke English. As noted earlier, this study focused on those Mexican-origin students who were English speakers. Students in both the rural and urban schools were largely from low-income and working-class backgrounds, with the exception that some of the White students, especially in the urban school, tended to be more economically well off. The urban high school housed a well-known performing arts magnet program that attracted some White students from a nearby affluent neighborhood.

The study commenced when the students were freshmen in their respective schools and ended when the class of 2001 graduated. Initially, there were almost 500 students in the total sample. These numbers dwindled considerably over the course of the 4 years.

All English-speaking students in the class of 2001 who were present on the day the survey was administered each year were queried about their attitudes toward school, future plans, relations with parents and family, and social pressures they felt, as well as the kinds of things that influenced important decisions in their lives. Although both schools were cooperative, their faculties were also very reluctant to give up class time for survey administration. Thus we were able to negotiate only one day to administer surveys in the fall semester in grades 9 through 11 and the spring of grade 12. We administered the surveys in English classes because almost all students took that course across all grades. Students who were absent on those days were not surveyed because we were prevented from tracking the identity of students on the survey forms owing to human subjects restrictions. This also explains why sample size was larger in grade 10 than in grade 9—more students were missed in the initial survey.

These surveys were followed up with several interviews and focus groups each year with a subset of 120 students from the larger sample. These students were selected to represent a mix of gender, ethnicity, and achievement levels. Achievement data and coursework patterns were also collected on these 120 students, although by the end of 12th grade only 80 students with complete records remained in this sample. The purpose of the smaller group discussions was to make sense of the survey data, to have students explain for us what was meant by their responses. Some data were also collected on teacher and parent practices and attitudes, and ethnographic data were collected on the schools and student subgroups. The driving questions behind the study were related to understanding the ways in which students formed their post-high-school aspirations based on the multiple influences in their environments, and how these differed by ethnicity, gender, and age.

Table 3.1 shows the larger sample size over time. The sample size remained more stable in the rural school than in the urban school. It is notable, however, that the sample of Mexican-origin students in the rural high school was smaller than their overall percentage in the student population. Approximately half of the Mexican-origin students in this school were limited English proficient (LEP), and many had been in the country a short period of time. These students were segregated into a separate English language development (ELD) track where they had little or no contact with other English-speaking students in the school. Moreover, some portion of these students read neither English nor Spanish fluently, so for all of these reasons, they were not included in the peer influence study. On the other hand, although the urban school reported very modest dropout rates, the numbers of students in the 2001 cohort diminished dramatically by 12th grade. One explanation offered by school staff was that large numbers of students were reassigned to a continuation high school between 10th and 11th grade because of academic and behavioral problems. Another factor, however, was that some students every year did not pass enough classes to move on to the next grade.

Both of the high schools exist in old, established neighborhoods with relatively low mobility. Thus, as students exited at each grade level after the ninth grade, few new students entered the schools to replace them. Surveys over time represent, for the most part, the students who remained in these schools from the freshman year. We also assume that most of the students who left each year were disproportionately those who were having dif-

Table 3.1. Cohort Sizes, Grades 9–12

	Chicano/Latino			*All Others*			
	Urban	Rural	Total	Urban	Rural	Total	*Grand Total*
Grade 9	71	49	120	310	150	460	580
Grade 10	82	48	130	277	157	434	564
Grade 11	55	49	104	186	143	329	433
Grade 12	44	48	92	155	122	277	369

ficulty or who had become disaffected from school, based on staff explanations for the declining cohorts. Thus senior cohorts represent the "survivors"—those students who were doing well enough academically to continue on with their class, and who were dedicated enough to the goal of completing high school that they had stayed the course. This, of course, has implications for our findings as year by year the sample represents an increasingly select group of students.

SCHOOL ETHOS

The ethos of a school undoubtedly influences students' perceptions of who "other kids at this school" are. Although the urban school was very multiethnic, and no group constituted a majority, students at the urban high school routinely referred to it as a "ghetto school." A casual observer would quickly conclude that Black culture was pervasive on the campus—in dress and behavioral styles, in musical tastes, and in the way that Black students claimed important physical spaces at the center of campus life. Likewise, in the rural school, because the presence of Latino students was diminished so much by the segregation of Spanish speakers into a separate (and invisible) track, this school appeared to "belong" to the White students. The most celebrated events at the school revolved around sports and other activities in which White students were usually the central figures. Football rallies and school dances were the topic of announcements over the PA system in the morning. And, as some Spanish-speaking students noted, the announcements were always in English. The rural students were less likely than the urban students to aspire to go to college, and more likely to plan on going to work or into a local trade after high school. Consistent with this, a chi-square test revealed that there was a significant correlation between aspirations to go to college and the particular school that students attended (χ^2, 3, n = 282, 8.227, p < .04). Although the student composition and ethos of the two schools were distinct, many Latino students expressed a sense of not belonging in either school.

FINDINGS OF THIS STUDY

The Changing Shape of Aspirations Over Time

One of the most compelling findings of the study is that simply staying in school appears to influence students' academic aspirations in a positive way, as these shoot up significantly after the first year of high school.

Cognizant of the literature that shows a significant difference between students' "aspirations" (what they hope to do) and their "expectations" (what they expect will actually happen) (e.g., Mickelson, 1990), we asked the students what they "planned" to do upon finishing high school. Our assumption is that this question bridged the gap between hopes and expectations.

The pattern of growth of aspirations, defined as their postsecondary plans, is different for Chicano/Latino students than for all others (see Figure 3.1). Aspirations of non-Latino students are substantially higher than those of Latino students throughout high school. By the 11th grade, almost 30% more non-Latino students than Latinos intend to go to college. However, there is a dramatic shift in the senior year. The gap closes to within 5% between Latino and non-Latino students with respect to intentions to go to college. "Going to college" becomes the thing to do for most students by senior year. A persistent theme in focus groups with all students was the distorted perception that there were only two choices to make after high school—either go to college or spend the rest of your life working at Mc-Donalds. Most students had very little information about noncollege options, but "college" meant different things to different students. For some this meant going away to a 4-year university where the chances of completing a degree are relatively high. For others, it meant enrolling at the lo-

Figure 3.1. College Aspirations, Grades 9–12

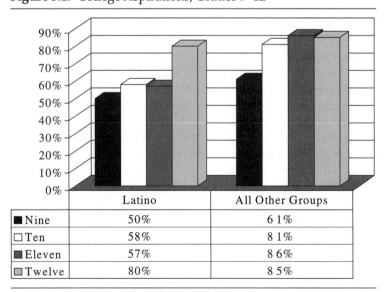

	Latino	All Other Groups
■ Nine	50%	6 1%
□ Ten	58%	8 1%
■ Eleven	57%	8 6%
□ Twelve	80%	8 5%

Table 3.2. College Choice: 2- vs. 4-Year College, Latino vs. Non-Latino, Grades 9–12

	Chicano/Latino		All Others	
	2 Year	4 year	2 Year	4 Year
Grade 9	13%	38%	14%	47%
Grade 10	13%	45%	21%	60%
Grade 11	16%	41%	27%	59%
Grade 12	45%	35%	29%	56%

cal community college where the vast majority quickly drop out and join the labor force.

Table 3.2 shows Latino and non-Latino students' responses to whether they intended to go to 2- or 4-year colleges, across grade levels. Surveys allowed students to report on a number of different post-high-school options, but here we focused just on what type of college the students who reported planning to go to college said they would attend.

Through focus group discussions we were able to understand what these patterns meant. Being in school exposes students to the idea of going on to college in a general way. Students hear teachers, counselors, and sometimes their peers talk about college. No matter which academic track or peer group students are in, they hear about college and come to see that it is the response that adults want to hear when they ask what they plan to do when they finish high school. To a large extent, students will say what adults want to hear. As one Chicano student noted, "Students say they are going to a 4-year college because it sounds good. It's the ideal thing to do after a student graduates." Thus we saw considerable growth in students' aspirations to go to college in their sophomore year. This was especially true for non-Latino students.

Aspirations remained relatively stable then until the senior year. By the spring of 12th grade when the students were surveyed, some had realized that a 4-year college was out of their reach, academically and/or financially. But the differences between what "going to college" meant for Latinos and non-Latinos were apparent. Whereas non-Latino students reported that they intended to enroll in 4-year colleges at almost double the rate they reported for 2-year colleges, Latino students were much more likely to head off to community college. Indeed, this is reflected in statewide data that show that more than three fourths of Latino students who go on to college after high school attend a 2-year institution (CPEC, 1999).

When queried in focus groups about the shift in aspirations over time, one Chicano student noted that some kids say they are going to college, but "they might get tired of school and end up dropping out, or they won't get the grades, or the money." Another added, "a lot of time students don't really know what it takes to get there." In other words, many students attached relatively little real meaning to their responses to this question on the survey.

The relatively low aspirations of Chicano/Latinos to attend 4-year colleges are consistent with the finding that these students lack information about college as an option (Kao & Tienda, 1998; Latino Eligibility Task Force, 1994). Thirty percent of Mexican-origin females in the rural school indicated in the ninth grade that they did not know what they would do after high school, compared with just 11% of non-Latino females. Not only were they not targeting college, they had no particular ambitions at all. This is especially worrisome because of the high percentage of Chicano/Latino students who drop out of high school because they see no link between schooling and their future occupations (Romo & Falbo, 1998).

At the same time that students' aspirations are generally rising, their grades are declining. Even with a disproportionate attrition among lower achievers, GPAs declined over time. Figure 3.2 shows students' grades over the 4 years of high school for the subset of 80 students who remained throughout the study period.

Each year, from grades 9 to 12, and in spite of the fact that many of the lowest performing students had exited school before graduation, grades declined. When queried about the gap between their aspirations and their grades in the 10th grade, students had many excuses; chief among these were the distraction of other students and their focus on developing stable friendship groups. These are key ways in which peers influence academic achievement without exerting any "pressure" in the normal sense of the word. Although they vowed they would raise their grades, they did not. Chicano/Latino students have among the lowest grades of all students, which is explained in part by their low commitment to homework and study. One out of five Chicano students in the urban school reported doing little or no homework at all in the 12th grade.

The Composition of Peer Groups

Most students tended to choose their best friends from among same-ethnicity peers, but this was especially true for Mexican-origin students. Two thirds to three quarters of them reported that their best friend was also of Mexican descent, compared with only a little more than half for all other groups. It is probable that there is an underestimation of the percentage

Figure 3.2. Latino vs. Non-Latino Students' Grades, Grades 9–12

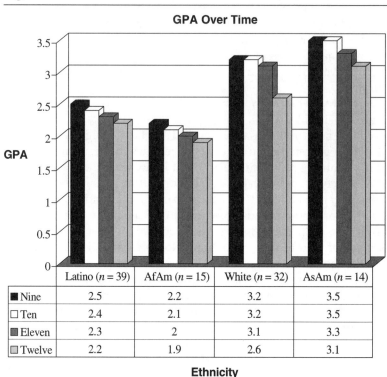

GPA Over Time

	Latino (*n* = 39)	AfAm (*n* = 15)	White (*n* = 32)	AsAm (*n* = 14)
■ Nine	2.5	2.2	3.2	3.5
☐ Ten	2.4	2.1	3.2	3.5
▓ Eleven	2.3	2	3.1	3.3
▨ Twelve	2.2	1.9	2.6	3.1

Ethnicity

of non-Latino students who also chose same-ethnicity best friends as we suspect that the concept of ethnicity was not as clear in the minds of many "White" students, and in fact many complained about being asked this question.

As one might expect, the greater racial and ethnic heterogeneity in the urban school appeared to have had an impact on the ethnicity of best friends, as only 66% of Chicano/Latino students in the urban school reported having same-ethnicity best friends (compared with 73% in the rural school) and only 41% of non-Latino students reported similarly (compared with 75% in the rural school). Latinas were also more likely than either males or other females to choose their best friends within their own ethnic group. Over subsequent years we asked students in what ways their close friendship groups had changed, if at all. Most students reported some change, and these changes often appeared to reflect a refocusing of their current interests and future goals. However, although best friends might have changed, their ethnicity usually did not. Most Latinos and rural students remained within enclaves of same-ethnicity peers for their most intimate friendships throughout high school.

The Changing Nature of Peer Influence

There is a consistent finding in the literature on peer influence that adolescent friends tend to develop similar attitudes about school and to perform more similarly in school over time. Thus researchers have concluded that peers do, indeed, influence each other academically (Coleman, 1961; Epstein & Karweit, 1983; Mounts & Steinberg, 1995). Other studies have found that students are most vulnerable to peer pressure in early adolescence, and that this diminishes with time (Coleman, 1980; Steinberg, 1996). Assuming that friends had an influence on each other's attitudes toward school, we asked students how important it was to their best friends to get good grades. The majority of students from almost all groups stated that their friends think it is at least "important" (on a 5-point scale from "very important" to "don't care") to get good grades. This appears to be consistent with a general "inflation" in socially appropriate responses, such as we noted in the aspirations to go to college. However, no more than about one fourth of all students perceived that getting good grades was "very important" to their friends. This is especially pronounced in the rural school, where few Latinas or Latinos or White males believe their friends considered it very important to get good grades (see Table 3.3).

There appears to be a slight increase in the assessment of importance of good grades across groups from the fall of 11th grade to the spring of

Table 3.3. Percentage of Latino and Non-Latino Students Reporting It Is "Very Important to Their Friends to Get Good Grades," Grades 11 and 12

	Chicano/Latino		All Other Groups	
	Grade 11	Grade 12	Grade 11	Grade 12
URBAN				
Female	22% (n = 31)	24% (n = 20)	28% (n = 99)	31% (n = 82)
Male	3% (n = 23)	6% (n = 17)	24% (n = 87)	25% (n = 73)
RURAL				
Female	18% (n = 21)	21% (n = 18)	22% (n = 76)	25% (n = 64)
Male	8% (n = 28)	9% (n = 24)	5% (n = 67)	7% (n = 58)

12th grade (almost 2 years). This is probably due to impending high school graduation and the reported readjustment in aspirations to fit students' actual academic histories. But it is evident from these data that Latinos did not have many friends who held high standards for their grades. In fact, 27% of rural Latinos reported that their friends did not care about their grades at all. In focus groups, both male and female Chicano/Latino students reported a lack of discussion of school, classes, or future plans among friends. This was especially true among the lower achieving students. When asked why they did not talk with friends about school, one Chicana mentioned that "friends don't really care." Another added,

> It's not an everyday thing you talk about. Sometimes you'll talk about GPA, but you don't ask each other how you're doing academically. You want to spend time with friends; you don't want to talk about school. You spend most of the day in school so you just want to relax and hang out.

Theoretically, as adolescents mature, they become less susceptible to peer influence until at some point this is no longer an issue. We asked students about many kinds of pressures, including school, friends, parental conflict, curfew, driving privileges, jobs, and several "risky behaviors," among others. Pressure to earn money became increasingly salient for all groups and was the number one pressure reported overall by the 12th grade. For some students, the pressure to earn money came from a desire to "wear the right clothes," have and maintain a car, and other personal expenses. However, some Latino students reported a direct pressure to contribute to their family's household income. The perceived pressure to get a job almost certainly dampened further academic aspirations. (Interestingly, very few Latino or Latina students reported a pressure to "wear the right clothes," whereas this was very salient for most other groups of students, especially among females.) On the other hand, pressure to engage in risky behaviors remained significant over time only for Latino males (see Table 3.4).

In focus groups students reported that they felt the most pressure to conform to the perceived expectations of their friends in the ninth grade as they were trying to find a place in the social structure of school. In fact, students reported doing things that they later regretted in order to be accepted by admired peers. But over time peer influence may take many forms that affect different aspects of behavior and indirectly affect achievement. Students also acknowledge that their peers influence their behavior in more indirect ways. When asked how much they believed that "other students in this school influence the way you dress and act" in the 11th and 12th grades, a surprisingly high percentage of students reported "a lot." Stu-

Table 3.4. Percentage of Latino and Non-Latino Students Reporting "A Lot" of Pressure to Engage in Risky Behaviors, Grades 9–12

| | Chicano/Latino | | All Other Groups | |
Ethnicity	Female	Male	Female	Male
Grade 9	22% ($n = 65$)	35% ($n = 55$)	20% ($n = 231$)	21% ($n = 217$)
Grade 10	12% ($n = 61$)	22% ($n = 63$)	11% ($n = 166$)	15% ($n = 196$)
Grade 11	8% ($n = 53$)	20% ($n = 51$)	7% ($n = 125$)	10% ($n = 106$)
Grade 12	5% ($n = 40$)	19% ($n = 42$)	5% ($n = 107$)	8% ($n = 96$)

Table 3.5. Percentage of Students Reporting They Are Influenced "A Lot" by Other Students in the School, Grades 11 and 12

| | Chicano/Latino | | All Other Groups | |
	Grade 11	Grade 12	Grade 11	Grade 12
URBAN				
Female	48% ($n = 31$)	50% ($n = 20$)	51% ($n = 99$)	57% ($n = 82$)
Male	44% ($n = 23$)	47% ($n = 17$)	55% ($n = 87$)	55% ($n = 73$)
RURAL				
Female	66% ($n = 21$)	67% ($n = 18$)	67% ($n = 76$)	67% ($n = 64$)
Male	15% ($n = 28$)	13% ($n = 24$)	54% ($n = 67$)	61% ($n = 58$)

dents' responses to this question were stable from 11th to 12th grade, although showing small increases in reporting a lot of influence; overall more than half of students reported a lot of influence by peers on how they dressed and acted (see Table 3.5).

Direct pressure to engage in particular behaviors, such as using alcohol or drugs, stemming from the clique or crowd to whom students belonged, tended to wane by the 12th grade. But indirect pressure to earn money in order to maintain an image (have a car, wear the right clothes, participate in social activities) continued to increase over time. The influence of the *reference group peers* ("other students in this school") on broader behavioral norms remained high for most students, and especially for females in the rural school.

For many students, the peer influence exerted by the clique or the crowd appeared to shift to the larger reference group at the school as they got older and their worlds expanded. Interestingly, however, rural Chicano males reported the opposite pattern of influence. Although pressure to engage in risky behaviors remained strong for many Chicano males, the pressure they felt from the broader reference group was relatively muted. This suggests to us that many rural Chicanos continued to feel more influence from the clique or crowd to which they belonged than from the broader social norms of the school peer group. We think this reflects a lack of sense of "belonging" in the wider school—something about which we heard in the focus groups. This could also be related to a narrower worldview. That is, these students' aspirations were likely shaped more by their smaller circle of friends (and family) than by any larger reference group that might have expanded their perspectives on life options and opportunities.

Because we hypothesized that how students wanted to be seen by others—and how they perceived that their friends wanted to be seen—was important in shaping their values toward schooling and their academic aspirations, we provided students with four options for how they might want others to see them, and they were asked to select only one. These forced-choice responses included: "Someone who is smart and a good student," "Someone who is funny and fun to be around," "Someone who is good looking and gets invited to all the best parties," and "Someone who is nice and always will listen to a friend" (see Table 3.6). Responses to these questions were generally stable over time, except that Chicanas in the 12th grade indicated in higher proportions than in the 11th grade that they would like to be viewed as "smart and a good student." Interestingly, when asked how they thought their friends would want to be seen, these Chicanas did not think their friends wanted to be viewed as "smart"; rather, they thought they would prefer to be known as "fun to be around."

Table 3.6. "How Would You Like Most Other Students to Think of You?" (Grade 12)

	Chicano/Latino				*All Other Groups*			
	URBAN		RURAL		URBAN		RURAL	
	Female	Male	Female	Male	Female	Male	Female	Male
Sample *n*	(21)	(18)	(19)	(24)	(80)	(73)	(64)	(58)
"Good student"	41%	10%	5%	0%	4%	17%	22%	10%
"Fun"	12%	36%	30%	75%	33%	46%	22%	64%
"Good looking"	7%	4%	5%	4%	14%	14%	2%	10%
"Nice"	40%	50%	60%	21%	39%	23%	54%	16%

We note that only urban Chicana/Latinas replied in large numbers that they wanted other students to think of them as "smart and a good student." Most females and Chicano/Latino students—with the exception of rural males—reported that they wanted to be viewed as "nice and good listeners," whereas males in general wanted to be viewed as "fun to be around." It is somewhat paradoxical that urban Chicana/Latinas rated being smart as highly as being nice, given that in the focus groups both Chicanas and Chicanos told us it wasn't "cool" to be seen as smart. One young woman had said, "It's more important that people think you are cool, pretty, or have a good personality. People don't really care about whether you are smart." And a Chicano student added his perception that good students weren't likely to be much fun. "Good students don't like to go out. Being a good student doesn't do anything for your social life." But the fact that so many of the urban Chicana/Latinas selected "smart" suggests that they were probably more aware than their rural sisters of other possible selves.

It appears they may have also underestimated their friends' aspirations. In separate analyses of variances (ANOVAS), we found no relationship between the ways that students claimed they wanted to be seen by friends and their reported aspirations. The fact that urban Latinas who wanted friends to think of them as "smart" did not aspire to any higher educational goals than their friends who wanted to be seen as "fun to be around" suggests that although they may have harbored a desire to be some other self, they lacked the social capital—socialization to the norms of the dominant class—to know how to realize those aspirations.

The degree to which students feel a part of the school also has an impact on their academic behavior. "Belonging" comes about largely by having friends who feel connected to the school, and by feeling accepted by others. Certainly, strong friendships, based on shared values lead to a greater sense of belonging. Recent research has shown a strong connection between sense of belonging and both student motivation and grades (Goodenow & Grady, 1993; Osterman, 2000; Chapter 7, this volume). Our data also suggest that lacking a sense of belonging may have been related to some students' lower aspirations (see Table 3.7).

One third of Chicana/Latinas in the urban school reported feeling "uncomfortable" or as if they "do not belong" at this school. When we investigated which females among the "all others" group in the urban school lacked a sense of belonging, we found that it was primarily White females who reported this alienation. But this was explainable by the fact that White females were disproportionately enrolled in the magnet school on campus and the magnet was highly segregated from the rest of the school. Thus many of the White young women were kept in a separate academic track at the school. Their infrequent interchanges with other students on the cam-

Table 3.7. Percentage of Students Who Report Feeling "Uncomfortable" or Like "I Don't Belong at This School," Grade 12

	Chicano/Latino	*All Other Groups*
URBAN		
Female	33% (*n* = 21)	21% (*n* = 82)
Male	8% (*n* = 18)	19% (*n* = 73)
RURAL		
Female	16% (*n* = 19)	16% (*n* = 64)
Male	17% (*n* = 24)	17% (*n* = 58)

pus were often the source of some discomfort because White students were a clear minority on the rest of the campus. Chicana/Latinas, on the other hand, reported feeling alienated at the school because of a more pervasive sense of being marginalized. These young women also appeared to be out of step with the prevailing ethos of their school, preferring to be viewed as "nice" or "smart" while they perceived others to be more interested in being "fun to be around."

IMPLICATIONS

Forms of Peer Influence

The findings from this study suggest that there are three ways in which students experience peer influence that may affect their academic achievement. The first is direct peer pressure to engage in "risky behaviors" that, by their nature, reduce students' focus on schooling and increase their chances of getting into trouble in school and out of school. This appears to peak early in high school and to wane thereafter, except for Chicano/Latino males in whom it remains salient throughout high school. The second form of peer influence appears to operate through normative control of behavior, by pegging one's behavior according to "others" in the school with whom one either wishes to identify or wishes not to identify. One way this is manifested is in the increasing pressure to earn money to sustain an image (e.g., to support a car, to have the "right" clothes). Of course, to the extent that work competes with schooling, this can have a detrimental effect on achievement. Normative pressure is also evidenced in students' perceptions of the academic standards held by other students in their school. This is reflected in the significant correlation between the specific school and the level of postsecondary aspirations of the students. The reference group exercises its control without ever necessarily coming into contact with the student. This form of influence appears to endure over time, except once again for Latino males who claim to be relatively unaffected by these broader normative influences in the school. The third form of peer influence occurs through creating a sense of belonging or alienation toward fellow students. A sense of belonging has been shown to be an important factor in students' engagement with schooling, and this is related to their desire to do well and achieve academically. Aspirations appear to be shaped, at least in part, by the degree to which students feel a part of the enterprise of schooling. Most students appear to feel some alienation at the beginning of high school, hence their vulnerability to peer pressures as they seek to find a niche in the school. But most do find a niche and the sense of alienation subsides. However, for many Latinas this feeling of *not* belonging appears to endure over time.

The Distinctive Patterns of Influence for Mexican-Origin Students

Chicano/Latino students as a group tend to have lower academic aspirations than other students, and this is reflected in their grades, which are also lower. Importantly, while all students may profess that "being a good student does nothing for your social life," most non-Latino students—with the possible exception of African Americans—are much more likely to find reinforcement for high academic aspirations among peers who may be reluctant to acknowledge their interest in school but who nonetheless continue to keep their academic options open by performing academically at acceptable levels. The fact that Mexican-origin students remain especially ethnically segregated, even within diverse high schools, means that they are not often privy to the support and information networks (social capital) that other students, who are headed for college in much greater numbers, share. Thus there is little opportunity to counter these low aspirations through day-to-day encounters with other more knowledgeable and academically motivated students.

The differences between male and female Latinos are also striking. Whereas significant percentages of Latino males profess that their friends do not care about grades at all and few report wanting to be known as a good student, a startlingly high percentage of urban Latinas reported wanting to be known as a good student. Of course, national data bear out the fact that Latinas are outperforming Latinos by large margins with respect to college going (Harvey, 2002). However, neither the males nor the females reported believing that their peers wanted to be known as a good student in these schools. This lack of support is reinforced by the high percentage of Latinas in the urban school who reported feeling that they did not belong there. It is especially ironic that these young women, stereotyped as low achievers and feeling marginalized by their school, may have harbored higher ambitions but felt that friends did not support such aspirations. Of course, because these young women reported seldom discussing school or future plans with their friends, there was little opportunity to correct these impressions.

It is also of significant concern that Latino males—and especially those in the rural school—were so unlike other students in their patterns of influence and the degree to which they cared about school. Many of these young men reported strong and continuing pressure to engage in risky behavior, many were unsure of what they wanted to do after high school, and many did not care at all about how well they did in school. Surrounded by peers with a similar malaise, they had few opportunities to change direction. Whereas other students appeared to be less influenced by the friends in their clique or crowd over time, these young men experienced comparatively little reduction in pressure from friends to engage in risky behaviors. While others began to develop an identity independent from their cliques, Latinos reported being significantly less influenced by the norms established by school peers. They appeared to maintain a closer psychological tie to their clique or crowd, which almost certainly limited their access to broader information networks and knowledge of other possible selves. As Stanton-Salazar in Chapter 2 argues, peers may constitute social capital by helping to socialize their fellow students to the dominant norms of achievement, or they may play a mediating role in providing access to powerful adult agents. But neither of these roles is possible in situations where Latino students are isolated from mainstream social contact and behavioral norms.

Our data suggest that the generally accepted view of peer influence as a bell-shaped curve in which influence increases through early adolescence, peaking at around age 14 and steadily declining thereafter, may not only misrepresent the actual pattern of influence for many Chicano/Latino males but also, in fact, misrepresent the nature of peer influence altogether. Peer influence may be even more complex and far-reaching than much of the literature, based on White, middle-class students, may lead one to conclude. We find that peer influence is developmental, but that it does not necessarily diminish over time. As students develop a more stable identity, they may be less inclined to act precipitously in order to fit in with a particular clique or crowd. Thus they may be less vulnerable to peer pressure to engage in risky behavior. However, by their own admission, most students in the 12th grade believe that other students in their school influence their behavior "a lot." This broader reference or normative group appears to be distinct from the clique or crowd and continues to exert influence well into late adolescence, and possibly beyond. As students get older and develop a more stable identity, independent from their close friends, the source of influence may come increasingly from the more abstract peers of the reference group who represent desired traits and behaviors rather than from the intense relationships of early adolescence that are so closely associated with identity development. This is further supported by the strong relationship already noted between students' aspirations and the particular school they attended.

Latino students tend to select best friends from their same ethnic group and to organize themselves into same-ethnicity cliques and crowds. Nonetheless, there was a significant correlation between the school *as a whole* and student aspirations. In school, the larger reference group may be "kids in general at this school" or, where highly differentiated groups are found, such as in diverse high schools, it may be the Mexicans, the jocks, or the skaters. But, taken together, they appear to affect the changing shape of adolescents' aspirations. Clearly, there are differences in this process between Latino students and all others. Some Latinas—especially those in urban areas where there is greater consciousness of opportunities—may harbor higher aspirations than they convey, and many Latino males may harbor even lower ones. However, neither group appears to have much access to close peers who can provide the peer social capital that Stanton-Salazar (see Chapter 2, this volume) describes as encouraging and sustaining high academic achievement. Moreover, the lack of a sense of belonging for many Latinas may further diminish the range of possible selves they can envision. If schools want to change the patterns of aspirations of Latino students, then they would do well to find ways to break down ethnic and academic barriers, increase a sense of belonging for all students, and encourage a culture of high achievement throughout the school. To do so, however, they must consider that there are very real differences among groups with respect to the ways in which attitudes and aspirations are influenced and supported by peers.

ACKNOWLEDGMENTS

The authors wish to thank the CREDE Center and the Office of Educational Research and Improvement (OERI) for the funding to support this study. This work was supported under the Education Research and Development Program, Center for Research on Education, Diversity, and Excellence (CREDE), administered by the Office of Educational Research and Improvement.

REFERENCES

Brown, B., & Theobald, W. (1998). Learning contexts beyond the classroom: Extracurricular activities, community organizations, and peer groups. In K. Borman & B. Schneider (Eds.), *The adolescent years: Social influences and educational challenges* (pp. 109–141). Ninety-seventh yearbook of the National Society for the Study of Education. Chicago: University of Chicago Press.

Coleman, J. C. (1980). Friendship and the peer group in adolescence. In J. Adelson, *Handbook of adolescent psychology* (pp. 408–431). New York: Wiley & Sons.

Coleman, J. S. (1961). *The adolescent society.* New York: The Free Press.

Cooper, C. R., Jackson, J. F., Azmitia, M., Lopez, E. M., & Dunbar, N. (1995). Bridging students' multiple worlds: African American and Latino youth in academic outreach programs. In R. F. Macías & R. G. García Ramos (Eds.), *Changing schools for changing students: An anthology of research on language minorities* (pp. 211–234). Santa Barbara: University of California Linguistic Minority Research Institute.

California Postsecondary Education Commission (CPEC). (1999). College-going rates of California public high school graduates, by racial/ethnic group, fall 1996 to fall 1998. Higher Education Performance Indicator Report. Sacramento: Author.

Csikzentmihalyi, M., & Schmidt, J. (1998). Stress and resilience in adolescence: An evolutionary perspective. In K. Borman & B. Schneider (Eds.), *The adolescent years: Social influences and educational challenges* (pp. 1–17). Ninety-seventh yearbook of the National Society for the Study of Education. Part I. Chicago: University of Chicago Press.

Eccles, J., Midgely, C., Wigfield, A., Buchanan, C., Reuman, D., Flanagan, C., & MacIver, D. (1993). Development during adolescence. The impact of stage-environmental fit on young adolescents' experiences in schools and in families. *American Psychologist, 48,* 90–101.

Eckert, P. (1989). *Jocks and burnouts.* New York: Holt, Rinehart, Winston.

Epstein, J., & Karweit, N. (Eds.). (1983). *Friends in school.* New York: Academic Press.

Erikson, E. (1968). *Youth, identity and crisis.* New York: Norton.

Foley, D. E. (1990). *Learning capitalist culture: Deep in the heart of Tejas.* Philadelphia: University of Pennsylvania Press.

Fordham, S., & Ogbu, J. U. (1986). Black students' school success: Coping with the burden of acting White. *Urban Review, 18*(3), 176–206

Gamoran, A. (1992). The variable effects of high school tracking. *American Sociological Review, 57,* 812–828.

Gándara, P. (1995). *Over the ivy walls: The educational mobility of low income Chicanos.* Albany: State University of New York Press.

Gándara, P., Gutiérrez, D., & O'Hara, S. (2001). Planning for the future in rural and urban high schools. *Journal of Education for Students Placed at Risk, 6,* 73–94.

Gibson, M. A., & Ogbu, J. U. (Eds.). (1991). *Minority status and schooling: A comparative study of immigrant and involuntary minorities.* New York: Garland.

Goodenow, C., & Grady, K. E. (1993). The relationship of school belonging and friends' values to academic motivation among urban adolescent students. *Journal of Experimental Education, 62,* 60–71.

Harvey, W. B. (2002). *Minorities in higher education, 2001–2002.* Washington, DC: American Council on Education.

Ide, J., Parkerson, J., Haertel, G., & Walberg, H. (1981). Peer group influence on educational outcomes: A quantitative synthesis. *Journal of Educational Psychology, 73,* 47–484.

Kandel, D. B., & Lesser, G. S. (1969). Parental and peer influences on educational plans of adolescents. *American Sociological Review, 34*(2), 213–223.

Kao, G., & Tienda, M. (1998). Educational aspirations of minority youth. *American Journal of Education, 106,* 349–384.

Latino Eligibility Task Force. (1994). *Latino eligibility study* (Report No. 4). Santa Cruz: University of California.

Marcia, J. (1976). Identity six years after. *Journal of Youth and Adolescence, 5,* 145–160.

Markus, H., & Nurius, P. (1986, September). Possible selves. *American Psychologist,* 954–969.

Matute-Bianchi, M. E. (1991). Situational ethnicity and patterns of school performance among immigrant and nonimmigrant Mexican-descent students. In M. A. Gibson & J. U. Ogbu (Eds.), *Minority status and schooling: A comparative study of immigrant and involuntary minorities* (pp. 205–247). New York: Garland.

McDill, E., & Coleman, J. S. (1965). Family and peer influences in college plans of high school students. *Sociology of Education, 38,* 112–126.

Mickelson, R. A. (1990). The attitude–achievement paradox among Black adolescents. *Sociology of Education, 63,* 44–61.

Mounts, N., & Steinberg, L. (1995). Parenting practices and peer group affiliation in adolescence. *Child Development, 64,* 467–482.

Ogbu, J. U. (1978). *Minority education and caste.* New York: Academic Press.

Osterman, K. F. (2000). Students' need for belonging in the school community. *Review of Educational Research, 70*(3), 323–367.

Peshkin, A. (1991). *The color of strangers, the color of friends.* New York: Holt, Rinehart, Winston.

Phelan, P., Davidson, A. L., & Cao, H. T. (1991). Students' multiple worlds: Negotiating the boundaries of family, peer, and school cultures. *Anthropology and Education Quarterly, 22,* 224–249.

Phinney, J. (1989). Stages of ethnic identity development in minority group adolescents. *Journal of Early Adolescence, 9,* 34–49.

Romo, H., & Falbo, T. (1998). *Latino high school graduation.* Austin: University of Texas Press.

Rumbaut, R., & Cornelius, W. (1995). *California's immigrant children: Theory, research, and implications for educational policy.* La Jolla: Center for U.S. Mexican Studies, University of California San Diego.

Schneider, B., & Stevenson, D. (1999). *The ambitious generation: America's teenagers, motivated but directionless.* New Haven, CT: Yale University Press.

Steinberg, L. (with Brown, B., & Dornbusch, S.). (1996). *Beyond the classroom: Why school reform has failed and what parents need to do.* New York: Simon & Schuster.

Swanson, D. P., Spencer, M. B., & Petersen, A. (1998). Identity formation in adolescence. In K. Borman & B. Schneider (Eds.), *The adolescent years: Social influences and educational challenges* (pp. 18–41). Ninety-seventh yearbook of the National Society for the Study of Education. Chicago: University of Chicago Press.

Trueba, H. (1988). Culturally based explanations of minority students' academic achievement. *Anthropology and Education Quarterly, 19,* 270–287.

Valverde, S. (1987). A comparative study of Hispanic high school dropouts and graduates: Why do some leave school early and some finish? *Education and Urban Society, 19,* 320–329.

4

"Acting Out" and Being a "Schoolboy": Performance in an ELD Classroom

Clayton A. Hurd

A great deal has been written recently about the barriers Latino immigrant students face in both learning English and achieving academic success in U.S. public schools. Ethnographic studies point to a number of factors limiting the classroom learning of English-language learners, including low expectations of teacher and school staff for Latino students (Valdes, 1996, 2001); teachers' negative attitudes about students use of Spanish and other code-switching varieties (Urciuoli, 1996; Zentella, 1997); bureaucratic tracking into an unchallenging, "basic skills" curriculum (Mehan, Villanueva, Hubbard, & Lintz, 1996; Romo & Falbo, 1996); and limited and inadequate English language development (ELD) instruction rather than effective bilingual instruction (Vasquez, Pease-Alvarez, & Shannon, 1994). Out-of-school factors have undermined school success as well, including society-wide disparagement of Latina/o students and their families through racist public discourse (Suarez-Orozco & Suarez-Orozco, 1995; Urciuoli, 1996) and a widespread public misperception that immigrant parents lack an appreciation of the value of education. A host of studies (Delgado-Gaitan, 1990; Olsen, 1997, among others) have demonstrated that low levels of parent involvement are often less a matter of disinterest than the lack of a welcoming environment offered by schools for interaction, a lack of translation resources for communication, and Latino parents' insecurity about their own low levels of educational attainment.

This chapter means to contribute to this important and growing body of scholarship about Latino students by offering an ethnographic account of some of the critical challenges facing Mexican-descent English-language learners at a comprehensive, bimodal (Mexican-descent/Anglo) suburban high school in northern California called Hillside High. (All names of people and places are pseudonyms.) Hillside High School has the rather unusual status of being the only truly racially and ethnically mixed school (approximately 60% Anglo, 40% Mexican-descent) in an otherwise largely segregated school district. (See Chapter 7 for a more detailed description of the high school.)

The analysis here draws from one full academic year's observation of the only three ELD classes at the high school—a combined beginner-intermediate class (27 students) and two advanced classes (22 students each). With the exception of one female student from the Punjab, all ELD students were of Mexican descent. Nearly all of these ELD students were children of working-class parents employed in the local agriculture economy, many as field laborers. Though the majority (58%) were recent immigrants from Mexico (arriving in the United States within the last 5 years), the variation in years since arrival was wider among the boys than the girls (see Table 4.1). In fact, a significant number of the boys (45%) had received most if not all of their schooling in the United States.

This study is not primarily concerned with ELD pedagogy, curriculum, or curriculum application, though the analysis may have relevance to those interested in such fields. What I offer is a student-centered ethnography of the ELD classroom, focusing on Mexican-descent students' interactions and behaviors as well as their own accountings of their experience within and outside of the class.[1] A central focus of attention is on the interpersonal and emotional factors that shape student behavior in the classroom context and that influence their experience of learning English at the

Table 4.1. Hillside High ELD Students: Years Since Arrival in the United States

Years Since Arrival	Males		Females		Total	
	n	*%*	*n*	*%*	*n*	*%*
0–3	15	32	16	53	31	40
4–5	7	15	7	23	14	18
6+	21	45	6	20	27	35
No Data	4	8	1	3	5	6
Gender Total	47	100	30	100	77	100

school. Here I stress emotion as a social phenomenon and focus on the interpersonal aspects of emotional experience (Lutz & Abu-Lughod, 1990). I
consider how peer-sanctioned norms of behavior shape relations between
students and teachers and among students themselves and examine how
these norms make academic engagement and creative learning in the ELD
classes difficult to sustain. There is, I suggest, a complex peer-mediated interpersonal politics that creates difficulty for students in the ELD class to
comfortably practice English and to demonstrate active interest in class lessons. These politics affect both boys and girls in the class, but the situations
and challenges are somewhat different.

In theory, ELD classes at Hillside High are designed to offer structured, English-monolingual instruction to English-language learners and
to provide them with a sheltered and "safe" environment to further develop second-language skills. Yet the realities in ELD classes at Hillside
High seemed to be in sharp contrast to these ideals. The classes, which
many students described as "disastrous and disorganized," tended neither
to provide a "safe" place for students to further develop their skills in English nor to offer a comfortable environment for engaged academic behavior. In fact, the ELD classrooms I observed were characterized by students'
virtual nonuse of spoken English, except when reading aloud or—among
some boys—when making jokes related to the teacher or the lesson.

Analysis in this chapter focuses on two phenomena in the ELD classes
that seem to suggest student noncompliance or disengagement from learning. The first is the prevalence of classroom "acting out" practices by some
male students. These classroom performances, and the way the teacher responds to them, severely limit the quality of classroom instruction in Hillside High ELD classes. The second phenomenon concerns the way in which
some male students invoke the term *schoolboy* as a teasing measure against
other boys who are perceived to behave in ways that signal engagement
and/or interest in what is deliberately being taught. Both the acting out
and teasing practices must be understood in relation to dominant forms of
masculinity that—taken together with conditions of class and racial sub-
ordination—put some of these boys at odds with formal classroom teaching and learning.[2]

These acting out phenomena as well as teasing about being a "schoolboy" exist, I argue, as *meaningful cultural practices* developed by some
Mexican-descent youth to create a sense of inclusion in a school and larger
social context of racial and class stratification. Yet these practices are not un-
contested among Mexican-descent youth; they are constantly under negotiation, and it is precisely this negotiation that leads to anxiety and ambiva-
lence for many English-language learners in relation to language learning

and demonstrations of academic engagement. In each of the cases to be considered, broader forces of discrimination and exploitation play out in internal relations of power, status, and privilege among Mexican-descent students themselves. These interpersonal battles severely shape these students' schooling experience and impact how they orient themselves to schooling resources.

ACTING OUT IN HILLSIDE HIGH ELD CLASSES

The following field-note excerpt is from an advanced ELD class taught by Laura Babcock. To indicate how long each ELD student has lived in the United States, I use the notation [YSA- (x)], signifying years since arrival. Hence YSA-1 indicates that the student has been in the United States for 1 year. The notation [US] indicates that the student was born in the United States.[3] This particular ELD class is extreme but not atypical of those I observed at Hillside High. The classroom environment is fraught with constant disruptions by some male students, managed in turn by teacher threats, and results in a shift of attention from the class lesson to discipline.

> Mrs. Babcock begins a lesson reading a story about a Chinese immigrant teenager, Shirley, and the experiences she goes through in an American school. "Shirley was a girl whose mother wanted her to become an 'ist'."
> "What the fuck is an 'ist'?" implores Emilio [US] in a low tone of voice, his face resting on the table.
> Mrs. Babcock apparently doesn't hear Emilio, but many other students do. Mrs. Babcock continues. "Does anyone know what becoming an 'ist' means?" A moment of silence passes as no one responds.
> "A waitress," Emilio says, when in fact his book is closed.
> "No, it's not a waitress, anybody else?"
> Emilio keeps answering with whatever word comes into his head.
> "Stop it *now!*" says Mrs. Babcock, looking somewhat upset.
> "Okay, an 'ist' is a profession such as Chemist, Physicist, Pianists, etc. But guess what?" adds Mrs. Babcock emphatically.
> "What happened Miss Laura [nickname for teacher]?" replies a female student.
> "Shirley failed a chemistry class!"
> "She sucks," shouts Emilio with his head still resting on the table.
> Mrs. Babcock walks up to him. "If you continue misbehaving,"

she warns Emilio, "I will ask you to go outside." She goes back to the front of the class and continues reading.

Beto [YSA-1], who is sitting next to Emilio, reaches over to one of the computers and turns it on, which consequently disturbs the class. Mrs. Babcock quickly turns to him and asks him to leave the classroom.

"I didn't do nothing," Beto complains.

"Get out! . . . please," Mrs. Babcock answers.

As Mrs. Babcock escorts Beto outside, another boy, Jaime [YSA-6], begins slamming his book on the table. Mrs. Babcock approaches him and aggressively takes the book from his hands. The student mumbles something inaudible to her in Spanish, but Mrs. Babcock ignores him.

After spending several minutes disciplining her male students, Mrs. Babcock begins reading again. After a few minutes, the class seems to be developing an interest in the story. Most of them are taking turns at reading, and the rest of them are listening attentively to Mrs. Babcock. Emilio, who is becoming impatient, resumes his complaining.

"I read this book already last year, Miss Laura."

"All right," Mrs. Babcock replies angrily, "Enough. That's your problem. It is not my fault you weren't here half of the time."

"Whatever," replies Emilio and begins to chat with those at his table.

With so much disciplining going on, the students begin losing interest in the story. The boys begin to talk out loud, while some of the girls begin laughing at what the boys are saying or doing. Looking very upset and fed up with what is going on in her classroom, Mrs. Babcock closes her book, making enough noise to catch everyone's attention, and angrily shouts:

"Okay! I'm trying to help you with the story and obviously you don't care."

"That's right, Miss Laura," replies Emilio, "we don't care."

"Since you don't seem to need my help," she says as she walks around the room, "you can complete these questions on your own." She begins handing out a photocopy assignment.

Three females and one male student sitting together at a table seem disappointed at Emilio for not allowing Mrs. Babcock to finish the story. As I walk up to them, one of the girls [YSA-2] angrily says to me, *"No más se la pasan jugando todo el tiempo"* [All they do is play around all the time]. Emilio, looking at the handout, says out loud, "This is easy, Miss Laura, you are just wasting our time."

The bell rings. Within seconds, the students desert the classroom, completely ignoring Mrs. Babcock's instructions to remain in their seats.

Here, classroom disruption practices carried out by a handful of boys included arguing with and insulting the teacher, making nonsense comments while the teacher was presenting the lesson, socializing and talking loudly with peers after being told multiple times not to do so, and ambling about the room. Beyond the antagonisms between the teacher and a few of the male students, the ELD classroom was characterized by an almost nonuse of spoken English by students, except when making jokes related to the teacher or the lesson or when reading aloud. The girls typically remained quiet, alternating between being on task, writing notes, sharing pictures, or putting on makeup. Despite the distractions, a small percentage of girls and boys did remain attentive. Overall, the environment in these classes made academic engagement and creative learning difficult to sustain. As a result, lessons moved very slowly.

How are we to understand these classroom dynamics? Are they a form of conscious resistance? If so, what is being resisted and why? Or are they simply a response to bad teaching? As shown through the field-note excerpt, the behavior of some boys impacts the quality of teaching and learning in the ELD classes. However, according to the students—both male and female—the blame for these disruptions falls as much on the *teacher* as on the boys. Despite the fact that Mrs. Babcock is well liked by most of the students—many stay in her class during lunch and before school—there is unanimous agreement about her lack of effectiveness in classroom management. As a 10th-grade beginning ELD student puts it: "Because she is such a good person, we cross the line with her. If she were more strict, we wouldn't be doing it [misbehaving]." A group of girls in the intermediate ELD class see it in a similar way.

> *Maria* [YSA-1]: The truth is, poor her, she cares about us a lot, but we haven't shown that we care about her. It is the worst class, but it is also the one where she does the most things for us, the most field trips and stuff. It is because she does not want to send us to the office. In order not to get us into trouble in the office, she tells people to calm down, but they do not understand.
>
> *Paola* [YSA-3]: In Miss Laura's class, if she, the third time she told them to calm down and they don't calm down, she sent them to the office, I'd say the class would be a lot more calm and everyone would pay more attention, but since she does not send them

> to the office, they interrupt, interrupt. . . . And with all the shouting, all the shouting that is going on, I mean, it is better to shout than to have to listen to it—It drives you more crazy listening to it than doing it.

Students see Mrs. Babcock as a "caring" person and say she is a "good" teacher, but they do not necessarily see her as a "caring teacher" (Noddings, 1992; Valenzuela, 1999).

The problems in the ELD classes may seem particular to Mrs. Babcock's class-management shortcomings, but student commentaries suggest than many of their classes are similar in character. The conditions for learning are extremely difficult, and the frustration has a profoundly limiting effect on the engagement of students, particularly recent arrivals, as indicated by student commentaries drawn from a group interview:

> *Adriana* [YSA-1]: How can I explain this? Here they tell you [that you] have to learn English. Like in jobs, they will always prefer a person who knows how to speak English. And for me it is very hard, you know, [because] here they stress education, and tell you that if you keep studying you can get a good career. You feel like you want to do well in school, [but] then you go to class and see how disorganized and disastrous is it, and it sticks to you.
> *Maria* [YSA-1]: Yeah, it's contagious.
> *Researcher:* But what do you mean by "disastrous and disorganized"?
> *Adriana:* Like when you come to class eager to learn, but the rest aren't paying attention.
> *Lupe* [YSA-5]: And you lose your concentration by watching others.
> *Adriana:* I listen up, but the others aren't.
> *Researcher:* What classrooms have you thought this way about?
> *Adriana:* In all of them.
> *Maria:* In all.

As this commentary indicates, acting-out practices at Hillside High are not limited to the ELD classes. Yet English-language learners are perhaps more impacted by such behaviors than other students because they tend to be scheduled in classes with the highest concentration of the most disruptive boys. These boys are the most disruptive when together, performing.

Further conversations with the ELD girls suggest, interestingly, that though teachers' gender, ethnicity, and language orientations may influence their ability to create a more manageable class environment, that influence is often only negligible.

Angelica [YSA-1]: Yeah, like in health class [taught by Ms. Ortiz, a Mexican-descent bilingual Latina], the teacher calms them down, but still there is disorder.

Lupe: Yeah, you see it everywhere.

Researcher: Yeah, but isn't she, the health teacher, really strict?

Angelica: Yeah, but they [the boys] are always interrupting her and interrupting her. There isn't a day where she doesn't take a student out.

Adriana: That also happens in Spanish class [taught by a Spanish-speaking Anglo male].

Researcher: And nobody says anything to the guys—the teachers—they don't say anything to them?

Adriana: Ms. Ortiz is the only one that would say something. Like when a kid calls another kid dumb, Ms. Ortiz right away asks him to apologize.

Maria: And the other kid just says "why me?"

Angelica: Yeah, 'cause she's always like "apologize, say sorry," and she sends them to the office, but still it never changes.

Lupe: It's like they are already used to it and as if they like it as well [going to the office].

These girls, like other students I talked with, claimed that the boys' acting-out behaviors can effectively disrupt classes regardless of the racial and gender backgrounds of teachers, though they admit that such behaviors tend to be exaggerated if the teacher is disliked. Teachers, for their own part, are limited in how they might respond to such disruptions. The situation tends to be one in which the teacher either tolerates the boys' behavior or responds to it by sending them to the office. Either response has significant drawbacks.

GENDERED ACCOUNTS OF DISRUPTIVE PRACTICES

Though the ELD girls' narratives demonstrate an acute frustration with the disruptive actions of the boys, I never witnessed a girl publicly address a boy about his behavior. Instead, many girls made concerted efforts to ignore the boys' actions or to remain unresponsive to their attempt at humor. Though girls might occasionally react to boys' actions with a laugh, more predominant responses were to strike expressive postures of annoyance or to voice muted frustrations to a girlfriend—or in some cases, the researcher—like: *"No más se la pasan jugando todo el tiempo"* [All they do is play around all the time!].

I was surprised and perplexed that the girls interviewed tended not to blame the disruptive boys for the problems in the class. Rather, they tended to put the onus of blame on the teacher—or on a collective "us." The use of "we" and "us" to name those at fault is intriguing (see Maria's first commentary earlier in this chapter), particularly given the girls' comments about the significance of the boys' behavior and the teachers' response to it. They were frustrated by the boys' actions, yet they admitted "it's contagious" and that "it is better to shout than to have to listen to it." In this sense, they understood themselves as participating as well, though not through public displays of disruption but by not paying attention [*no poniendo atención*] in class. Boys' acting-out performances were considered somewhat "natural," a perception that also naturalizes the privilege boys enjoy in making it difficult for others to learn.

Lisa Dietrich (1998), in her work on Latina girls and schooling, discusses how socialization to conservative gender roles and behavioral expectations can create a situation in which young Latinas are "expected to take responsibility for situations yet not take control of situations" (p. 38). They are bestowed with the role of "moral gatekeepers," yet are expected not to challenge male control. This may help explain ELD girls' lack of active response to the boys in class, their unwillingness to pin blame on the boys, and their feeling of guilt and shared responsibility for the "disastrous and disorganized" nature of the classes. "We," as some girls put it, are to blame.

Unfortunately, getting the boys to reflect on acting-out behavior was difficult despite the multiple contexts of interaction I and other research assistants had with them. The few tangible explanations we did get for acting-out episodes portrayed them as reactions to class assignments they did not understand, to boredom, and/or to unresponsive and sometimes perceived-to-be racist teachers. Without downplaying the legitimacy of such statements, what became clear from extended observation is that the acting-out behavior of some boys demonstrated a much more significant investment in the social experience of the class than in the academic experience.

Following popular typologies in educational research that distinguish between recent immigrant and later generation ("castelike") youths' responses to U.S. public schooling, one might expect the students acting out in the ELD classes to be those born in the United States or those who received most or all of their schooling here. However, such a framework is limited in its inability to account for situations in which ethnic "communities" are neither purely immigrant nor purely castelike minorities. The community from which Mexican-descent students at Hillside High come, for example, includes both recent immigrants and second- or third-generation Mexican families. The immigrant/castelike typology is less useful in explaining this sort of primary/secondary cultural milieu.

Though members of the U.S.-born group did tend to be among the leaders in acting out performances, they were not alone. Over the course of the year, a number of the more recent immigrant male students became quite active class performers as well. The inclination to act out plays strongly on many of the recent male immigrants who find themselves compelled to coperform in solidarity with their peers. Narrative from a ninth-grade recent immigrant student, Hector, provides a good illustration. Since middle school, Hector [YSA-4] has struggled to balance his friendship with a second-generation student, Jose [US], also in the ELD class, with his own desire to excel academically.

> *Researcher:* So you guys think that by knowing people in your
>   classes, you get distracted?
> *Hector:* Yes, [looking at Jose] like with him. I've been suspended and
>   given in-house because of this guy. I have him in four different
>   classes. Ms. Laura gave us a 3-day in-house because of him. In
>   my referral, Mrs. Babcock wrote that I was a good student, but
>   when I get together with him [pointing at Jose], I am bad.
> *Researcher:* [Looking at Jose.] And why do you distract him so much?
> *Jose:* I don't know. I just want to tell him things so that they [teachers]
>   get mad at him.
> *Researcher:* [Looking at Jose.] So you distract him on purpose?
> *Hector:* [Answering instead] Yes, that's why my grades are so low.
>   Sometimes he does it on purpose. He gets jealous that I am
>   graduating. Sometimes he sees me doing my work and he tells
>   me that I will not graduate, and because he will not graduate,
>   he's also trying to prevent me from graduating. Last year, during
>   Middle School, I graduated and he didn't. So he went to my
>   graduation and he was very jealous because I was graduating
>   and he was just watching me, and he is trying to make sure it
>   doesn't happen again here.

In this situation, emotion pulls both ways, on Hector to decide how to balance friendship with schoolwork and on Jose to maintain a bond of solidarity even though he is faltering in school.

CHOLEANDO, PERFORMANCE, AND BELONGING

Diego Vigil (Chapter 5, this volume, 1999, 1988), in his work on gangs and schooling, sees classroom acting out as a result of what he calls "street culture"—socializing children into norms and values that reward antiauthoritative and defiant behaviors—entering the classroom. Although none of the boys in Hillside High's ELD classes were "jumped-in" gang members and only a few identified themselves as having affiliations, they are growing up in neighborhoods where gang relations and affiliations shape their everyday realities and expressive styles (see Mendoza-Denton, 1996, for an apt description of how gangs can shape Mexican-descent youth's realities and styles, even for those not involved or affiliated). For this reason, Vigil's insight remains important in that it shifts attention away from simply asking questions about why students act out in class (which they tend to talk about in negative terms) to considering the kinds of meaningful and pleasurable activities in which they are invested and that might account for their behavior in class. If these boys do not seem to be engaged in classroom learning, what other kinds of meaningful social activities and associated systems of status and value might they be invested in?

Undergraduate research assistant Efren Ponce and I interviewed a number of boys from the ELD classes—both those who regularly acted out and those who did not—about what it meant to be "cool" and popular at school. These interviewees made explicit the ties between being perceived as "cool" and the value of not seeming to be invested in excelling academically in school. Consider these interview discussions:

> *Researcher:* If I were a student here, why would I want to be in a popular group?
>
> *Juan* [YSA-5]: Because you want to feel "bad."
>
> *Researcher:* Bad? How so?
>
> *Juan:* That you have friends and all that.
>
> *Researcher:* What is the difference between being in a popular group and a nonpopular group?
>
> *Juan:* That some [in the popular group] think they're all that and don't do homework and those [in other groups] do their homework. The ones that don't do their homework, they think that they are *muy fregones* [really tough]. And they get girls. Some of them don't listen to the teacher; they do not care about school. And some don't care what their grades are like.
>
> *Researcher:* Why do you think this is so? Why do they not care about their grades? Why do they not listen to their teachers or anything like that?
>
> *Juan:* Because they think they look good. Because in their minds they are "bad."
>
> *Researcher:* As far as school goes, does hanging around with these friends help you or mess you up?
>
> *Juan:* It messes you up.

Juan speaks of the allure of being "bad" as a way of "feeling" high status among larger groups of peers. Being "bad" includes being tough, having a social network of friends who will "back you up," and not doing your homework. Juan's commentary suggests that what attracts boys to certain social groupings is both a particular ethos of sociability and a social support network. Ideally, it is about a group of friends who are "cool" with you, who make you feel "bad," who do favors for you, and who help you get girls. The other side of this attraction is that it "messes you up" in that it compels "some people" not to do homework, not to "care about school," and not to care "what their grades are like."

Others boys talked about how popular groups had to be to be "gangsterlike" in their actions *(choleando)*, dress, and comportment. Popularity was about getting girls, getting back up, and having access to tangible social rewards, as Beto [US] explains:

> [One joins a popular group] to get chicks, to get girls. That is one. To back them up, that's two. And what else? Like the good groups, they give advice; they let you borrow the homework when you don't have it, like I know people that let you borrow it. Some will do their homework, you know?

Some of those interviewed expressed how popularity meant having visibility, commanding social power, and having a "whatever" attitude toward things:

> *Researcher:* Okay, so here you have a group that is always fighting, that is disruptive in class, and doing things that are not respected [by many people in the school]. Why do you think there are more people wanting to join in?
> *Javier* [YSA-4]: Because some say they are stronger. Like if they fight, then one is going to say they are strong, and I'm going to leave my studies, or I'm going to get in to see what it feels like, to see what they are like.

Juan also offered a telling insight about those who in his opinion are not "cool" and would not be accepted as popular:

> *Researcher:* What makes some groups unpopular?
> *Juan:* They are passive. . . . And they think more.
> *Researcher:* They think more?
> *Juan:* More. They think more than us.
> *Researcher:* How can that be, more?

> *Juan:* Well, they look ridiculous, they *think* better.
> *Researcher:* And why does that make a person unpopular?
> *Juan:* Because they think they are better than others.

What this exchange illustrates is that a person who is not perceived as tough and who tries to put himself above others, which in turn makes him "look ridiculous," cannot make a legitimate claim for inclusion in a high-status peer group.

Many of the boys interviewed talked about the appeal and allure of the "cholo"/"gangster" identity. But overall, the boys gave diverse meanings to these terms, from offering ways to be "cool" and "popular" to assuring that one will not go to college or even finish high school. These boys play and struggle with the "gangster" identity, and acting out seems in some ways a reaction to the perception of being seen as a "gangster" as well as an effort to position them favorably in relation to the social rewards that come from being associated with being a "gangster."

How, then, do these student commentaries make us rethink some boys' acting-out behaviors and why they are sustained despite the overwhelming risk of academic failure or low achievement? Herbert Kohl's (1994) notion of acting-out behaviors as kinds of "not-learning" practices is helpful. Kohl distinguishes not-learning from failure, arguing that failure is "the frustrated will to know," whereas not-learning involves the will to refuse knowledge in such a way that may "strengthen the will, clarify one's definitions of self, and provide inner-satisfaction" (p. 6). Kohl, however, places this concept of not-learning in an idiom of individuality, best understood through the biographical experiences of certain students. What is missing in his discussion is an appreciation of not-learning practices as kinds of performances, as shows of solidarity with a community of peers, imagined or real, immediately present in the classroom or not. In this sense, acting out may be better seen as a way of asserting group membership in larger social worlds in and around school (see Chapter 5, this volume, for similar observations).

D'Amato (1993), in his ethnographic work with Hawaiian schoolchildren, sees classroom acting out as a form of collective resistance among students who, because of sociostructurally determined beliefs about the lack of value of school, are more likely to test teachers' authority through coordinated efforts of "playful peer contention" (p. 183). However, among the Mexican immigrant students who are "acting up" in the current study, the value of schooling is essentially undisputed; all those I interviewed saw the importance of getting a high school diploma, and most of those interviewed entertain ideas of attending at least some college. Moreover, all students do not collectively "share" an engagement in disruptive behaviors in the class; some students become extremely frustrated by the behavior of others. Nor are those participating necessarily doing so in an equally conscious manner—for example, for the girls it is clearly not a situation of conscious resistance but rather one of tortured guilt.

Taking the gendered aspects of this phenomenon seriously, the boys' acting-out practices—and the way such practices influence the behavior of others—must be seen in relation to hegemonic constructions of (working-class) masculinity. The ethnographic data I present suggest that processes of peer-based socialization produce and constantly reestablish—through everyday performances and interaction—particular hegemonic sensibilities about masculinity that compel some Mexican-descent boys to be at odds with classroom learning. Many boys are invested in or allured by a particular set of meaningful cultural practices—"*choleando,*" being seen as "bad"—which, though pleasurable for the high status they confer, limit the range of expressions boys can exhibit and remain in good standing (of high status) within important social networks. In this sense, tropes of resistance are not the best way to account for these boys' actions; rather, behavior is more accurately understood in its relation to norms developed through a differential socialization in a social context of racial, class, and gender stratification. Acting-out performances are tied to a unspoken understanding of how boys are to behave to sustain meaningful, inclusive bonds of belonging (see Chapter 5, this volume, for a similar analysis).

THE "SCHOOLBOY" PHENOMENON AMONG ELD STUDENTS

> During a math lesson, the teacher asked the students to name opposite integers. Alejandro [YSA-1], sitting at a table with a group of other boys, volunteered a correct answer. Immediately, the boys in his group broke out in a chorus of "schoolboy, schoolboy" followed by the comment "now you think you are smart." [Field-note excerpt]

It was clear from participant-observation in the ELD classes that the boys who were acting out and not participating were quite bright and some, like Alejandro, quite knowledgeable. This fact is not lost on girls in the ELD class.

> *Lupe* [YSA-5]: [In Math class] it's usually the same student [who acts out], Julio.
> *Angelica* [YSA-1]: And even though he's smart, he doesn't show it.
> *Lupe:* Yeah, only when he wants to.
> *Maria* [YSA-1]: Yeah, he's only smart when he wants to be.

Adriana [YSA-1]: He's very intelligent and he thinks very clearly because he has given me a lot of advice.

Lupe: Because you see that he's a goof-off, you think that he's not smart.

In the ELD classes I observed, the term *schoolboy* was invoked exclusively
by boys to tease other boys; girls tended not to be active participants or the
targets of such teasing. This is not to say that Latina girls do not worry
about being considered a "schoolgirl" (e.g., see Mendoza-Denton, 1999) or
that some of these ELD girls were not subject to such teasing. Rather, this
phenomenon among girls did not take place in classes I attended nor did it
come up in extensive interviews with the girls. It would seem that such
teasing was not prevalent among the recent immigrant girls perhaps because, as Dietrich (1998) suggests, some of the behaviors prized by schools
and called "schoolgirl" behavior (deference and social peer supportive) conform to behaviors seen as properly feminine by girls themselves.

The schoolboy phenomenon shares some important features with the
acting-out practices explored above. Invocations of "schoolboy" point to
larger social meanings about the "correct" nature of social relations among
boys. They imply without having to be said: "Don't try to be better than others." The censure is framed as a call for egalitarianism, yet the boundaries of
this "community" are extremely limited. Central to this egalitarianism is a
sense of "others" against whom this community *ethos* is made meaningful—those who are "passive," those who think they are better than others,
those who "look ridiculous" for "thinking more." One's social status is evaluated through one's willingness and/or ability to conform to localized social norms that mark certain behaviors as appropriate [being "bad," being
aggressive, holding one's ground, not putting oneself above others] and others as endangering masculine status [passivity, putting oneself above oth-
ers]. What makes the censure on "being smart" and being a "schoolboy"
effective is not the way in which some boys exercise direct authority over
others; rather, through the rhetorical use of sentiments of derision, one or
more boys are able to evoke locally valued notions of reciprocity that move
the targeted individual toward a desirable action (or inaction) and behavior. Here authority does not reside so much in one who speaks or controls
others but rather is made manifest by way of calling attention to largely unspoken but locally understood conditions of inclusion/exclusion, leaving
it up to the perceived "schoolboy" to construct an appropriate set of meanings on which to base his subsequent behavior (Brenneis, 1995).

I have focused on the practices of acting out and "schoolboy" teasing
in relation to dominant forms of masculinity not because this relationship
is the only or necessarily the primary one that explains the phenomena, but
because this connection is less developed in the literature on student non-

compliance. Certainly, class and race factors frame these practices as well. Ethnographic work on the experience of working-class youth in schools has demonstrated how groups of students—both White and racial minority—have employed diverse forms of cultural practice to produce a sense of belonging and solidarity against White middle-class norms required in the schooling context. For example, Paul Willis's (1977) well-known ethnography of working-class boys in Britain describes how they demonstrated an oppositional style against school authority to preserve their working-class cultural style while relegating themselves to school failure (see also Eckert, 1989; Foley, 1990; Philips, 1983). Similarly, Ogbu (1993) and Fordham and Ogbu (1987) argue that for some African American students, the fear of being perceived as "acting White" is felt so strongly that it compels a refusal to assent to learning or to establish relationships of trust with teachers, both prerequisites for schooling success. Sanctions against being a "schoolboy" among ELD students at Hillside High resonate with sanctions against "acting White" that Ogbu and Fordham identify among African American students. These forms of teasing compel particular classroom behaviors and stigmatize others. In terms of school practice, these sanctions limit the ways academic tasks can be approached and how some students value such tasks.

What is interesting in both Ogbu's and Willis's ethnographies is their attention to how intergroup conflicts—developed from historical relationships of racial and class subordination/exclusion—play out *within* subordinated groups themselves. The students in Ogbu's study accused those who did well in school of being disloyal toward their "race." Similarly, Willis's ethnography of White working-class boys in Britain describes how their oppositional style against school authority was also waged significantly against the "ear'oles," a group of students who conformed to the school norms. This censorship against "acting White" or "being a schoolboy" brings up the important consideration that intergroup oppositions can be projected onto the intragroup level through the way in which social categories become salient to youth as they affect their sense of status and belonging. Expressions and appeals to be true to one's "community" or "race" work to create affective bonds of solidarity between people as well as make operative powerful forms of inclusion/exclusion, perhaps in order to affirm particular ideas about what constitutes proper personhood and its attendant modes of self-representation (Fordham, 1996; Morgan, 1996) or locally valued notions of the "educated person" (Levinson & Holland, 1996).

Among Mexican-descent populations in the United States, however, these understandings of proper and "educated" personhood are variable and highly contested. The aggressive forms of cultural prescriptivism regarding language and culture in the United States have not created a unified Mexican immigrant subject. Mexican immigrants in the United States use their social relations and multiple attachments to accommodate, endure, and resist the difficult circumstances and dominant representations they encounter in school and community. Intraethnic differences among Mexican-descent youth have resulted from various pressures to acculturate to dominant, Anglo norms of language and behavior and take root through the way youth position or identify themselves along a continuum from recent immigrants to more established and acculturated Mexican Americans. The meanings youth themselves give to these differences, however, are quite complex, and the labels used to mark differences not only indicate levels of acculturation to dominant Anglo norms; they also act as mutually defining categories that both youth and adults associate with particular styles, symbols, and values that (are assumed to) signal and explain various "ways of being" and behaving in the school context (Eckert, 1989; Mendoza-Denton, 1999).

For Mexican-descent students, these labels are connected not only to prestige but also to a sense of dignity, well-being, and respect—as particular responses to persisting negative stereotypes of Mexican youth and to subordinate status in U.S. schools and society (Rosaldo, Flores, & Silvestrini, 1994). Intragroup differences are perhaps best understood as competing ways of claiming rights to first-class citizenship in "an economic and political context that relegates cultural group members to static and disparaged ethnic, racial, gender, and class identities" (Zentella, 1997, p. 13). In this sense, local understandings of intragroup differences are not easily accounted for in terms of generation or class; it is often the perception of class or generational difference—rather than any empirically identifiable difference itself—that makes a difference. They are constituted in the cultural poetics of everyday encounters through interpersonal battles over power, status, and privilege among Mexican-descent youth.

At Hillside High, the process of ascribing and embodying labels of intraethnic difference—for example, whether one is seen as a Mexicano, Mexican American, or "cholo"/"gangster"—are extremely significant to Mexican-descent youth. The negotiation of such labels is central to how students relate and position themselves to one another as well as how they orient themselves to schooling resources. Unfortunately, though, attempts of Mexican-immigrant boys to succeed in school necessarily means engaging the "cholo"/"gangster" identity, even if the attempt is to try to shed or get around it. Consider the following interview with Carlos [US], a relatively high-achieving senior Mexican-descent student and also a member of the school's Migrant Student Association. Though he is not an ELD student, Carlos's commentary is telling in its description of how achieving relative success—even in advanced placement classes with White students and teachers—does not entail a separation from the negative perceptions and expectations associated with being young, male, and Latino.

> [All] the little gangs [around here] are Mexican, and I get pretty embarrassed. It's my race, you know. And you know how some people can stereotype you? I don't want to be stereotyped as a gangster or nothing. . . . Like in classes [he has AP classes with White students], you don't want to be judged as a stupid person, like a gang [member]. Like, maybe you wear the color, or you ask a stupid question—"oh, he is gang member." Saying [that you are] "a gangster" doesn't seem like an insult right now, but it's the thought of "oh, he is Mexican, he's gotta do this," . . . that "he is ignorant and stupid just like the other Mexicans that are in gangs." You don't want to be compared like that. [spoken in English]

For Carlos, not being seen as a gangster is extremely important because it allows room to develop an identity as a successful student, or at least to develop an identity that is not inconsistent with being a good student.

Although students like Carlos may characterize "cholos," "gangsters," or "wannabe" students as undesirable and "stupid," other students may in turn describe academically successful Mexican students derisively as "schoolgirls" or "schoolboys." Juxtaposing Carlos's words with some of the commentaries from male ELD students earlier brings into relief the fault lines that exist among Mexican-descent students at the school. In both cases, struggles over social difference have consequences for students in their effort to engage with school activities and achieve school success. In terms of Stanton-Salazar's social-capital framework (Chapter 2, this volume), some peer networks—including those within which many of the ELD students in this study find themselves—may function to moderate rather than mediate access to important sources of institutional support. That is, those students whose social-categorical membership compels them to define themselves against schoolmates who exhibit proscholastic norms are often cut off from access to authentic social capital and may remain less receptive to the forms of social support extended by adult institutional agents.

THE ROLE OF THE SCHOOL

Although the analysis in this study suggests that the school is not wholly responsible for the difficulties ELD students face in learning English and achieving academic success, it is significantly implicated in perpetuating these difficulties. Schools are not innocent in the processes of differentiation that separate Mexican-descent students (see Valenzuela, 1999). Though I have highlighted the processes of peer-based socialization that inform both the acting-out practices and "schoolboy" teasing of some Mexican-descent boys, the school must be understood as playing a central role in affirming the particular sensibilities about masculinity that compel these sorts of performances. Schools, by providing vast resources and high visibility to sports programs and their associated activities, contribute to the production of what Holland and Eisenhart (1990) call "gender regimes," which validate particular versions of masculinity that legitimate aggression, domination, and sexist discourse. These institutional practices influence interactional discursive practices among boys and girls, producing in turn limited and essentialist subject positions that many boys and girls are compelled to inhabit—some more comfortably than others (Eder, 1995). At the same time, though the school promotes the sporting mentality as an "ideal" for all boys, it offers a "safe" place (and accompanying resources) for exercising the forms of aggression and domination it legitimates to only a limited and elite group of students. For the boys in the ELD classes, one might say that the classroom is their playing field as well as the terrain on which status is gained and lost.

Students' negotiations of social difference within the schooling environment are intimately linked to the relationship between school resource providers and student status groups. Schools can exacerbate the inequalities that mark intraethnic differences by the way in which they accord differential status through policies of ability grouping, tracking, and other forms of "disciplinary measures" that communicate implicit judgments about students as individuals and as members of identifiable groups. Placement of students in groups through policies of ability grouping and tracking has a double effect of influencing students' choices of peer groups, while implying a normative judgment about the group's future prospects and perceived intellectual abilities (Eisenhart & Graue, 1993). Dress codes, security and surveillance measures, and behavioral prohibitions all differentiate students. In this way, institutional power shapes students' fields of action (Davidson, 1996). In other words, when teachers or other school staff members categorize students, it affects how students understand and define themselves within the context of the school.

It is important to understand that the teasing and intraethnic dynamics that create difficulties for some students do not sprout somehow organically from within the Mexican community or "culture"; nor should it be argued that school underachievement can be located in the forms of social relations that exist among Mexican-descent students. At the same time, intraethnic differences do not constitute or explain the variability in the schooling performance of Mexican-descent students; in fact, it is often the perception of such differences that leads to dangerous stereotypes that are used by school personnel to "explain" the relative motivation or interest of certain groups of students to do well in school and to assess their "educatability" (Valenzuela, 1999). It is exceedingly important that schools acknowledge and come to an informed understanding of their own role in perpetuating difficulties for Mexican-descent students by recognizing the dialectic relationship between how they separate and classify students (including informal ways of categorizing students and more formal tracking practices) and students' own "choices" to segregate themselves along lines of social difference, particularly along lines of race, language, and gender. At Hillside High, the school is complicit in the social marginalization of English-language learners given its utter failure to provide opportunities for meaningful interaction between students from different racial and linguistic backgrounds, through either curricular, cocurricular, or informal activities.

CONCLUSION

The analysis in this chapter suggests that understanding the academic challenges facing Mexican-descent English-language learners requires taking seriously the way in which broader forces of gender, class, and racial discrimination and exploitation play out in internal relations of power, privilege, and status among Mexican-descent students themselves. Student behaviors that might seem to suggest noncompliance or disengagement—acting out in class or not actively participating—do not constitute a collective "Mexican" response or resistance to schooling; rather, they result in part from processes of differentiation (forms of inclusion/exclusion) among Mexican-descent students along lines of gender and (perceived) class and generational difference. The acting-out and teasing behaviors in ELD classes are meaningful social practices and performances that have the potential to set effective limits on what appears acceptable, say-able, or do-able while simultaneously maintaining important bonds of both solidarity and sociality with other Mexican-descent classmates. I distinguish between solidarity and sociality because the issue may not necessarily be one of standing together with others but rather one of feelings of belonging in very local and visceral terms. Yet the "inclusionary" aspects of acting out and teasing are not innocent of the same kinds of "othering" processes that have characterized intergroup relations in the United States (between Anglos and people of color and, in this case, immigrants of color) and have historically generated inequalities in the larger society along lines of race, gender, and class.

This analysis in this chapter also suggests that understanding the behaviors of some Mexican immigrant students with regard to formal learning requires an appreciation of the various levels and forms of peer socialization at work in the school. In other words, formal classroom-based learning is only one of the many forms of learning taking place in the school environment; students are learning to become members of particular social worlds. This is a social and interpersonal process rather than a primarily psychological or linguistic one for the ELD students. For many of them, the process of learning to become members of particular social worlds has a tenuous and sometimes antagonistic relationship to practices of formal learning.

Of course, students' actions and behaviors in the schooling context relate to their experiences not only in particular peer worlds but in family and community worlds as well. Students' schooling orientations are supported considerably by socially negotiated rationales (D'Amato, 1993) that draw from the various and often conflicting expectations put upon them by larger social collectivities of which they are a part—family, peer group, and community. For Latino students in U.S. schools, academic success is predicated to a large degree on how these students come to value and negotiate both intraethnic (gender, generational, socioeconomic) and interethnic differences (self-perceptions of being a Latina/o youth in a racially biased and racially politicized setting). How one "chooses" to act or behave in schooling contexts has to do with how one is able to manage these affiliations. Yet the behavioral "choices" students make need to be understood as highly susceptible to constant evaluation according to standards held by peers, whether they be close friends or simply other classmates. It is this interpersonal process in which forms of social interactions are rendered meaningful through negotiation and display that has been the interest of this chapter.

If schools have a sincere interest in creating environments that facilitate learning for Mexican-descent English-language learners, they would benefit greatly from a working understanding of the variable relationships at play within the school that challenge these students to make difficult adaptations to cope with incongruities in expectations, values, and beliefs. Too often, Mexican-descent failure or underachievement is related to students' cultural backgrounds and families, or is understood to result from falling in with the "wrong" peers. Focusing on these sorts of accounts—locating the source of the problem in students' families or peer networks—not only is inaccurate but functions to exonerate schools from their responsibilities to change and transform schooling practices to fit the linguistic and cultural realities and identities of diverse student bodies. Schools' institutional and discursive practices have the ability not only to perpetuate the segregation and marginalization of many Mexican-descent students within the school but also to shape power dynamics within and among peer groups in ways that reinforce forms of student identification that separate students from one another and, consequently, create social and cultural borders that limit school engagement for a significant number of Mexican-descent students (see Chapter 6, this volume). The analysis in this chapter suggests that in order to more effectively serve Mexican-descent students, schools must both recognize the mutually constituted forms of social difference that exist among their students and take active steps to mitigate the schooling practices that perpetuate those differences.

ACKNOWLEDGMENTS

The research discussed in this chapter was made possible through generous grants from the University of California Linguistic Minority Research Institute, the Spencer Foundation, and the U.S. Department of Education/OERI (Margaret A. Gibson, Principal Investigator). I also wish to acknowledge all the students and staff from Hillside High School who have contributed to this work, and most especially the students and teachers in the ELD classes.

NOTES

1. In addition to classroom observation, I conducted regular semistructured individual interviews as well as relatively unstructured group interviews with members of the classes. My participation observation also included informal interactions with students in class and outside of class, both within the schooling context (lunch, between classes) and outside of school (students' workplaces, neighborhoods). All student quotes in this paper were originally made in Spanish and translated to English, unless otherwise noted. An exception is field-note excerpts that provide direct transcriptions without translation. Spanish phrases are kept in the transcript when they seem to convey a sentiment that might be lost in the translation.

2. A third phenomenon in the ELD that I lack space to discuss in this chapter was a prevalent form of teasing and "making fun of" among ELD students—both boys and girls—in relation to their "correctness" in the use and pronunciation of spoken English. This teasing created obstacles for English-language learners, both in terms of their willingness to speak English in class and their ability to practice speaking it outside of the classroom. I address this phenomenon elsewhere (Hurd & Gibson, 2002).

3. This system of designating time in the United States is somewhat limited because it does not account for those students who may migrate seasonally to Mexico or another region in the United States. Although few of the ELD students' families actually migrate seasonally for work, many return to Mexico for a few months each winter owing to a lack of availability of work, closure of the local labor camp, and/or to rendezvous with extended family. During this period, Hillside High ELD students may miss anywhere from a few days to a few weeks of school.

REFERENCES

Brenneis, D. (1995). Caught in the web of words: Performing theory in a Fiji Indian community. In J. A. Russell et al. (Eds.), *Everyday conceptions of emotion* (pp. 241–249). Netherlands: Kluwer Academic.

D'Amato, J. (1993). Resistance and compliance in minority classrooms. In E. Jacob & C. Jordan (Eds.), *Minority education: Anthropological perspectives* (pp. 181–208). Norwood, NJ: Ablex.

Davidson, A. L. (1996). *Making and molding identities in schools: Student narratives on race, gender, and academic engagement.* Albany: State University of New York Press.

Delgado-Gaitan, C. (1990). *Literacy for empowerment: The role of parents in children's education.* New York: Falmer Press.

Dietrich, L. C. (1998). *Chicana adolescents: Bitches, 'ho's, and schoolgirls.* Westport, CT: Praeger.

Eckert, P. (1989). *Jocks and burnouts: Social categories in the U.S. high school.* New York: Teachers College Press.

Eder, D. (1995). *School talk: Gender and adolescent culture.* New Brunswick, NJ: Rutgers University Press.

Eisenhart, M., & Graue, M. E. (1993). Constructing cultural differences and educational achievement in schools. In E. Jacob & C. Jordan (Eds.), *Minority education: Anthropological perspectives* (pp. 3–15). Norwood, NJ: Ablex.

Foley, D. (1990). *Learning capitalist culture: Deep in the heart of Tejas.* Philadelphia: University of Pennsylvania Press.

Fordham, S. (1996). *Blacked out: Dilemmas of race, identity, and success at Capital High.* Chicago: University of Chicago Press.

Fordham, S., & Ogbu, J. (1987). Black students' school success: Coping with the burden of "acting white." *Urban Review, 18*(3), 176–206.

Holland, D., & Eisenhart, M. A. (1990). *Educated in romance: Women, achievement, and college culture.* Chicago: University of Chicago Press.

Hurd, C., & Gibson, M. A. (2002). *Different paths taken: The divergent academic experiences of English language learners during high school.* Final Report to University of California Linguistic Minority Research Institute.

Kohl, H. (1994). *I won't learn from you and other thoughts on creative maladjustment.* New York: New Press.

Levinson, B., & Holland, D. (1996). Introduction: The cultural production of the educated person. In B. A. Levinson, D. E. Holland, & D. C. Foley (Eds.), *The cultural production of the educated person* (pp. 1–51). Albany: State University of New York Press.

Lutz, C., & Abu-Lughod, L. (1990). Introduction: Emotion, discourse, and the politics of everyday life. In C. Lutz & L. Abu-Lughod (Eds.), *Language and the politics of emotion* (pp. 1–23). New York: Cambridge University Press.

Mehan, H., Villanueva, I., Hubbard, L., & Lintz, A. (1996). *Constructing school success: The consequences of untracking low-achieving students.* New York: Cambridge University Press.

Mendoza-Denton, N. (1996). "Muy macha": Gender and ideology in gang-girls' discourse about make-up. *Ethnos, 61*(1–2), 47–63.

Mendoza-Denton, N. (1999). Fighting words: Latina girls, gangs, and language attitudes. In D. L. Galindo & M. D. Gonzales-Vasquez (Eds.), *Speaking Chicana*. Tucson: University of Arizona.

Morgan, M. (1996). Conversational signifying. In E. Ochs, E. Schegloff, & S. Thompson (Eds.), *Grammar and interaction* (pp. 405–434). London: Cambridge University Press.

Noddings, N. (1992). *The challenge to care in schools: An alternative approach to education*. New York: Teachers College Press.

Ogbu, J. U. (1993). Variability in minority school performance: A problem in search of an explanation. In E. Jacob & C. Jordan (Eds.), *Minority education: Anthropological perspectives* (pp. 83–112). Norwood, NJ: Ablex.

Olsen, L. (1997). *Made in America: Immigrant students in our public schools*. New York: New Press. (Distributed by W. W. Norton).

Philips, S. U. (1983). *The invisible culture: Communication in classroom and community on the Warm Springs Indian Reservation*. Research on Teaching Monograph Series. New York: Longman.

Romo, H., & Falbo, T. (1996). *Latino high school graduation: Defying the odds*. Austin: University of Texas Press.

Rosaldo, R., Flores, W., & Silvestrini, B. (1994). *Identity, conflict, and evolving Latino communities*. Stanford, CA: Stanford Center for Chicano Research.

Suarez-Orozco, C., & Suarez-Orozco, M. (1995). *Transformations: Immigration, family life, and achievement motivation among Latino adolescents*. Palo Alto, CA: Stanford University Press.

Urciuoli, B. (1996). *Exposing prejudice: Puerto Rican experiences of language, race, and class*. Boulder, CO: Westview Press.

Valdes, G. (1996). *Con respeto: Bridging the distances between culturally diverse families and schools: An ethnographic portrait*. New York: Teachers College Press.

Valdes, G. (2001). *Learning and not learning English: Latino students in American schools*. New York: Teachers College Press.

Valenzuela, A. (1999). *Subtractive schooling: U.S.–Mexican youth and the politics of caring*. Albany: State University of New York Press.

Vasquez, O. A., Pease-Alvarez, P., & Shannon, S. M. (1994). *Pushing boundaries: Language and culture in a Mexicano community*. New York: Cambridge University Press.

Vigil, D. (1988). *Barrio gangs: Street life and identity in Southern California*. Austin: University of Texas Press.

Vigil, D. (1999). Streets and schools: How educators can help marginalized gang youth. *Harvard Educational Review, 69*(3), 270–284.

Willis, P. (1977). *Learning to labor: How working-class kids get working-class jobs*. Westmead, England: Saxon House.

Zentella, A. C. (1997). *Growing up bilingual: Puerto Rican children in New York*. Malden, MA: Blackwell.

5

Gangs and Group Membership: Implications for Schooling

James Diego Vigil

Gangs are ubiquitous on the streets of urban America, especially in Los Angeles, the gang capital of the world. In the most marginalized and socio-economically stressed sectors of the inner cities and metropolises, the urbanization of Chicanos, or Mexican Americans, has generated a process of street socialization and a gang subculture. Since the 1940s, many second-generation Chicano youth have struggled to adapt to the city, and their multiple sense of marginality has given birth to a street culture, that of the gang. For these youth, both the pervasive effects of marginality—poverty, crime, and violence in neighborhoods—and gang peer influence attenuate the guidance of other socializing agents, such as parents and schools.

The peer pressure exerted on the streets directs the youths' participation in school, profoundly affecting their learning and classroom experiences. It often manifests in disruptive behaviors—such as "backing up" a fellow gang member, refusing to acknowledge the teacher, and not participating—that interrupt or slow learning for the gang youth (Burnett & Walz, 1994). Because teachers and school staff frequently interpret such behavior as simply the disruptive behavior of nongang youth (see Chapter 4, this volume), the connections between gang influence and classroom behaviors, as well as gang youth's lack of access to conventional supportive resources, are left unexamined. Therefore, although school officials and policy makers may be able to address more conventional disruptions and acts of nonlearning associated with the larger student body, they remain in the dark with only limited information on how to approach the multiple-aged gang peer group and their gang-influenced school behaviors.

Mistaking gang-influenced behaviors as more generally encountered classroom disruptions further compounds the challenges already faced by Chicanos who, with other ethnic minorities and low-income students, have historically been ill-served in public schools (Kozol, 1992). Common school policies—such as tracking by ability group and the use of standardized tests as the ultimate measures of educational performance and ability—have tended to work against minority students (Valencia, 1991). Traditional and ongoing school policies, both formal and informal, might also evoke feelings among at-risk students and gang members that school is an unwelcome place for them. For example, a 14-year-old gang member from central Los Angeles complained to me that he was always assigned a seat in the back of the classroom:

> I always thought, how could I learn when I'm always sitting in the back away from all the teaching in the front where the good students sit? In back with me were all the other mess-ups. So what did we do? Mess-up.

Inferior schools (Kozol, 1992; Oakes, 1985), funding inequities, cultural insensitivity, and an ethnocentric curriculum have accentuated the problems.

Thus, for "at-risk" marginal gang youth, who are overwhelmingly male, schooling in places like Los Angeles is particularly problematic (Vigil, 1997, 1999). Yet very little research on gangs has been conducted that can inform educational practitioners and policy makers. This chapter addresses this lacuna and extends the analysis of my previous ethnographic work in the greater Los Angeles area, in which I examined the behaviors and academic performance of Mexican American high school students (Vigil & Long, 1981, Vigil, 1982, 1988a, 1997), specifically that of the male students who are gang members and/or who have a street identity and allegiance (Vigil, 1999). Augmenting my earlier fieldwork, I draw also from more recent observations and interviews conducted at four high schools in Los Angeles.[1]

As I have discussed elsewhere (Vigil, 2002a; Vigil & Yun, 1996), gang phenomena are a complex cluster of strands that are interwoven, involving social as well as personal elements—and in this chapter I further probe the ways in which peer-influenced street behaviors and attitudes guide learning and school performance. As in previous work, I use a multiple marginality framework, in which multiple marginality refers to the complex and persistent historical and structural forces that tend to destabilize a significant sector of urban ethnic minority populations (Moore, 1978, 1991; Vigil, 1988a, 1988b, 1999). This framework highlights the ways in which events, times, places, thoughts, and people are related to ecological, socioeconomic, cultural, and psychosocial factors that push (or "pull") a youth into a gang. Furthermore, it underscores how access to social and cultural resources that would promote educational success is outside the purview of street-gang populations who are the pariahs of most working-class Chicano neighborhoods (see Chapter 2, this volume). Of particular relevance to this volume are the ways in which peer gang members, through ties connecting the street and school behaviors, influence one another's academic performance.

MARGINALIZATION, PEERS, AND IDENTIFICATION

Among Chicano youth the sense of cultural marginality is most profound for those who join gangs and become gang members (Vigil, 1997). Where they live, what work their parents have,[2] how they experience their social world, their interactions with peers and peer groups, and their self-identification with the barrio (neighborhood) reflect a state of marginality that involves both broad historical factors and ongoing ecological and socioeconomic forces in their lives. Today, the youth gangs who originate in the economically marginal areas of Los Angeles continue to be fueled by the persisting marginal socioeconomic conditions of these areas (Vigil, 2002b). Racial and ethnic discrimination and cultural differences continue to lead to economic insecurity and lack of opportunity, fragmented social control institutions, and both psychological and emotional barriers in broad segments of the Chicano community in Los Angeles. These segments are consistently challenged by inadequate living conditions, stressful personal and family lives, and ongoing institutional racism and cultural repression.

Drawn at an early age to the public spaces of the streets in order to escape households severely affected by this multiple marginality, Chicano street youth are often left unsupervised by adults. Their socialization—that is, "the process by which children learn to do, and want to do what is required and expected by others . . . [and which results in] the desire for approval" (Edgerton, 1978, p. 446)—takes place on the streets where learning, expectations, and approval are deeply embedded in peer relations and identification with a peer group. Especially for adolescents, peer dynamics become exceedingly salient and influential (Vigil, 1988b). These youth are guided by the behaviors of the multiple-aged peer group and their identification becomes situated within an age-stratified street subculture and delineated by their connection to their street peers. Their gang peers can provide them with particular forms of capital associated with the power and membership of gang hierarchy, but they lack connections with peers who can act as agents for or sources of the forms of peer capital that orient them toward academic achievement (see Chapter 2, this volume).

Of the youth in any barrio, 4% to 10% undergo street socialization to the point that they join gangs (Vigil, 1988a). Youth as young as 7 or 8 years old have been known to join gangs, but the usual age when this process intensifies is at age 12 or 13. It is the multiple-aged peer group of the gang that is especially influential on new novitiates, acting as a substitute for the family in many ways—a substitute for most conventional institutions and pathways. Thus street youngsters must contend not only with peers their own age but also with those who are older, sometimes in their mid-20s. When these youth join the gang, it becomes more a convoy than a peer group, as the older members often call the "shots," with the destroyers deploying in support of the battleships. The identity of the younger gang members then becomes established through their participation in gang practices established by behaviors of the older members. A 17-year-old from an East Los Angeles barrio summarized it this way:

> When I joined the barrio I was jumped in [initiated with a beating].[3] I remember the older guys looking me over real hard. When they started hitting me from all over, the older guys gave me the best shots to make sure I could take it. But after, they made me feel like I belonged and every time I'd see them I felt good because of it. I was part of the barrio. I belonged. I was somebody.

The bonding that occurs among street children during their early street experiences becomes solidified during adolescence, often leading to more intense bonding with the peer group and to destructive gang activities.

Many street youth, like the one quoted, recognize older gang members as the legitimate "authorities" and operate within a set of rules and regulations established by the older members that are incongruent with those instituted by dominant organizations, like schools. As Stanton-Salazar notes in Chapter 2, social resources can be appropriately analyzed only within the hierarchical divisions of particular communities. As a result of the conflict between the street norms gang youth strive to live by and those of the school, many street-socialized children either drop out or are kicked out of school in the eighth or ninth grade. Most of the gang members, both hardcore and peripheral, who initially enter high school leave by the end of tenth grade (Vigil, 1988a).

School officials have, for the most part, taken a "zero tolerance" attitude toward gangs, gang members, and all that they represent, and regularly expel or suspend gang youth, in essence ending their school careers

(Vigil, 1997). As explained to this author by one principal of an East Los Angeles high school: "Gang members never show up to school the first day, and when they don't, they lose their seat. We are so crowded that it's easy to make latecomers go to another school in the district." Thus, of the relatively few gang members who manage to stay in high school, most are hanging on at continuation or alternative high schools, referred to by some observers as "soft" jails (Munoz, 2001; Raywid, 1990). The rest are on the streets, usually at barrio hangouts, whiling the time away talking, smoking "bud" (a potent flower from the marijuana plant), selling drugs (usually rock cocaine) to outsiders, and catching up on intergang news about conflicts with other barrios as well as the past and future social gatherings that dot the week's activities.

RESISTANCE OR DIFFERENTIAL SOCIALIZATION?

For those gang members and other street-socialized Chicano youth who remain in school, the peer relations formed and negotiated on the street transcend the street–school border. These peer dynamics and their associated behaviors often place the street-socialized students at odds with not only the social structure of their schools but also the Mexican-descent students who avoid the streets and form peer alliances within schools that promote school engagement and belonging (see Chapter 7, this volume). The social resources articulated in gangs are of a different sort and from a different reality than those accessed by Mexican-descent students who are not street socialized. Among the complex of factors that determine peer dynamics in student associations, school–student interactions, and student–teacher power relations, two are central to this discussion. One, well described by Hurd (see Chapter 4, this volume), is the disruptive behavior or lack of participation by students, often led by a small number of boys, that interrupts or slows learning. The second refers to the teaching and organizational practices within classrooms that fail to engage students in learning (Valenzuela, 1999). Exploration of the student–teacher classroom dyad encompasses both sets of factors and is central to our understanding of the relationships between gang-influenced socialization and school behaviors.

Some researchers (Darder, Torres, & Gutierrez, 1997; Ogbu, 1987) assert that the defiant, acting-out attitudes and behaviors displayed by students at school are motivated by a more-or-less conscious resistance to authority (Giroux, 1983). Other researchers (Cromwell, Taylor, & Palacios, 1992; Curry, Fox, Ball, & Stone, 1993; Goldstein, 1994; Kodluboy, 1994; Valencia, 1991), including myself, suggest that such matters as particular socialization routines that shape thinking and behavior irrespective of ideology also need to be considered in dealing with minority youth's educational experiences. Resistance to a dominant culture is not, we argue, the same for one who is a part of that culture as it is for youth socialized to an alternative culture, in this case, that of the street or gang. Multiple marginality forces have directed gang members away from proacademic goals.

In Chapter 4, Hurd raises questions about the resistance explanation that imbues students with a premeditated, conscious attitude to thwart learning from an oppressive schooling system that harbors racist practices and teachers. Following Kohl (1994), Hurd maintains that deliberate "not-learning" makes more sense than resistance; it involves the will to not learn and thus will "strengthen the will, clarify one's definitions of self, and provide inner-satisfaction" (p. 6). In short, it is a conscious decision. However, Hurd adds an important element; he notes that Kohl's explanation does not go far enough because, in many cases, "not learning" is not just a one-person act; the "community of peers" is an essential ingredient in students' acting-out performances rendered by the students.

My past research on street gangs and youth subgroups supports a group rather than an individual orientation, as illustrated by the following observation:

> At one evening gathering I observed a newly inducted East Los Angeles gang member respond in a very nonchalant way to mention of the death of an important older member. An older gang member gave him a moderately stern look and replied: "He's from the barrio, *ese* (you)." The message was simple: Anyone in the barrio is important, and you should feel what we feel about him.

Identification is thus established through allegiance to the gang, which also both reflects and reinforces the individual's relational role within the group.

We ask, therefore, whether in dominant institutions, such as schools, street behavior associated with group peer approval can be interpreted as "resistance" to the institution, as suggested by Yinger's (1960) "contra-culture," Willis's (1977) "oppositional culture," and even Cohen's (1955) "reaction-formation" theories? These frameworks suggest that students who flout authority to gain peer approval have the same lived experiences as those who conform. But are the students really resisting, countering, and rejecting something if, in fact, they haven't really experienced the culture they're resisting? Or is it strictly in their minds, as Cohen has suggested in his reaction-formation theory, where working-class youth invert middle-class values? For some observers, resistance makes sense because it lends a politicized voice to the downtrodden and the powerless. But the evidence for such a "voice" is thin, and it is a facile, speculative explanation for the abysmal schooling patterns of marginalized minority youth. The school behavior of street-socialized youth is not so much a reaction to and resistance to a dominant culture and group as it is the reflection of the absence of mainstream influences in the lives of the youth. Gang youth have learned different values in a quite different cultural milieu; in short, their behaviors in school reflect their socialization to a street culture rather than to the dominant culture.

An essential part of the explanation for unconventional classroom behavior for gang members, and perhaps other youth subgroups, is the street socialization they undergo to conform to the patterns and behaviors that are readily accessible to them as members of their group. Sometimes the street-socialization and peer-influenced behavior is supported directly or at least reinforced from home. One story of an older, former gang member from East Los Angeles conveys this. As a young child, he was beaten by a child his own age and ran home crying for comfort and pity. When he arrived and blurted out his story, his father immediately led him back outside by the arm and demanded that the boy return to fight the other child so that he could learn to take care of himself. The father, a street fighter himself, thus was pushing the second generation to *"no te rajes"* (don't be a chicken).

In this alternative culture, there exists a tendency toward "reckless" behavior, a mix of mischief and deviance, with some youth, especially the "loco" gang members with the earliest, harshest, and most continuous trauma-ridden lives, enjoying lives of seemingly abandoned, impulsive behavior. Gang youth comments seem, at first, to support that it is just plain fun to disobey, do your own thing, and live on the edge. When I asked one member why he was in a gang, he succinctly responded: "Adventure, money, and besides it was fun." The heady sense of excitement is a strong current in gang lore; it has even become a core cultural construct known as *locura*, the art of acting wild or maintaining a state of quasi-controlled insanity. This idea of *locura* is ingrained in the subculture and invested into nicknames, such as "Cycho," "Psycho," "Loco," and "Loca," that glorify craziness and in which gang members typically invest great pride. One youngster, when questioned by the police about his involvement in a shooting that accidentally wounded a 5-year-old child, showed no remorse; instead he boldly said: "I don't give a fuck. Why do you think they call me Psycho!" Another 17-year-old explained that when he gets in fights or in an aggressive mood: "My head goes crazy like a T.V. that has static."

Upon deeper analysis, it seems that the "reckless" behavior of gang members emerges not from conscious commission but rather from the many omissions in their lives; they see acting "loco" as their only recourse. According to Flores-Gonzalez (2002), "pressure to prove oneself to one's gang peers during street socialization leads some to exhibit extreme, nearly crazy, behaviors" (p. 41). Psycho is just one example of those who have experienced soul murder, in which early childhood traumas have overwhelmed and emotionally "killed" them, setting them on a life of *locura* where suicidal pathways abound irrespective of dominant cultural norms and practices. Voids left by parents and schools, coupled with street socialization, have led to a street culture fashioned by gang members to aid in their survival. As part of the gang pact, fellow gang members fashion a very supportive, interactive, reciprocal relationship that collectively helps these youth strive for something they never had. A gang member from Chino, a rural barrio, said it best when he offered this observation: "No one cared except these guys, so why should I?" Hence it was through his affiliation with and participation in the gang that this member experienced a sense of belonging, an overwhelming connection to his gang peers. Social integration into the gang is what marks most gang members' lives.

Peer-group identification and solidarity are central in the lives of Chicano gang youth, and how these operate in the social organization of the student world both within and outside the school needs to be considered. To understand gang-influenced behaviors in schools, we must consider how larger social and community forces affect classroom décor and mediate peer relations in schools. For example, gang members are regularly on guard against the police, breeding a paranoia that infects other social settings. Law enforcement often generates strong antipolice sentiments and actions by barrio residents. Mirande (1987) cites numerous cases of this tension and conflict, which sometimes lead even to riots. Gang members have several times told me of incidents involving police fanning gang rivalries by picking up gang members from one barrio, dropping them off in an enemy neighborhood, and announcing the youths' presence on their public address systems as they drive away. As a result of these experiences, gang youth are wary of most adult authority figures, including school personnel. Even when lower school officials, such as noon aides, take issue with gang youth for minor transgressions, they begin to call them "narcs."

Further, the personal histories of gang members overwhelmingly show that learning difficulties entered their lives quite early (Belitz & Valdez, 1994; Catteral, 1987; Rumberger, 1991; Vigil, 1988a, 1999, 2002a), and only later did peers of like ilk nurture and solidify an antilearning, antischool attitude. Thus much of the discussion about resistance and not-learning as explanations might benefit from another perspective: Particular students "never have learned" (and are embarrassed to say they "can't" learn), so in order to sidestep failure, they act out and disrupt and thus give the appearance of commission and not omission (Cox, Davidson, & Bynum, 1995;

Curry et al., 1993; Valencia & Aburto, 1991). Their behavior signals the schools as sites of failure.

PEER COHESION, GANG DYNAMICS, AND GROUP MEMBERSHIP ROLES

Gang identification, norms, functions, and roles are enmeshed in peer relations and dependent on peer support networks. Peers provide the role models for following the rules, regulations, routines, and rhythms of the gang. In the gang case, members belong to a multiple-aged peer group, with older, experienced peers providing examples and lessons far beyond the world of the young gang member. The glue that holds the peers together is the avowed sense of egalitarianism espoused by gang values. It is the group before the individual. This belief and practice actually has two components, one from the recent past and the other from earlier times. First, growing up in a barrio, usually an isolated, visually distinct enclave, tends to engender a group orientation early in life (Vigil, 2002b). Moreover, there is a constant aura of fear and apprehension in areas that are rife with gangs, each with a particular barrio association. Thus, when asked where they are from, gang members know to respond with their barrio (read: group), not family, ethnic group, or nation.

Second, a common cultural thread in rural, peasant Mexico (Foster, 1988), and perhaps a contributing factor for marginalized Chicanos, is a social leveling where no one shows off or strives to get markedly ahead. This prevents group envy *(envidia)* and preserves the community ethos. On the edges of American society in practically every conceivable area, including cultural identity, Chicano youth adopt this cooperative group or egalitarian orientation. Culturally marginalized—in a personal or group state of "betwixt-and-between" where two cultures are in continuous contact— Chicano gang youth are caught in a linguistic and cultural bind, inadequately fluent in English or Spanish, and equally at odds with the deeper customs and values of both American and Mexican culture. Thus identification with the group and allegiance to the group ethos become increasingly salient for Chicano gang youth.

With these constructs as a foundation, it is clear that street socialization has additionally worked to submerge personal interests to those of the group. Indeed, gang rituals often involve activities to help clarify and/or solidify group cohesion. As noted earlier, gang initiation rites usually require a novitiate to show that he can stand up to the blows inflicted in a timed fight where gang members pummel the prospective gang candidate.

In addition, other more spontaneous instances help test the commitment and dedication of a gang member. An 18-year-old from Ontario provided this example of such an experience:

> We got together to talk about how we were going to plan it. It wasn't too hard. We had a .22 automatic rifle with 18 shots and one 4-10 shotgun with only two shots. We got together in a pickup truck. I was the driver or elected driver, but I didn't mind. . . . I can still recall what happened that night. As we got closer, my heart started thumping faster. As soon as we made a left . . . a white '64 Chevy started chasing us. I still don't know who exactly fired the gun from the truck. I just kept going faster. . . . The '64 caught us and started ramming us. . . . I couldn't make the truck go any faster, but the '64 kept pushing, trying to make us wreck, which is exactly what happened.

Participating in a gang activity—moreover, playing a particular role in the activity or ritual, as did the above youth—can solidify a member's identification with the group.

School misbehavior, or showing a withdrawn or delinquent attitude, has also become a posturing ritual of sorts, part of the previously mentioned complementary role set that a person and group need for performances. Performances are guided by the expectations of the group, and implicit and explicit role expectations are associated with the group (see Chapter 4, this volume). When enacted, role behaviors show the merging of a person into the larger identity of the group (Goffman, 1959). Acting bad, indifferent, reckless, and anti-authority fits into the role expectations of the gang, as various members of the multiple-aged peer group are the audience and act as prompters or coaches for the role an individual seeks.

Many *veteranos* strike an uncaring, aloof attitude that devalues school and education in general. As the younger members strive to measure up, the older ones become the audience for the performances. It is only in the retelling of the performances that the older member gets to nod approval by chuckling and affirming that the youngster did right, for although the older members are not in school, the power of group relations and solidarity carries over to school settings. A 15-year-old gang member from Chino poignantly makes this point:

> The art teacher was always telling me I was good, that I should go to art school. My grades in art were better than any other classes. When I was in her class I tried real hard to make her happy because she

made me feel so good. The thing that was good is that none of the other guys from my barrio were in the class. Nobody from any barrio was in either. I would act all regular with her, and she would joke with me about my baggy pants, and wasn't I afraid they would fall off. One time she saw me out by the restrooms where I hung out with the guys from my barrio, and she smiled and said hello. The guys looked at me all surprised because teachers never talked to us that way with respect and everything. I felt bad later, but I didn't smile back and just stayed there looking straight ahead.

This boy's reaction illustrates how performances vary for a changing audience. By himself, and with the teacher's compliments, he acted one way, but in view of his peers and their influence and evaluations, he acted another way.

The role expectation and performance dynamics illustrated above can be divided into two main categories. The first entails role learning and enactments for the group (read: gang), or perhaps other students whom gang members might want to impress, and the second involves behavior aimed toward learning in general, irrespective of the teacher, but certainly exaggerated if the teacher is disliked. Younger members learn how to talk, walk, and dress in uniform (even uniformed!) ways by modeling street elites who strike a mood and posture to which younger members aspire. Conforming to the standards of the gang peer group is expected, and teaching and instruction by older gang members are readily applied when the rules and routines are violated. For example, dress styles have changed over the years, and recently it is fashionable to wear cut-off khakis or Levis just below the knee with long, white, soccerlike socks up to the knee. A 17-year-old from Maravilla further illustrates both the significance of the particular audience and the influence exerted by older gang members:

When I'd visit my girlfriend in Montebello, I would dress all regular, straight pants and a regular shirt, like with designs on it. But when I'd come back to the barrio, I would dress right away in my *cholo* outfit—khakis, white tee shirt, and everything. I never wanted the guys to see me in those clothes.

Another gang member was told that his socks were too short, and he should raise them to just show the kneecap and no leg; the aversion to showing leg is taken from prison-facility customs to always maintain a manly presence. Although the dress style is a street habit, it is clear that a synergistic prison-to-street interaction affects what gang members do (Moore, 1978). However, informal learning continues apace on the streets as gang members keep abreast of the history and deeds of the barrio gang, the cultural customs and habits of the streets, the modes of marshaling resources, and the problem-solving abilities to negotiate through violence-infested neighborhoods (Vigil, 2003).

Older and particularly influential gang members who have taken stock of school as *"no vale"* (it is no good, useless) and have instead earned their spurs, so to speak, by doing prison time set the standards on the streets. Not so surprisingly, gang members take pride in doing time. A 17-year-old from Pico Viejo once told me: "I got more respect from the guys after I was *torcido* [twisted, i.e., arrested]. Before, they acted as if I was not around. Later, the *vatos* [guys] would ask me how it was. I even walked around all proud." This suggests that a great deal of instruction and learning takes place on the streets, and what is seen as important in schools is a reflection of what is given importance on the streets (Vigil, 1999).

With learning difficulties often already a problem, gang members become frustrated and take the path of least resistance, a path of the street learning that does not necessarily include academic achievement. Difficulties in early reading and/or ability-grouping experiences within elementary or middle school help gang members bond with those who have similar learning problems, strengthening the tendencies toward group orientation (Vigil, 1999). In fact, the practice of creating learning groups based on "ability" or "competency level" increases the consistency and strength of the group bonding, reinforcing the connections, and making it more difficult to break them. In a cyclic way, such peer-based practices of the school reinforce the solidity of gang peer allegiance. Students learn and practice ways set by the group to avoid or disrupt learning; status is gained in this way by the role performance that shows allegiance to the group but is often incongruent with an interest in academic learning and respect for teachers and institutions.

SCHOOLING UNDERMINED

Disruptive classroom behavior takes many forms—talking out of turn, throwing objects at another student, verbally or physically engaging another student, not responding to instruction, and being unprepared. Students recounted: "If I took a book home, I would have to walk in a long direction home to not let my homeboys see me"; "I would just get my books and throw them in the locker"; "no one wanted to be seen with books"; and "it didn't look *firme* [cool] to be with those big backpacks, full of books, so I always left them at school." Similarly, in order to exhibit a nonstudent attitude, with an eye toward the streets, opposition to being prepared (i.e., having pencils, paper, assignments, and so on) was cultivated. Gang students are always without something.

Although the main audience for antilearning activities is primarily other gang members, there are obvious instances when the audience is expanded to include the teacher and other students. Indeed, oftentimes the teacher is the essential prop (see Chapter 4, this volume). A common practice is that of showing disinterest and evincing no response to teacher instructions or directives. Something as simple as "please take out your books" meets with either no movement to do so or a lackadaisical placement of the book on the desk. Upon further instruction, "turn to page _____," the book is flipped through to any page to fake conformity. Although more a gesture to thwart learning than to strike a defiant attitude, a type of passive rebellion, this observable but "silent" behavior allows the teacher to continue with the lessons of the day without disrupting the classroom flow.

classroom behaviors that do not interupt

Still other gang-influenced and gang-directed behaviors in classrooms and schools do interrupt instruction. Gang lore has it that when a member gets in or finds trouble, the rest of the gang will back him up. This backup mentality is readily apparent when someone misbehaves or disrupts the classroom proceedings and, before the teacher can direct admonishments toward the offender, another student follows suit (see also Chapter 4, this volume). For example, a teacher from East Los Angeles reported that a student began to talk to a fellow student and across the classroom his friends chimed in, "ignoring" the teacher's request for quiet and order. Soon two other friends added to what became a cacophony of voices. Classroom decorum deteriorated as other students added their voices to the crescendo. Angry and frustrated, the teacher sent the culprits to the office for discipline.

Classroom behaviors that do interupt

Unfortunately, more violent disruptions by gang members often involve physical fights on campus grounds and classrooms. In one school, a minor incident between two females from different East Los Angeles gangs during a physical education class ended with dozens of students prepared to "back up" their individual "homegirls" at a scheduled location after class. Another time, a rival gang member threatened another gang member and, before they could square off after school, the word of the impending conflict spread to both barrios. Thus what was a personal thing evolved into a "rumblelike" affair. Police broke up this altercation, but not before several injuries and minor damage to property had occurred.

Other gang altercations at schools have ended fatally. One East Los Angeles high school rampant with gangs experienced a murder that was witnessed by only a few gang members. A 16-year-old who was knifed crawled into the bushes and died, and it was only after a day or two when his family missed him that the campus was searched and his body recovered. Previously, at the same campus, a food vender, accused by gang-affiliated students of regularly and disrespectfully "hitting-up" (i.e., making insulting overtures, harassing) some of "their" girls, was beaten unmercifully.

Disturbingly, incidences of gang members attacking teachers are becoming more widespread nationwide (Noguera, 1995; Stromquist & Vigil, 1996). Fortunately, most teachers have learned to avoid "fronting-off" (embarrassing or confronting) gang members. However, this reifies teacher apathy toward such students' abridged learning activities, for even passive, silent behavior is tolerated as long as the classroom remains quiet for the other students. Too many teachers, unwilling or unable to devise strategies to reach these students, accept this passive behavior. On the other hand, some teachers attempt to counter this behavior by taking the student aside to work one-on-one; removed from the peer audience in a classroom setting, a gang member, usually prone to disruptive performances, may engage in a learning activity with the teacher (Vigil, 1999).

Other teachers recount how the role-playing façade of gang members can be both challenged and utilized. One high school teacher in Whittier noticed that one of her students sat in the back of the room and seldom participated either verbally or mentally in classroom activities. The teacher's opinion of this student's behavior was, of course, suspect until the day she observed him on the schoolyard with his friends, all of whom were dressed in gang attire. Six or eight males were interacting with him, and he seemed to be accorded great respect and deference as they bantered back and forth. She concluded that he must be someone "important," at least amongst that group, and she then approached the student in an entirely different way, first by talking to him with respect and later by cajoling him to join in some of the classroom exercises that required only his eye contact to show that he was following the discussion. Although the student gradually displayed more willingness to join in activities in this class, in other classes, unfortunately, teachers were not as perceptive or respectful as the one who had attempted and succeeded in reaching him.

Gang members often tell stories of at least one teacher whom they liked and who engaged them in learning. Further, they report instances where one school employee reached not only one but a number of gang youth. A high school administrator from Pico Rivera identified one male student as a gang leader of sorts and approached him during morning breaks and lunchtime, striking up conversations on any number of topics. Inevitably, the dialogue would turn to what school activities and programs the student and his friends might like to see. Initially, the student kept a low profile in these engagements, but over a few weeks he invited other friends to join in these discussions with a "cool" principal. What resulted after a few months was the beginning of a boxing program that the gang youth felt addressed their interests. The principal followed through with both parent involvement and fund-raising campaigns for the boxing club and established the Boys Council, a leadership group composed mostly of street gang members. The initial leader eventually became active in school politics and was elected to student body positions.

CONCLUSION

Despite the efforts and good intentions of some school personnel, school structures, contexts, and practices also add to the socialization of youth as gang members; students who lack connections to school often become "street kids" who adopt street identities. Too often, in schools, street-socialized youth have marginal status "due to the lack of social support, prestige, and rewards; their inadequate performance of the student role; and the absence of meaningful relationships" (Flores-Gonzalez, 2002, p. 42). Thwarted not only in their homes but also in their educational experiences, street-socialized youth become increasingly disruptive and disenfranchised.

Thus the influence of one teacher or principal rarely competes successfully with the multiple marginalization and street socialization of Chicano gang youth. Once poverty and marginalization have taken their toll in low-income, ethnic-minority communities, a small but significant number of children grow up under the purview and guidance of the multiple-aged peer group of the street gang and learn the rules and regulations of the street subculture. In the absence of formal social-control tethers, such as families and conventional neighborhood caretakers, the gang begins to replace nurturing and counseling sources and acts as a social resource for its members. Street-gang subculture and peer influence direct what is learned and valued, strongly influencing school routines and practices for gang youth.

Acting out is not only a response to school but a reflection of the students' marginalized social positions and experiences in other aspects of their lives (Flores-Gonzalez, 2002). Street socialization played out in the interactions between gang-affiliated students and schools is largely a result of a cultural transitional process undergone by second-generation youth in many ethnic-minority communities (Waters, 1999). In their adaptation and accommodation to American life, second-generation Chicanos navigate between two cultures and ways of life. *Choloization,* a process in which Chicanos acculturate (or not) to the dominant culture, involves multiply marginal aspects of the impoverished lives of immigrant populations (Vigil, 2002a) and speaks to the pressures and strains from which the gang subculture is born.

When gang youth find themselves on the streets and adapt to the cultural cues and rules of the street elites, they surrender their individuality and become immersed in the "group psychology" of the gang (Vigil, 1988b). Even though most barrio youth are able to avoid serious street-gang involvement, the most marginalized individuals become gang members, and in the absence of traditional influences, it is they who are most in need of direction and guidance. Unfortunately, this need is met in the streets where the presence of a street culture provides a direction to explore and to become "somebody" with supportive others.

Street socialization dictates that survival requires affiliation with a gang for protection, security, friendship, emotional support and affection, and, of course, instructions on how to think and behave. Multiple marginalization has taken such a toll in the lives of gang members that learning and behavioral difficulties surface quite early and set them on a weakened and often shortened educational path. By the time they reach the early teen years and join a gang, their educational careers worsen. Never able to catch up with their early shortcomings, these youth find sanctuary in the gang and adopt a group orientation that helps legitimize anti-authority behavior in school, as elsewhere.

How do schools address these gang-related influences, especially the effects of street socialization and the bonding that unites the group against authority institutions and figures? One strategy, the creation of alternative and continuation schools, designed to remedy the abysmal educational record of street-gang and other disaffected youth, in the early years was quite successful (Munoz, 2001). Over the decades, however, many such schools have come to function as warehouses for their disaffiliated, disenfranchised students where these youth further cement their anti-authority attitude. Nonetheless, barring a transformation of society and schooling to eliminate the worst effects of multiple marginality by eradicating the situations and conditions that compel youth to become street socialized, there are some small things that might bear fruit in a schooling strategy. A major starting point is to recognize how and why street socialization unfolds among low-income, ethnic-minority populations. If school administrators and teachers could better understand this process, they might generate strategies to harness the power of the group that drives gang youth. Several changes might be possible if this were accomplished. For one, school personnel might be able to co-opt gang values and norms; for another, such gang beliefs and practices as loyalty, respect, egalitarianism, and a kinlike friendship, among others, can be explored. As noted in some of the accounts above, approaching gang members one-on-one helps break the group façade that each member carries in his or her presentation to the outside world, bringing the role-performance configuration onto a new stage where the teacher can enter the drama. Developing more personal contact and opportunities for interaction helps identify the interests and concerns of gang members, some of which might be integrated into school or community activities and programs. Of utmost importance in this regard is showing respect to the student.

ACKNOWLEDGMENTS

My thanks to the editors, and to Jill Koyama in particular, for insightful feedback on earlier versions of this chapter, and also to John M. Long for helpful editorial advice.

NOTES

1. The observations and interviews cited in this article are mostly from the late 1990s but also include episodes from earlier work that considered educational issues. My early work as a public school teacher in the 1960s informed and shaped a research agenda that emphasized educational issues and street-gang dynamics for the Mexican American population. There are three phases to my investigations. The first, dealing with acculturation and school performance, began in 1971 and continues to the present. An example of this research is a study of an urban high school in East Los Angeles (Vigil, 1997) and a suburban high school 14 miles east from the urban one. Students from different generations and various ethnic identities were observed and interviewed, providing the basis for a comparison of changes over 14 years. Since conducting fieldwork for that study, I have added two more high schools to my ongoing research on these topics. A direct derivation from the above work is my research addressing street-gang members and street gangs, the second phase that began in the mid-1970s, expanded in the 1980s, and continues to the present. This focus on Chicano street gangs later led to the third phase of gang work, a cross-cultural ethnographic study involving African Americans, Chicanos, Salvadorans, and Vietnamese in various neighborhoods in Los Angeles (Vigil, 2002a).

2. In my study of barrio gangs, there were some noteworthy socioeconomic differences between the average income of gang families, $11,843, and that of other Mexican families living in Los Angeles County, $15,531 (Vigil, 1988a, p. 28). There were also major differences between urban and suburban Chicanos over a 14-year span. In 1974, urban dwellers made an average of $7,500, whereas those living in the suburbs averaged $11,500. In 1988, those numbers increased to $23,000 and $33,300, respectively (Vigil, 1997, p. 12).

3. See Vigil (1996) for a discussion of "street baptism" or the initiation rite of gangs.

REFERENCES

Belitz, J., & Valdez, D. (1994). Clinical studies in the treatment of Chicano male gang youth. *Hispanic Journal of Behavioral Sciences, 16*(1), 57–74.

Burnett, G., & Walz, G. (1994). Gangs in schools. *ERIC Digest, 99*, 1–4.

Catteral, J. S. (1987). On the social costs of dropping out of school. *High School Journal of Sociology, 94* (Suppl.), 19–30.

Cohen, A. (1955). *Delinquent boys: The culture of the gang.* Glencoe, IL: The Free Press.

Cox, S. M., Davidson, W. S., & Bynum, T. S. (1995). A meta-analytic assessment of delinquency-related outcomes of alternative education programs. *Crime and Delinquency, 41*(2), 219–234.

Cromwell, P., Taylor, D., & Palacios, W. (1992). Youth gangs: A 1990s perspective. *Juvenile and Family Court Journal, 3*, 25–31.

Curry, D., Fox, R. J., Ball, R. A., & Stone, D. (1993). *National assessment and anti-gang information resources. Report to the U.S. Department of Justice.* Washington, DC: National Institute of Justice.

Darder, A., Torres, R., & Gutierrez, H. (Eds.). (1997). *Latinos and education: A critical reader.* New York: Routledge.

Edgerton, R. B. (1978). The study of deviance—marginal man or everyman? In G. D. Spindler (Ed.), *The making of psychological anthropology* (pp. 442–476). Los Angeles: University of California Press.

Flores-Gonzalez, N. (2002). *School kids/street kids: Identity development in Latino students.* New York: Teachers College Press.

Foster, G. (1988). *Tzintzuntzan: Mexican peasants in a changing world.* Prospect Heights, IL: Waveland Press.

Giroux, H. (1983). Theories of reproduction and resistance in the new sociology of education: A critical analysis. *Harvard Educational Review, 53*(3), 257–293.

Goffman, E. (1959). *The presentation of self in everyday life.* New York: Doubleday.

Goldstein, A. P. (1994). Aggression toward persons and property in America's schools. *The School Psychologist, 48*(1), 1–18.

Kodluboy, D. W. (1994). Behavioral disorders and the culture of street gangs. In R. L. Peterson & S. Ishii-Jordan (Eds.), *Multicultural issues in the education of students with behavioral disorders* (pp. 233–250). Cambridge, MA: Brookline Books.

Kohl, H. (1994). *I won't learn from you and other thoughts on creative maladjustment.* New York: New Press.

Kozol, J. (1992). *Savage inequalities: Children in America's schools.* New York: Harper Perennial.

Mirande, A. (1987). *Gringo justice.* Notre Dame, IN: University of Notre Dame Press.

Moore, J. W. (1978). *Homeboys.* Philadelphia: Temple University Press.

Moore, J. W. (1991). *Going down to the barrio.* Philadelphia: Temple University Press.

Munoz, J. (2001). *Re-examining the margins of public education: New models of analysis of alternative education for at-risk students.* Unpublished doctoral dissertation, University of California, Los Angeles.

Noguera, P. (1995). Preventing and producing violence: A critical analysis of responses to school violence. *Harvard Educational Review, 65*(2), 189–212.

Oakes, J. (1985). *Keeping track: How schools structure inequality.* New Haven, CT: Yale University Press.

Ogbu, J. (1987). Variability in minority responses to schooling: Nonimmigrants vs. immigrants. In G. Spindler & L. Spindler (Eds.), *The interpretive ethnography of education: At home and abroad* (pp. 255–278). Hillsdale, NJ: Lawrence Erlbaum.

Raywid, M. A. (1990). Alternative education: The definition problem. *Changing Schools, 18,* 4–10.

Rumberger, R. W. (1991). Chicano dropouts: A review of research and policy issues. In R. Valencia (Ed.), *Chicano school failure and success* (pp. 64–90). London: The Falmer Press.

Stromquist, N., & Vigil, J. D. (1996). Violence in schools in the United States of America: Trends, causes, and responses. In J. C. Tedesco (Ed.), *Prospects, 27*(2), 361–383. International Bureau of Education (Special Theme issue on school violence worldwide). Paris: UNESCO.

Valencia, R. R. (Ed.). (1991). *Chicano school failure and success: Research and policy agendas for the 1990s.* London: The Falmer Press

Valencia, R., & S. Aburto. (1991). The uses and abuses of educational testing: Chicanos as a case in point. In R. Valencia (Ed.), *Chicano school failure and success* (pp. 203–270). London: The Falmer Press.

Valenzuela, A. 1999. *Subtractive schooling: U.S.-Mexican youth and the politics of caring.* Albany: State University of New York Press.

Vigil, J. D. (1982). Chicano high schoolers: Educational performance and acculturation. *The Educational Forum, 47*(1), 59–73.

Vigil, J. D. (1988a). *Barrios gangs: Street life and identity in Southern California.* Austin: University of Texas Press.

Vigil, J. D. (1988b). Group processes and street identity: Adolescent Chicano gang members. *Ethos, 16*(4), 421–445.

Vigil, J. D. (1996). Street baptism: Chicano gang initiation. *Human Organization, 55*(2), 149–153.

Vigil, J. D. (1997). *Personas Mexicanas: Chicano high schoolers in a changing Los Angeles.* Ft. Worth, TX: Harcourt Brace.

Vigil, J. D. (1999). Streets and schools: How educators can help Chicano marginalized gang youth. *Harvard Educational Review, 69*(3), 270–288.

Vigil, J. D. (2002a). *A rainbow of gangs: Street cultures in the mega-city.* Austin: University of Texas Press.

Vigil, J. D. (2002b). Community dynamics and the rise of street gangs. In M. M. Suárez-Orozco & M. M. Páez (Eds.), *Latinos: Remaking America* (pp. 97–109). Berkeley: University of California Press.

Vigil, J. D. (2003). Urban violence and street gangs. *Annual Review of Anthropology, 32,* 1–51. Palo Alto, CA: Annual Reviews.

Vigil, J. D., & Long, J. M. (1981). Unidirectional or nativist acculturation?—Chicano paths to school achievement. *Human Organization, 40*(3), 273–277.

Vigil, J. D., & Yun, S. C. (1996). Southern California gangs: Comparative ethnicity and social control. In R. Huff (Ed.), *Gangs in America* (2nd ed., pp. 139–156). Thousand Oaks, CA: Sage.

Waters. T. (1999). *Crime and immigrant youth.* Thousand Oaks, CA: Sage.

Willis, P. (1977). *Learning to labour.* Farnborough, England: Saxon House.

Yinger, M. (1960). Contraculture and subculture. *American Sociological Review, 25,* 625–635.

6

The Influence of Intergroup Relations on School Engagement: Two Cases

Heather Lewis-Charp, Hanh Cao Yu,
& Diane Friedlaender

When I was a freshman I participated in the Freshman Challenge Day and the Freshman Transition Program, and I really enjoyed that these kids would take time from their classes to help the new kids who were coming in from junior high to high school . . . [I learned how] to make friends. At first it was a little uncomfortable—sometimes I can be very shy so I was a little uncomfortable, but then afterwards I felt very comfortable around my peer leaders. . . . I give credit to this Students Supporting Achievement program [for the good intergroup relations at this school] because the students and teachers get involved in the cultures—that helps a lot as well.
—*Mariella, a student at Woodrow High School*

The expectations of the students weren't there. If any teacher had high expectations for students, then it was felt that they were setting them up for failure. . . . Students weren't told that they didn't have the skills when it was obvious that they didn't have the skills for something. The fact that they just showed up in class was considered worthy of credit. . . . We were just supposed to be happy that students showed up.
—*Jose's teacher at North Vernon High School*

Mariella Contreras and Jose Rodriguez are Mexican-descent students who came to high school with similar levels of high academic promise. Despite their similarities, their academic paths diverged in high school—Mariella built positive relationships with peers and teachers who challenged her to take risks and to excel, whereas Jose encountered peer groups and teachers who did little to push him beyond his "comfort zone." As the above quotes by Mariella and Jose's teacher illustrate, school climate and context played a critical role in framing the nature of the relationships and expectations available to each student.

This chapter uses a comparative case study approach to examine the influence of peer and intergroup relations on the coping strategies of Mexican-descent youth as they navigate between their school, family, and peer worlds. We seek to untangle the factors influencing these students' attitudes about self, peers, and academic engagement. Further, we address contextual factors within high schools that inhibit or enhance their ability to effectively manage or navigate the barriers they face. Key research questions that frame our inquiry include:

- How do intergroup relations influence students' ability to form diverse peer affiliations and engage academically?
- How does school context (i.e., leadership, policies, programs, and practice) influence students' ability to border cross and engage in school?
- What can schools do to promote positive relationships among students of different racial groups?

THEORETICAL PERSPECTIVE

Our study builds off the Students' Multiple Worlds Study (SMW), which created a theoretical model of the interrelationships between students' family, peer, and school worlds, investigating how meanings and understandings derived from these worlds combine to affect students' engagement with schools and learning. The SMW model directs our attention to the nature of boundaries and borders as well as processes of movement among different worlds. By *worlds,* we refer to the cultural knowledge and behavior found within students' peer groups, families, and schools. Each world contains its own sets of values and beliefs, expectations, actions, and emotional responses familiar to insiders (Phelan, Davidson, & Yu, 1998). *Borders* arise when knowledge, skills, and behaviors in one world are more highly valued and rewarded (e.g., by members of the dominant group) than in another. *Border crossing* is the movement and adaptation youth must make to cope with incongruities in expectations, values and beliefs, and actions across worlds (Erickson, 1987).

In U.S. schools, Mexican-descent students face numerous borders, many of which are sociocultural, structural, and socioeconomic. *Sociocultural borders* arise when cultural components in one world are viewed as less important than those in another (Delgado-Gaitan & Trueba, 1991; Erickson, 1987; Erickson & Bekker, 1986). *Structural borders* are features of school environments that prevent, impede, or discourage students from participating fully in social or academic learning. Three types of conditions give rise to structural borders: (a) inadequate resources and supports to meet students' needs, (b) lack of bridges to connect students with available resources, and (c) lack of match, that is, structures and services are available and visible to students but either do not match students' needs or impede students' ability to connect with the school or peers. *Socioeconomic borders* arise when economic circumstances create limitations on a student's ability to fully engage in schooling or when students of different socioeconomic backgrounds come into contact (Phelan et al., 1998).

Although cultural differences do not necessarily create barriers to school learning, sociocultural and socioeconomic borders between predominantly White, middle-class teachers and largely working-class Mexican-descent youth can give rise to subtle prejudices, creating miscommunication in student–teacher interactions and at times leading to lowered academic expectations (Cummins, 1996; Erickson, 1987). Similarly, structural barriers within the school, such as academic tracking and a shortage of Spanish-speaking teachers and counselors, leave many Mexican-descent youth without access to crucial information (e.g., on college admission or high school graduation) and sources of support (Oakes, 1985; Stanton-Salazar, 2001).

Within youth cultures, sociocultural and socioeconomic borders may lead to what Allport (1954) characterizes as "in-groups" (usually students of White or middle-class backgrounds) and "out-groups" (usually students of ethnic minority or poor backgrounds). Adolescent identity formation is integral to this process, as during adolescence, youth often distance themselves from youth of other ethnic, cultural, and socioeconomic backgrounds to assert their own identity (Tatum-Daniel, 1997). This process, which typically begins in junior high, can intensify cultural and socioeconomic differences between peer groups, perpetuate stereotypes and prejudices, and limit students' opportunities to learn from and draw strength from each other. For Mexican-descent and other ethnic-minority students, such peer-enforced borders can create obstacles to achievement, causing them to feel intimidated about participating in classes and activities where "in-group" peers are the majority (Lee, 1996). On the other hand, same-race or same-ethnic peer support is often pivotal to the formation of a positive ethnic identity among Mexican-descent youth, who frequently seek out peers for validation of their ethnic and cultural self.

We define peers on multiple levels, focusing most prominently on how students get along across racial and ethnic groups. We consider issues of intergroup relations to be integral to students' access to social capital, as peer affiliation across socioeconomic and racial groups can prove to be a powerful mediating factor, leading to the increased distribution of institutional knowledge and the reinforcement of proscholastic norms and identities (see Chapter 2, this volume). Within this larger "intergroup relations context," we define peers as friends, classmates, those who share extracurricular activities, and schoolmates. In keeping with critical social-capital theory, we understand that the context for interaction between students of different racial and socioeconomic groups occurs most often within structural borders that regulate students' access to both institutional resources and the mediating role of peers (i.e., academic tracking and segregated schools). Within diverse school settings, however, we also see students' of all economic and racial backgrounds having some agency in regulating and enforcing socioeconomic and sociocultural borders between students via their attitudes about "in-group" and "out-group" members. Thus our analytical framework assumes that a school climate that facilitates peer relations within and across groups, addressing both structural borders and peer-enforced differences, can enhance students' social-capital network and, ultimately, their engagement in school.

Further, it's important to point out that students' identities are multilayered and that the intersections of these identities situate students' differently in relation to structural, sociocultural, and structural borders. Most prominently, for instance, we recognize that there are differences in how males and females perceive and are able to draw on supports across their peer, family, and school worlds. In particular, as has been described in Chapters 3, 4, and 5 of this volume, Latino males spend less time on schoolwork, act out more in classes, are more pressured by peers into gang involvement and/or high-risk behaviors, and receive less monitoring from parents than do Latinas. Thus the process of gender identification, so central to adolescence, creates additional barriers for young Latino males who, in their search for independence, find it more difficult than Latinas to reach out to others in school for the help they need.

Lastly, our theoretical perspective suggests that the more adept Mexican-descent and other students become at border crossing, the more intergroup hostilities will decrease, as status divisions between in-groups and out-groups are minimized. Moreover, increased border crossing by students strengthens the affiliation of diverse peers across multiple social networks, as well as the potential for peers to act as resources to one another (see Chapter 2, this volume). Through increased trust and relationship building, students are more likely to draw from each other's institutionally based forms of knowledge to help each other overcome the structural borders that impede their ability to engage in academic learning.

ABOUT OUR STUDY

The case study data for this chapter are drawn from a longitudinal research study involving five rounds of data collection extended over 3 1/2 years (1996–2000). The purpose of the longitudinal study was to investigate the influence of peers, family, and school on students' ability to border cross. We focused on the graduating class of 2000 within six racially diverse California high schools. We selected two urban, two rural, and two suburban schools, so as to maximize variability in the socioeconomic and social context. In the first 2 years we conducted individual interviews with 72 randomly selected youth and conducted four monoracial student focus groups at each school. Within this sample, we conducted up to three interviews with a total of 23 youth who identified as Latino, and engaged approximately 50 Latino young people in focus-group discussions. In the third year of our study, we used purposeful sampling to identify 24 case study students for observation and more in-depth interviews and the development of profiles because they were representative of themes or attitudes emerging from our student focus groups. We developed case studies of seven students who identified as Latino, two of whom we profile in this chapter.

In addition to student case studies, we developed in-depth school profiles. These descriptions draw from a variety of data sources, including interviews with administrators and teachers at each school, same-race student focus groups, a teacher survey, and two waves of student surveys with the entire Class of 2000. These data help define the contextual factors influencing students' development, level of academic engagement, and perceptions of racial and ethnic differences within the school setting.

The following vignettes are illustrative of themes we heard and observed from Latino students throughout the 3 1/2 years of our study. Although we emphasize the themes that emerged from our entire data set, we have preserved the nuances and integrity of each student's individual experience. Rather than focus exclusively on peers, the vignettes present a balanced view of school, family, and peer influences, as each is pivotal to understanding the context in which peer relations occur. We highlight Jose and Mariella because their test scores and academic records indicate that they began high school with a similar level of academic achievement. We define achievement broadly, as a combination of grade point average, enrollment in academic track classes, standardized test scores, and attitude about school. Both had parents with high expectations, a history of academic success, plans to attend college, and both were placed as freshman into high track or college preparatory courses. The divergence of their stories in high school speaks to the powerful role of schools and of peers in shaping life choices. Later in the chapter, we link Jose and Mariella's individual stories to findings from our larger study and articulate the implications of this work for school policy and practice.

NORTH VERNON HIGH SCHOOL

This whole area is poverty stricken, sad, and [has] given up lots of hope . . . I think there is a general hopelessness, not a striving, like why bother?

—*Ms. Jones, North Vernon Teacher*

Rising immigration in the late 1980s and early 1990s transformed North Vernon High School, which serves a rural and predominantly working-class student body, from a school that was 80% White to one that, by 2000, was 33% White and 56% Latino. As Ms. Jones communicates, teachers' expectations for students are low. For example, only 52% of North Vernon teachers agreed that "teachers [at this high school] hold high expectations of students regardless of the students' race or ethnicity." This percentage is significantly lower than our six-school average of 82%. In 2000, North Vernon ranked in the lowest 20% of high schools statewide and was formally designated an "underperforming school" within the state accountability system.

Teachers and students alike reported that North Vernon has a "bad" reputation, due in large part to Mexican and African American gang activity on campus. Twenty-six percent of students reported that they did not feel safe at the school, compared with our six-school average of 19% and the national average of 8%. North Vernon administrators have taken a passive approach to addressing intergroup relations problems on campus, often denying that tensions exist, and employing strategies focused on the reduction of negative behaviors rather than the creation of a positive school climate. For instance, at the beginning of our study administrators instituted a school dress code and a more comprehensive discipline policy, installed fences around campus, revoked student breaks in response to fighting, and instituted a $400 fine for anyone involved in a fight, regardless of cause.

With little support from the administration, North Vernon teachers have developed several programs designed to reduce intergroup tensions. Students Creating a Difference (SCAD) began as a program where youth facilitators collaborated with the local police department to resolve gang conflicts and evolved into a community service program. North Vernon also has a Peer Advocate (PA) program, which trains youth as peer educators and counselors. Unfortunately, SCAD and PA reach only a small proportion of North Vernon's student population and, lacking full buy-in from the administration, they have only a limited effect on the overall school climate.

Jose Rodriguez: Assimilating to Working-Class Values

Jose Rodriguez is a soft-spoken, second-generation Mexican-descent student. Jose's parents both completed high school; his father is a dockworker and his mother is a high school bilingual aide. According to Jose, his parents tell him, "If you don't work hard, you're not going to go anywhere in life. Don't expect anything to be given to you. . . . Make sure that you get a good education." The Rodriguez family has been intentional in supporting Jose's Mexican identity, taking him to visit relatives in Mexico, celebrating Mexican holidays, and establishing "Spanish only" days in the house. He says, "As long as you know [Spanish], you can get somewhere in life. That's part of my family history that you can't change. . . . I am going to pass it down to my kids and their kids after that." Partially because of his parents' support, Jose stayed out of gangs and maintained an excellent academic record through the beginning of high school. When asked as a freshman what was most important to him, Jose replied: "Making my mom and dad proud, getting a diploma and going to college."

Jose's focus on academics decreased when, as a freshman, he began working in his grandfather's liquor store. Jose's parents believed work experience would help Jose learn "how to be an adult" and "how to balance" his time. His mother said, "It makes me very happy and proud because he helps my dad a lot." Balancing school and work responsibilities, however, proved difficult for Jose, who ultimately withdrew from most of his college preparatory courses and from AVID, which stands for Advancement Via Individual Determination. (AVID students take a course that provides study and note-taking skills, information, and emotional and practical academic support for students [see Mehan, Villanueva, Hubbard, & Lintz, 1996].) Jose said, "It got too hard. I didn't have enough time. [AVID was] putting a lot of load on me and while that was happening my mom and dad were telling me . . . that I have to start about thinking about if I want a job." Jose and his family's emphasis on work is not unlike that of other working-class students whom we interviewed at North Vernon. Students seek employment to relieve some of the economic strain on their families and, at the same time, are provided few models within their school for visualizing academics as a route to social mobility.

Learning to "Relax and Take It Easy"

Jose came to North Vernon with aspirations to graduate from high school and attend the University of California. As a freshman he said, "Mostly I'm quiet and I get my work done. . . . First off, goes my school work, and that's how my mom likes it, too." Jose's teachers in elementary and junior high school uniformly described him as an "excellent" student and his standardized test scores placed him at the 80th percentile in math and the 68th percentile in reading. Jose's grades were good through junior high school, where he earned a 3.6 GPA in the seventh grade. His GPA declined, however, to a 3.0 in the eighth grade, a trend that continued in high school. As a North Vernon freshman, Jose was placed in AVID, advanced English, biology, Spanish I, and algebra I. He struggled in these classes, failing AVID and two semesters of biology, and earning two Ds in advanced English. At the beginning of his sophomore year, Jose withdrew from all his challenging courses except for math.

From Jose's perspective, the decision to withdraw from challenging classes was due to competing work responsibilities and his desire to "relax a little and take it easy." By the end of his junior year, Jose's GPA was 2.40 in what he described as an "unchallenging" course load. Although Jose's grades remained higher than those of many of his Mexican-descent peers, they were disappointing given his previously demonstrated academic promise.

Peer Intergroup Relations Climate: Learning What *Not To Be*

The peer intergroup relations climate at North Vernon, particularly the prevalence of rival Mexican-descent gangs, played an important role in how Jose and his friends identify themselves. As his English teacher said, "Jose has every chance in the world to be involved in a gang because of where he lives and what school he goes to. And I guess it's self esteem and his family life that keep him out of that." The struggle against the perceived inevitability of gang involvement, captured in this quote, runs throughout Jose's interviews. Although we did not ask any questions about gangs, all conversations with Jose about his friends led back to his desire to resist gangs and their stigma. For instance, he said of his friends, "They don't want to do stuff like get into gangs, and then they say they feel sorry because a lot of other Mexican kids are getting into gangs. [Gang-involved peers] are putting a label onto us, but we're not like that." It is clear that, although Jose and his friends do not participate in gangs, they nevertheless feel stigmatized by them.

The peer climate at North Vernon, one where many Mexican-descent males are involved in gang activity, makes Jose's association with like-minded friends particularly important. His friends, like him, are focused on graduating high school, pleasing their families, and staying out of trouble. The following two quotes, gathered in his freshman and sophomore year, illustrate the importance Jose places on these qualities in his close friends.

> My friends are just like me . . . they're not into gangs. They say [gangs] are a waste of life. They say that they'd be pretty sad because their mom [and rest of their family] would pretty much disgrace them [if they were to get involved in gangs].

> I'm not in gangs, and I don't think I'd ever want to be. I've seen news reports on how they're killing people and they just end up in jail. It's not worth it, I guess. It doesn't appeal to me very much. That's why I like the friends I hang out with. They're just like me.

In this latter quote, Jose reveals the allure of gangs through the tentativeness of his assertions, qualifying his statements by saying he "guesses" it's "not worth it" to be in a gang and that gangs don't "appeal . . . very much." Several of the Mexican-descent young men we interviewed across our six schools talked about their struggle to resist gang involvement and the role that their parents and like-minded peers played in helping them to do so. As both Hurd and Vigil argue in Chapters 4 and 5, working-class Mexican-descent males, like Jose, face peer pressure to prove their masculinity by acting out in their schools and in their communities. Successfully avoiding such pressure, as Jose did throughout high school, is a measure of his success.

It is striking, however, that young men like Jose direct so much energy at resisting negative peer influences that they don't define a positive vision for what they can accomplish and achieve. Jose's shift from a student who wanted to "work hard" and attend college to one who wanted to "take it easy" reflects a culture of peer-enforced masculinity that limits individual achievement by contributing to downward leveling norms (Portes & Rumbaut, 2001). In such a climate, school and families come to define success for Mexican-descent males more by what they *don't* do than what they do.

Jose's story illustrates how family, peers, and school worlds can shift toward increased congruency, over time. The very high expectations of the AVID program sent Jose's worlds out of balance, and he did not, for numerous reasons, receive the kind of support from his parents, peers, or teachers he needed to meet that challenge. Instead, he downgraded his expectations in a way that would bring his worlds to a state of equilibrium, thus minimizing his discomfort as he navigated from one world to another.

In contrast to Jose's story of underachievement, the following description of Mariella Contreras and Woodrow High School offers a picture of a challenging and supportive academic and peer environment.

WOODROW HIGH SCHOOL

Woodrow High School, located in an affluent semiurban community, faces challenges very different from those faced by North Vernon. Unlike North Vernon's primarily working-class population, Woodrow's student body is socioeconomically bifurcated. Woodrow was primarily upper-middle-class White until the 1970s, when the closing of a high school in "Eastside," a neighboring city, resulted in busing of working-class and poor students of color to the school. In 2000, Woodrow's school population was 45% White, 41% Latino, 7% Black, and 7% Asian and Pacific Islander. Total enrollment was about 1,800 students.

Although the academic education for students who persist in high-track classes at Woodrow is excellent, White students receive a disproportionate amount of this benefit. The official 12.6% dropout rate for Latino students is misleading, in that only approximately half of incoming Latino freshmen make it to graduation. Of those, 20% complete the full set of courses required for admission to the University of California or a state university, compared with an overall senior class rate of 43%. A high percentage of Woodrow graduates go on to college—38% attend 4-year colleges and 53% attend 2-year colleges. Woodrow ranks in the top 40% of high schools in California on state performance measures.

Despite the challenges they face, Woodrow has the most positive racial climate of the six schools studied. School administrators and teachers alike emphasize the importance of intergroup relations, saying that, "without it, the rest just doesn't work." In keeping with this philosophy, Woodrow High has focused on creating a connected school environment. For instance, it has developed a "house" structure where groupings of students in their freshman year share common teachers in English, social studies, and science. Woodrow also offers a program called Students Supporting Achievement (SSA), whose goals are to increase grades, decrease dropout rates, increase attendance, and increase graduation rates by providing students with peer and adult advocates. Teachers refer students to peer counseling if a student experiences a problem in class, and entire classes sometimes receive conflict mediation counseling. As will be discussed in more detail in Mariella's case, Woodrow has also made efforts at detracking and has created a freshman transition program. Other efforts include two different parent outreach programs, *El Apoyo del Padre* and Building Success, which recruit and support parents of underrepresented students.

In addition to these forms of support, Woodrow has reacted assertively when faced with racial incidents. For instance, in 1997 racial epithets were spray painted on campus. With administrative endorsement and leadership, students and parents of all races came together with antiracism signs and chants to demonstrate against racism and paint over the graffiti. One student said, "We handled it pretty good, like we were family." In combination, these efforts represent a comprehensive approach to intergroup relations that help students, like Mariella Contreras, find the support they need to succeed.

Although Woodrow's school district is less poor than North Vernon's, with a per pupil expenditure of $7,794 compared with North Vernon's $5,801, this doesn't fully account for the differences between the two schools. Another school in the same district as Woodrow, with an equally bifurcated student body, had a very negative intergroup climate. As was the case for the school described in Chapter 7, intergroup relations and achievement for poor students was complicated, rather than ameliorated, by the socioeconomic class divisions between students. Thus we believe that Woodrow's positive climate can be attributed primarily to the school's proactive approach to engaging students.

Mariella Contreras: Embracing Diversity and Striving To Do Her Best

Mariella is a 17-year-old Latina who navigates incongruent worlds with relative ease. She is the daughter of a third-generation Mexican father, who works as the manager of food services for a prestigious hospital, and a first-generation El Salvadoran mother, who trained to work as a nurse. Much of Mariella's inner strength comes from her close-knit family, which raised her to have a sense of pride in herself and supported her goals for the future. Through stories and values passed on by her extended family, Mariella developed an appreciation for her family's struggles and successes, giving her the confidence that she, too, can overcome the challenges she faces. It was this network of familial support that helped Mariella manage the death of her mother, who died when she was 10 years old. Mariella explains, "It made me look at myself and [motivated] me to get ahead in life, basically. I guess that it has taught me to value what I have."

Mariella has a supportive father, who as an only parent articulates his high expectations for Mariella and her younger brother. Mariella often talks with her father about coursework, grades, and college. She says, "He really pushes me to get ahead so I can get into the university. . . . He expects a lot from me." Mariella's father reiterates this sentiment, saying, "I have devoted 100% of my time except for work . . . to helping them study." The consistent support of her family has helped Mariella to achieve academically.

Achieving as a Latina

Woodrow students come from five elementary school districts, which vary in their heterogeneity. Although many students who attend Woodrow High School self-segregate, students like Mariella—from Pine City, the most ethnically and socioeconomically diverse feeder district—are more likely to have diverse friends. Mariella has maintained many of her diverse friendships since elementary school. These students, like Mariella, are very focused on academics. In her words, "My friends are very motivated."

The curriculum in Woodrow's college track classes is challenging for Mariella, and although she does not always get high grades, she nevertheless pushes herself to do her best. For example, she enrolled in 3 years of lab science, 3 1/2 years of college preparatory math, and 4 years of English, social studies, and foreign language. After completing all the levels of Spanish offered at her high school, including 1 year of AP Spanish, Mariella enrolled in 1 1/2 years of French. Although she received mostly Ds and Fs in her algebra II and precalculus classes, she remained undaunted and repeated them over the summer at the local junior college. In contrast, Mariella has done well in English and social studies, achieving nearly a 4.0 in these subjects. Her English teacher comments:

> Mariella is great. She is definitely a high achiever and takes her responsibility in class very seriously. . . . She always works hard. She's always in class. She's always prepared. She's a model student.

In addition to enjoying positive relationships with her teachers, Mariella has benefited from the school climate at Woodrow High School. For example, from her sophomore to senior year Mariella was a student leader in the freshman transition program, giving presentations to freshmen, sometimes in Spanish, on how to succeed in high school. Through this program, Mariella became well known on campus by her peers, thus giving her a sense of value and importance at school.

Mariella also benefited from Woodrow's academic policy to limit tracking, which allowed any interested student to take college preparatory courses. This policy enabled her to remain in advanced math classes despite low grades. Although Mariella does not blame others for her low math grades or internalize them as a measure of her self-worth, she does, at times, marvel at her own persistence, especially given how few Latinos there are in her classes. She says: "I'm proud of myself but sometimes I wonder why I took the class. I would love to see more Hispanic people in higher classes." Mariella, however, insists that she does not feel "isolated" or that she does not belong. She says, "I feel like one of them, that we are all in the same class. Whenever I need help I go to the teacher. I have a lot of friends. Whenever I need help I can ask them." Thus support from friends and teachers help create a nonjudgmental environment where Mariella can risk failure, challenge herself, and achieve to the utmost of her ability.

PEER WORLD: LEARNING ABOUT DIFFERENCE

Mariella attended schools that exposed her to diverse peers and cultures, and she has embraced this diversity by developing close friendships with Latino, Laotian, Chinese, White, and Filipino students. Her father and brother modeled cross-ethnic friendships, and several of her aunts married White men. Mariella also has strong roots in her own culture. She is immersed in the cultural celebrations, religious life, and daily interactions of her extended family, most of whom live nearby in Pine City. Mariella believes it is her knowledge of and security in her own identity as a Latina that has contributed most to her curiosity about other cultures and her ability to maintain diverse friendships. She explains:

> Because I know so much about my culture, I want to learn more about other people's culture. I have a variety of friends of different cultures because I want to learn more about . . . what they like to do and what . . . customs they have.

Hence Mariella and her friends talk openly about culture and invite each other to participate in cultural events. For instance, Mariella invited two of her Chinese and Filipino friends to attend her confirmation, where they felt comfortable asking questions about her religious and cultural practices. Mariella feels confidence that her friends respect her ethnic self, and this confidence frees her to learn more about their cultures and traditions.

Mariella's peer group, whom she describes as "serious" and "motivated" students, help support Mariella's academic achievement and engagement. Mariella's friends are in her classes and help each other with homework and studying for tests. Although she is aware that Latinos are underrepresented in her classes, their absence does not make her feel that she does not belong because she feels comfortable interacting with students of other races and backgrounds. Mariella's diverse peer group and facility with border crossing open up avenues for her to explore her own abilities at the same time she is being confirmed in her Latina identity.

Mariella's peer group and supportive family have mediated the barriers to college track classes and interethnic interaction that many Latino students at Woodrow High School face. Her experiences attending ethnically mixed schools since elementary school enabled her to build lasting friendships with a diverse group of friends, while her strong sense of self enabled her to maintain these friendships throughout high school.

FINDINGS FROM OUR STUDY

Effective Intergroup-Relations Efforts

Our overarching finding is that efforts to enhance intergroup relations within high schools are not just about making students feel good about themselves and each other. If done effectively, intergroup-relations efforts have the potential for opening up new academic spaces for diverse youth. A systematic focus on intergroup relations can help create opportunities for cross-peer interaction and build the trust necessary for students to engage one another on multiple levels (socially, culturally, and academically). Further, students' accounts of their high school experiences, like those of Mariella and Jose, suggest that there are strong relationships between students' ability to navigate structural, sociocultural, and socioeconomic borders and their access to social capital. Thus intergroup relations involves both equalizing structural borders that isolate students from one another and explicitly teaching students the skills they will need to navigate sociocultural and socioeconomic borders when they encounter them. Further, we argue that incongruencies in expectations across students' worlds can lead students, like Jose, to turn their back on what Stanton-Salazar (Chapter 2, this volume) describes as "tangible forms of academic support" (e.g., that offered through AVID). That is, we argue that efforts to address structural borders that do not involve parents, or more broadly affect the school climate, are more likely to fail because they do not take into account the various influences on students' lives. In this section, we discuss the influences of family and peers on students' values, beliefs, and actions. We then turn to the implications of this research for educational policy and practice.

The Central Role of Families

Our research indicates that, of all the potential actors in adolescent lives, families continue to play *central* socializing and support roles. Most students in our sample, like Jose and Mariella, cited repeatedly the powerful role of family members on their attitudes, values, life decisions, and coping strategies. The emphasis on family was particularly strong among our Mexican-descent students, who were the most adept in our sample at recounting their family histories and the relevance of cultural traditions. Unfortunately, working-class families do not always have the institutional knowledge to help their children successfully navigate school settings. For instance, although Jose's family communicated a strong *value* in academic achievement, they could not tutor him in his challenging coursework or guide his selection of courses. Further, pressing economic needs within the family precluded Jose from fully engaging in school just at the time—that is, his freshman year—when he was most vulnerable. For students, like Jose, whose families face economic hardship and who do not have the institutional knowledge to help them succeed, the role of schools and peers becomes even more important. It is to the role of these two forces that we now turn.

Diverse Peers and Academic Achievement/Engagement

The question of whether peer groups drive the development of specific coping strategies or vice versa is a complex one. We believe that in most cases peer-group affiliation is an ongoing process of negotiation that, in an iterative fashion, both shapes and is shaped by individual coping strategies, values, and beliefs. Peers are just one piece of a much larger puzzle that includes families and schools. Students form friendships and identify with peers largely because of the way institutional spaces within schools are organized; typically, they form relationships with students with whom they share classes or activities. Similarly, friendships, as is illustrated by Jose's and Mariella's cases, are often rooted in relationships developed in early childhood within students' neighborhoods and elementary schools. Moreover, families, through their communication of values and the types of social controls they place on their children, play a powerful role in students' selection of friends and identification with peer groups. Thus our discussion of peers is rooted in a consideration of the larger context in which peer relations occur.

Among the students of color in our study, the social capital of students' peer groups proved to be an important indicator of academic success. Like Mariella, academically successful students of color are often adept border crossers, demonstrating the ability to form connections with peers of different racial and socioeconomic backgrounds. We cannot say that having border-crossing skills leads to high achievement, but our research does indicate that the two are linked or correlated in interesting ways. Moreover, we found that students, like Jose and Mariella, who have an affirming sense of what it means to be Mexican are better able to resist negative peer influences. Again, although we cannot make a causal link between these qualities, we believe that it raises interesting questions for future studies.

We hypothesize that border crossing plays a part in academic achievement within multiethnic high schools by contributing to the sense of "belongingness" described in Chapter 7. It opens up settings and contexts within the school that could be perceived as exclusive or not welcoming. We found this was especially important for the Mexican-descent and African American students in high-track classes in our study, because they were most likely to be underrepresented within those contexts. In Mariella's case, for instance, a sense of belonging to the larger school learning community helped her persist in high-track classes despite academic difficulties. Mariella genuinely felt that she belonged, despite the fact that most of her classmates were not of Mexican descent. Further, through her involvement in the freshman transition program, Mariella became a sort of "institutional agent" whose responsibility was to help other students within the school navigate structural and sociocultural borders. This not only helped Mariella develop self-confidence but also acted as a formal medium within the school through which students could act as resources for one another. Within our sample, we found that students do not necessarily have to have close friends within other racial groups to succeed; however, successful students of color were able to form alliances with classmates and key institutional agents (i.e., teachers or counselors) of other races.

Although gender was not a focus of our study, it did emerge as a factor in students' peer relations, border crossing, and academic engagement. In keeping with national trends, most high-achieving Latino students we interviewed were female. Like Hurd in Chapter 4, we found that the young Mexican-descent males in our study sample, even those who successfully avoided gang affiliation, were profoundly influenced by the "*cholo*" or "gangster" identity. Further, our research resonates with issues raised in Chapter 3, that Latino males, though often having very loving relationships with their parents, are given more autonomy from their home world and, thus, have more unmonitored time with peers than Latinas. For instance, Jose's parents, though highly supportive of school, still believed that it was important that Jose work in order to develop more financial independence and responsibility. The autonomy of Latino males may account, in some degree, for their increased vulnerability to school failure and gang involvement.

In addition to highlighting the relevance of interethnic and interracial border crossing, our study revealed a few central lessons regarding what fosters diverse peer affiliation. Students of all races who attended racially and socioeconomically diverse elementary and middle schools, as Mariella did, have more diverse friends and feel more comfortable in contexts where they are a minority. We found, by comparison, that most students who attended racially and socioeconomically homogeneous elementary and middle schools had difficulty, at least initially, navigating sociocultural barriers within their diverse high school. Thus it would seem that border-crossing skills, like any others, are developed through contact and experience. Moreover, students who attended racially diverse but homogeneously working-class or poor schools, as did Jose, did not benefit as much academically from their contact with diverse peers. We presume that diversity in these cases does not lead to enhanced social capital networks, because few youth in these contexts are privy to middle-class forms of social support (see Chapter 2, of this volume). Moreover, Jose's case illustrates that in some cases the ethos of working-class families and schools may privilege early financial independence, in the form of a part-time jobs for teenagers, and in doing so unintentionally impede school engagement. Further research on these topics is warranted.

At the heart of our study are issues of intergroup relations; we have investigated how school programs and policies contribute to a climate where diverse youth can participate freely, with peers and teachers, in an exchange of ideas without feeling they need to compromise their sense of ethnic or racial self. In Mariella's words:

> The ideal high school setting would be a high school that is very integrated. Everybody would know their culture, nobody would look upon each other like they are different, and everybody would be aware of who they are . . . [School administrators and teachers] wouldn't leave it up to students [to create a positive peer climate] but [would] take it upon themselves that, "Maybe we should do something about it."

It is to that "something" that we now turn our attention.

IMPLICATIONS FOR SCHOOL POLICY AND PRACTICE

There is little doubt that most of us would agree with Mariella's vision of what an ideal high school setting would look like and that most schools are striving, in their own way, toward this ideal. However, the process of building a positive racial climate and addressing the needs of a diverse student body is a challenging one, often complicated by socioeconomic forces, housing segregation, and entrenched racial tensions. Schools staffed by primarily White teachers find themselves unprepared to deal with rapid demographic shifts because a majority of teachers suddenly find that their cultural knowledge does not match that of their students. As one teacher at North Vernon said sadly, "[Students'] experience is so much different from what I am used to, I sometimes feel so very inadequate." Our six schools illustrate that there are no easy cookie-cutter solutions or programs for creating a positive racial climate or addressing the needs of diverse students: What works most effectively within one context may fail in another. However, we do believe, like Mariella, that teachers and administrators need to take responsibility for the intergroup climate within their school and the implications that climate has for students of diverse backgrounds. Further, we believe that lessons gleaned from contrasting the respective approaches can guide schools as they engage in their own unique change process. Schools can draw on generalized diversity principles to guide praxis within their own school community. Below we highlight two such "principles" emerging from our analysis that we hope can inform the way schools address peer intergroup relations.

Generating Positive Intergroup-Relations Goals

The importance of developing discrete and positive intergroup-relations goals emerged as a major finding of our study. One piece of establishing such goals is developing a proactive stance toward diversity; specifically, the focus of school interventions should include ongoing opportunities for *positive interaction* between students both inside and outside the classroom. North Vernon is illustrative of this point, as staff members focused so much on crisis management and on keeping fights under control that they did not have the time or energy left to imagine what positive intergroup relations might look like. In some cases, efforts to suppress student conflicts may have worsened the climate for learning within the school. For instance, security fences and gates were installed without consideration of how such physical barriers affect students' sense of psychological space and engagement. A proactive approach, in contrast, may have coupled the creation of gates for increased security with an explicit focus on creating open green space for students to congregate and hold student activities.

We also found that it is important that schools proactively address racial incidents *as a community,* rather than dismiss them as the act of individuals. Such conflicts provide opportunities for the school community to bind together and reinforce values of intergroup tolerance and respect (Miron, 1997; Walker, 1999). Further, schools that take such action model an effective strategy for confronting injustice. Woodrow's response to spray-painted racial epithets is an excellent example of how a school can turn a negative act into a positive one that reinforces rather than diminishes the school culture.

Like Woodrow, the other schools in our study that had the most positive intergroup climate took proactive efforts to create a personalized and connected environment for all students. As will be described in the next section, they developed strategies and programs that bring youth together in shared work and in celebration of each other's difference. A proactive approach was also distinguished by a school-wide commitment to equity, illustrated by holding high expectations of all students, disaggregating achievement data, and engaging in an ongoing assessment of academic tracking and climate issues that can potentially impede student learning (Baptiste, 1999; Katz, 1999; Keyes, Hanley-Maxwell, & Capper, 1999).

Building Inclusive Communities and Transformational Relationships

We found, as did Gibson and her colleagues in Chapter 7, that large comprehensive high schools often have small "schools-within-schools," like the Migrant Education Program or AVID. Although such programs vary considerably from school to school and do not work for all students (Jose is a case in point), when they do work, they promote a sense of belonging and connectedness. Such programs are an invaluable safe haven for students who without them would be disconnected from caring adults within the school. The drawback to such programs is that they often reach only a small portion of the school population, leaving most students to navigate the large comprehensive high school on their own. A focus on intergroup relations does not seek to replace such programs but rather seeks to use their lessons to transform the school climate as a whole.

A key aspect of creating inclusive communities is to *make relationship building a priority.* This includes relationships between teachers and students, but also student–student and teacher–teacher relationships. The "house" structure at Woodrow High School is an example of such an approach, as it provides a sense of continuity to students who stay with the same student cohort for three periods. Similarly, it provides a support structure for teachers who can collaborate on lessons and work together to support individual students. Relationships, in this sense, are imbued with an experience of caring and being cared for that research demonstrates is pivotal for student success (Beck, 1994; Gilligan, 1982; Hargreaves, 1994; Mitchell, 1990; Noddings, 1984, 1992).

In addition to establishing caring relationships, educators need to think of building relationships within the school environment that are *transformational.* Transformational relationships are highly purposeful connections between individuals and collectives of people that facilitate positive behavioral changes in individuals. Academically engaged individuals, like Mariella, who experience transformational relationships with their peers, family, and teachers, have others who advocate on their behalf, share knowledge of the education system for their advancement, bridge them to other social networks, serve as role models, and provide emotional and moral support. Moreover, these institutional agents regularly provide evaluative feedback, advice, and guidance as a way to hold individuals accountable for their actions and to help them realize their potential. These aspects of transformational relationships somewhat parallel the key forms of institutional support set forth in Stanton-Salazar's (1997) social-capital framework (see also Chapter 2, this volume). In Jose's case, the fact that teachers at North Vernon felt that they were "setting students up for failure by holding high expectations for them" suggests that Jose had few opportunities to develop transformational relationships that pushed him to enroll in classes that would increase his life options.

As a practice, the development of transformational relationships requires considerable investment of time and effort. An effective relationship requires mutually reciprocal investment and risk taking not only on the part of adults—especially teachers—to learn how to border cross into students' worlds but also on the part of students to exchange their own unique perspectives—with one another and with teachers—whether it be knowledge, cultural experience, or values. To be an effective member of a multicultural society, students of all backgrounds, including Whites, cannot adhere to what is most familiar or comfortable because little learning happens there. Students stand to gain much more when immersed in challenging school environments that are conducive to engaging in academic settings among diverse peers.

CONCLUSION

This chapter draws attention to the importance of students' affiliation with diverse peers and peers' role in either constraining or sustaining students' ability to navigate sociocultural, socioeconomic, and structural borders. Peers play a crucial role in students' lives by providing supportive relationships and fostering students' motivation to engage in schools. To the extent that young people can freely interact with peers who are different from themselves, they greatly expand their range of self and cultural expression, experiences, and opportunities for academic achievement and advancement. What peers cannot overcome, however, are school climates that do not value Mexican-descent students' unique cultural assets and experiences within and outside of the academic realm. Our study suggests that academic achievement among students of color increases in settings where school leaders take a proactive role in explicitly addressing issues of equity and creating natural and frequent opportunities for students of different races to interact with each other. The sense of belonging and competence in an inclusive school community may serve as the pivotal factor in Mexican-descent students' ability to succeed.

ACKNOWLEDGMENTS

The research discussed in this article was made possible through grants from the Carnegie Corporation of New York and the Spencer Foundation. We also wish to acknowledge all the students and staff from across the six high schools who have contributed to this work, and most specifically the students and parents that we case-profile in this article.

REFERENCES

Allport, G. W. (1954). *The nature of prejudice.* Cambridge: Addison-Wesley.

Baptiste, H. P. (1999). The multicultural environment of schools: Implications to leaders. In L. W. Hughes (Ed.), *The principal as leader* (2nd ed., pp. 105–127). Upper Saddle River, NJ: Merrill.

Beck, L. G. (1994). *Reclaiming educational administration as a caring profession.* New York: Teachers College Press.

Cummins, J. (1996). *Negotiating identities: Education for a diverse society.* Cambridge: Harvard University Press.

Delgado-Gaitan, C., & Trueba, H. (1991). *Crossing cultural borders: Education for immigrant families in America.* Philadelphia: Falmer Press.

Erickson, F. D. (1987). Transformation and school success: The politics and culture of educational achievement. *Anthropology and Education Quarterly, 18*(4), 335–355.

Erickson, F. D., & Bekker, G. J. (1986). On anthropology. In J. Hannaway & M. E. Lockheed (Eds.), *The contributions of the social sciences to educational policy and practice: 1965–1985.* Berkeley, CA: McCutchan.

Gilligan, C. (1982). *In a different voice: Psychological theory and women's development.* Cambridge, MA: Harvard University Press.

Hargreaves, A. (1994). *Changing teachers, changing times.* New York: Teachers College Press.

Katz, A. (1999, April). *Keepin' it real: Personalizing school experiences for diverse learners to create harmony instead of conflict.* Paper presented at the annual meeting of the American Education Research Association, Montreal, Canada.

Keyes, M., Hanley-Maxwell, C., & Capper, C. A. (1999). Spirituality? It's the core of my leadership: Empowering leadership in an inclusive elementary school. *Educational Administration Quarterly, 35*(2), 203–237.

Lee, S. (1996). *Unraveling the "model minority" stereotype: Listening to Asian American youth.* New York: Teachers College Press.

Mehan, H., Villanueva, I., Hubbard, L., & Lintz, A. (1996). *Constructing school success: The consequences of untracking low-achieving students.* Cambridge and New York: Cambridge University Press.

Miron, L. F. (1997). *Resisting discrimination: Affirmative strategies for principals and teachers.* Thousand Oaks, CA: Corwin Press.

Mitchell, B. (1990). Loss, belonging, and becoming: Social policy themes for children and schools. In B. Mitchell & L. Cunningham (Eds.), *Educational leadership* and changing contexts of families, communities, and schools: Eighty-ninth yearbook of the National Society for the Study of Education (pp. 19–51). Chicago: University of Chicago Press.

Noddings, N. (1984). Caring: A feminine approach to ethics and moral education. Berkeley: University of California Press.

Noddings, N. (1992). The challenge to care in schools: An alternative approach to education. New York: Teachers College Press.

Oakes, J. (1985). Keeping track: How schools structure equality. New Haven, CT: Yale University Press.

Phelan, P. K., Davidson, A. L., & Yu, H. C. (1998). Adolescents' worlds: Negotiating family, peer and school. New York: Teachers College Press.

Portes, A., & Rumbaut, R. G. (2001). Legacies: The story of the immigrant second generation. Berkeley: University of California Press.

Stanton-Salazar, R. D. (1997). A social capital framework for understanding the socialization of racial minority children and youth. Harvard Educational Review, 67(1), 1–40.

Stanton-Salazar, R. D. (2001). Manufacturing hope and despair: The school and kin support networks of U.S.–Mexican youth. New York: Teachers College Press.

Tatum-Daniel, B. D. (1997). Why are all the Black kids sitting together in the cafeteria? And other conversations about race. New York: Basic Books.

Walker, E. W. (1999). Conflict in the house: Interethnic conflict as change agent. Paper presented at the annual meeting of the American Educational Research Association, Montreal, Canada.

7

Belonging and School Participation: Lessons From a Migrant Student Club

Margaret A. Gibson, Livier F. Bejínez,
Nicole Hidalgo, & Cony Rolón

Contrary to popular assumptions that academic motivation is simply up to the individual (one student is motivated whereas another is not), current scholarship indicates that academic motivation "grows out of a complex web of social and personal relationships" and that a sense of membership in the school community directly influences student "commitment to schooling and acceptance of educational values" (Goodenow & Grady, 1993, pp. 60–61). Research points as well to a strong and positive link between students' subjective sense of belonging in school and both their participation and achievement (Goodenow & Grady, 1993; Osterman, 2000; Osterman & Freese, 2000; Solomon, Battistich, Kim, & Watson, 1997). *School membership* and *belonging* are similar constructs. They refer to "the extent to which students feel personally accepted, respected, included, and supported by others" in school (Goodenow & Grady, 1993, p. 61). Quite simply, students function better and participate more in school settings and situations where they feel they belong. Conversely, in contexts where students experience feelings of rejection or alienation, their participation and performance decline (Goodenow & Grady, 1993; Osterman, 2000).

As we show in this chapter, students' sense of fitting in and being comfortable in their surroundings during high school is strongly influenced by the nature of their connections with peers. By *peers* we refer to schoolmates and classmates irrespective of whether students are friends. *Peer relations* refers to associations between individual students and between groups of students. In the course of our research, we have found that both intra- and interethnic peer relations can have a powerful influence—either positive or negative—on students' feelings about belonging in school and on the ways in which they participate in the social and academic life of the high school. Moreover, we have found that students may report an overall sense of belonging in school but are highly uncomfortable in those school settings and situations that bring them into direct contact with peers who they feel neither accept nor respect them. This sense of discomfort directly affects the nature of their school participation and academic engagement.

In a study of 2,169 Mexican American high school students, Gonzalez and Padilla (1997) found that students' sense of belonging in school was the only significant predictor of academic resilience and achievement. That study, like much of the literature on school membership, focuses on students' overall sense of belongingness and gives little attention to whether students' sense of fitting in varies from one school setting to another, to why this is so, or to how this affects student participation and achievement. In addition, this body of work gives little attention to student–student relationships and their impact on school membership and participation, focusing instead on students' relationships with teachers and other adults at school.

Belonging and not belonging emerged unexpectedly from our data as significant categories used often by Mexican-descent students in talking about school. (We use the term *Mexican-descent* when referring to students of Mexican origin, regardless of birth country or generation in the United States.) In general, our study supports the links made in previous research between belonging, school participation, and academic achievement. To this it adds a more nuanced look at the factors that promote and impede students' perceptions of belonging and membership in school, with particular attention paid to the role of peer relations across a variety of school settings.

A sense of fitting in at school may be a major incentive for participation, and for some youth even a prerequisite, but this alone is not sufficient to promote academic persistence and achievement, especially among economically marginalized minority youth. It must be coupled with other forms of support and assistance, including access to the types of adult and peer social capital that can enhance academic performance. Much like the literature on belonging, the social-capital literature points to the necessity for a bonding or "we-ness" with school staff and with other students as a precondition to accessing school resources. Following Stanton-Salazar (Chapter 2, this volume), we define *peer social capital* as adolescents' connections to peers and peer networks that can provide the resources and other non-tangible forms of support, including proacademic norms and identities, that facilitate academic performance.

The concept of social capital dictates that supportive peer or adult relations lead students to the institutional resources and funds of knowledge that students need in order to "decode the system" and "participate in power" (Delpit, 1995; Stanton-Salazar, 1997). Not all students have the same access to the types of adult or peer interactions that facilitate academic success. Those whose parents are college educated and who come from middle- and upper-class households generally have greater access to and a greater ability to draw from the sorts of relationships in school that can aid their academic progress than do working-class children and children raised in poverty. The achievement gap, thus, stems not only from economic differences but also from differential opportunities in school to connect with those "others" who can open doors and provide the resources required for academic success.

In addition, while children from affluent households generally acquire this kind of social capital directly from their families, many working-class youth, particularly those from marginalized communities, may find it only through connections at school. It is through close and sustained association with adults who can guide and support their educational progress and with peers who are college bound that working-class minority youngsters come to possess forms of knowing and behaving that they can draw upon to advance academically (Gibson & Bejínez, 2002; Mehan, Villanueva, Hubbard, & Lintz, 1996; Stanton-Salazar, Vasquez, & Mehan, 2000). Often these connections are formed outside of the regular classroom, in clubs or sports or in other nonclassroom settings (Flores-Gonzalez, 2002; Quiroz, Flores-González, & Frank, 1996; Stanton-Salazar, 2001; Valenzuela, 1999).

Of importance to our analysis is the question raised by Stanton-Salazar in Chapter 2 as to whether working-class students can themselves be a source of social capital for one another. We address this question by examining the role that one school club—the Migrant Student Association (MSA)—plays in the lives of Mexican-descent students at a school we call Hillside High (all names of people and places are pseudonyms). MSA members consist almost entirely of children of Mexican-descent migrant farm workers. As we shall show, migrant students themselves broker social capital through their relations with one another and with the teachers who staff the Migrant Education Program. Through their participation in MSA, members come to value and nurture a culture of inclusiveness, information-sharing, and academic engagement.

In order to emphasize the educational impact of MSA on its members, we need first to provide some background information about our study and then describe the position of Mexican-descent students within the larger school structure, the nature of their relationships with their non-Mexican peers, and the profound sense of not belonging that many "Mexican students" experience on campus.[1] Our attention then turns to how the structure and practices of MSA help to contest the marginalization of Mexican students at HHS and provide opportunities for students of diverse academic abilities and preparation to interact with and influence one another toward school participation and achievement. We conclude with a discussion of the implications of this case study for school policy and practice.

ABOUT OUR STUDY

Hillside High is a suburban public high school located in the hills overlooking the California coast. HHS serves students from two very distinct communities, each with different needs and with sharply different school outcomes. The first is the town of Hillside, a mostly White, middle- to upper-middle-class professional community where the median family income is $73,515 (U.S. Census Bureau, 2002a). The second is Appleton, a predominantly Mexican and Mexican American working-class town whose economy is based largely on agriculture. The median family income for Mexican families living in and around Appleton is roughly $33,000, and many of the migrant families whose children are the focus of this chapter earn less.[2]

Hillside and Appleton are part of a large unified school district with only two comprehensive high schools, Appleton High and Hillside High. To relieve severe overcrowding at Appleton High—a school built for 1,500 students that now houses over 3,000—the district buses some 600 Appleton students each day to Hillside. As a result, HHS is also overcrowded, serving approximately 1,900 students in a school designed for 1,200. In the fall of 1998, when this study commenced, the ninth grade was almost equally divided between non-Hispanic White students, who comprised 44% of the Class of 2002, and students of Mexican descent (both parents of Mexican origin), who made up 43% of the freshman class; another 6% had one parent of Mexican origin. Asian Americans, African Americans, non-Mexican Latinos, and mixed-race students made up the remaining 7%.

We draw our findings from a larger longitudinal study of all members of the Class of 2002, in which we were able to follow students' academic performance from the time they entered HHS in ninth grade through to their graduation in June 2002. When students of Mexican descent left HHS, we also made every effort to keep track of their whereabouts and school progress. Our full research sample includes all 588 students in the Class of 2002 who completed our ninth-grade survey, including 248 students of Mexican descent and 256 White students.[3] Altogether 94% of the freshman class completed one or both parts of the survey.

In this chapter we focus on the school experiences and performance of the 160 migrant students in the Class of 2002, all of whom qualified for supplemental services provided by the federally funded Migrant Education Program (MEP).[4] Although most of these students live permanently in Appleton—only a small number of families follow the crops seasonally— close to half leave the area in December when their parents are unemployed, many returning to Mexico. About 20% of these migrant students are absent from school for at least some days in January.

In addition to drawing from students' academic records—to which we had full access throughout the 4 years of fieldwork—our findings come from student surveys and interviews, participant observation both inside and outside of classes, and student essays on key topics addressed in this chapter. We also conducted interviews with a wide range of teachers, administrators, counselors, coaches, and migrant education staff over the course of the 4 years.[5]

THE SCHOOL CONTEXT

Having attended separate elementary and junior high schools in their respective neighborhoods, students from Appleton and Hillside, generally, come together for the first time in ninth grade. Thus, for most of these students, HHS is the first ethnically mixed school they have ever attended. Beyond ethnicity, there are many other differences shaping peer relations and student performance. Eighty-one percent of the Mexican-descent students have two immigrant parents. Most of the Mexican parents have migrated to California from small towns and *ranchos* in northern Mexico where educational opportunities were limited, and more than half attended school for 8 years or less. In sharp contrast, 89% of the White students had at least one parent who had attended college. In ninth grade only one third of the Mexican-descent students had a computer at home compared with 90% of their White classmates. That same year 93% of the Mexican-descent students but only 26% of the White students rode the bus to school. More than 90% of the Mexican-descent students speak Spanish at home, and half of these students were designated limited English proficient (LEP) when they entered ninth grade. Social class differences also distinguish the two groups. Whereas many of the White students live in affluence, most of the Mexican students live in poverty or near poverty. Over half of the Mexican-descent students received a free or reduced-price lunch during ninth grade, and many more undoubtedly qualified based on the 80% free-lunch-eligibility rate at the elementary school that most of these students attended.

Academic Performance Patterns

Even though HHS is recognized for its solid academic programs, excellent cocurricular activities, and a strong teaching staff, it nevertheless reflects long-standing, disturbing national and state patterns of generally low academic attainment among students of Mexican descent (see Chapter 1, this volume). Only half of the Mexican-descent students at HHS go directly into college preparatory math and English classes upon entering ninth grade. The other half, mainly students with limited proficiency in English, take from 1 to 3 years of English language development (ELD) or sheltered English classes. Almost all White students, on the other hand, take algebra or geometry as freshmen, and 1 in 3 takes an accelerated English class. Grades offer another indicator of the performance disparities. At the end of ninth grade, the mean grade point average (GPA) for White students was 3.03 (a B average); for Mexican-descent students it was 2.09, or a C average.

The achievement gap persists through high school, and by the end of 12th grade just 20% of the Mexican-descent students had completed all courses required for admission to the University of California or California State University compared with 64% of the White students. It is notable, however, and important to the focus of this chapter, that 68% of migrant students stayed at HHS and graduated from 12th grade, compared with just 27% of the nonmigrant first- and second-generation Mexican-descent students and 58% of the third-generation Mexican-descent students. In addition, 9% of the migrant students finished elsewhere in the area, bringing the migrant student high school graduation rate to 77%. Not only do these graduation rates compare favorably with those of the nonmigrant Mexican-descent students at HHS, particularly the first- and second-generation students, but they also far exceed the nationwide graduation rate for migrant students, which is estimated to be about 50% (U.S. Department of Education, 2002).

 It is also noteworthy that among the most academically at-risk students—those with a ninth-grade GPA of 1.8 or lower—47% of the migrant students graduated from HHS, compared with 11% of the nonmigrant Mexican-descent students (all generations) and 13% of the White students with similarly low freshman-year marks. The roles of the migrant program and the migrant student club that it sponsors are key to the migrant students' comparatively high graduation rate, especially in light of the many obstacles that these students must overcome. Chief among these is a sense of not fitting in or not belonging to the larger school community.

Fitting in at Hillside High

In general, the gathering spots of White and Mexican students are very separate. Between classes and during lunch, large numbers of White students hang out in the school's central courtyard, commonly referred to as "the quad," and their occupation of this area is both contentious and privileged. Mexican students, on the other hand, generally gather in peripheral spaces where they are less visible, such as the cafeteria or the migrant education office. Many Mexican students describe feelings of nervousness and alienation, some even shame and inferiority, as key obstacles to their active participation in spaces and activities dominated by their more privileged White peers.

It is important for readers to understand that there is a historical context of contention at HHS fueled by the attitudes and actions of some parents, students, and community members from the Hillside area. For example, many Hillside parents believe that academic standards have suffered since the school district began busing Appleton students to HHS in the early 1990s. Over the years a vocal contingent of Hillside area residents has unified around a call for secession, pressing the state to permit them to form their own separate school district, a district that in essence would serve predominantly middle- and upper-middle-class White students. This history and its impact on the position of Mexican students at HHS are described elsewhere (Donato, 1987; Hurd, 2003).

When asked why they don't hang out in the quad, Mexican students explain that "The quad is only [for] White people." They also explain that White students "judge you a lot," "stare at you as you walk by," and on occasion "throw food at you." Even some third-generation students—those who identify as Mexican Americans and who speak English fluently—express discomfort about passing through the quad, saying they feel they "don't belong" there. Mexican students whose English is limited express even greater anxiety. Because most school-sponsored lunchtime activities take place in the quad, these turn out to be mainly White affairs, limiting Mexican students' access to and participation in school-wide activities. (When we pointed this out to the principal, she moved lunchtime activities to a more neutral space on campus.)

White students recognize the social divisions, observing that "the quad is English and the outskirts are more Hispanic." In addition, White students explain that they don't know many Mexican students because, for the most part, they take different classes and are not part of their social circles. They also express unease about hanging out or even passing through areas of campus where groups of Mexican students congregate, but their discomfort rarely seems to limit their social and educational opportunities at school. With the exception of AP Spanish, most Mexican-majority classes and clubs are of little interest either socially or academically to the White students.

In large measure, HHS belongs to the students from Hillside, and they form the dominant groups on campus. Their parents control the PTA and Site Council and have substantial influence over school programs and activities. Hillside students also fit easily into the social and academic life of the school. In addition, they benefit disproportionately from the school's advanced placement and honors classes, its extracurricular programs and activities, and its leadership clubs. Although some of these predominantly White students certainly recognize the alienation felt by Mexican-descent students, few have any real understanding of Mexican students' lives outside of school or the difficulties they encounter on a daily basis in school. Nor do they see any particular need to integrate socially with their Mexican peers.

A sense of not belonging and not being respected permeates many aspects of Mexican students' lives at HHS, including their decisions about whether or not to speak up in class or ask for help when needed, whether to participate in the social life of the high school, and ultimately whether to remain at HHS, transfer to another school, or drop out of school altogether. Some Mexican students, a small minority and mainly boys, consistently act out in class, disrupting learning for themselves as well as their classmates (see Chapter 4, this volume). More, however, simply remain silent in those classes where they do not feel comfortable, not wishing to draw attention to themselves.

As we explained earlier, students who fail to attain a sense of full membership in the school community are likely to be less engaged in school, less motivated academically, and at risk for psychological and perhaps even physical withdrawal from school (Goodenow & Grady, 1993; Osterman, 2000). Such is the case at HHS. Many of the students we interviewed and "shadowed" through a school day spoke of being intimidated or embarrassed in classes where they are in the minority (for similar findings, see Davidson, 1996; Phelan, Davidson, & Yu, 1998; Valenzuela, 1999). An interview with several Mexican students, all cheerleaders, all high achieving, and all on track for college, illustrates how student discomfort impacts academic engagement. One, Gaby, mentioned her fear that she might mispronounce some word in English or otherwise show some lack of knowledge that middle-class White students take for granted. "It's scary," she explained. Another, Marisol, added, "They'll probably laugh at you," and "they just think we're little Mexicans." Marisol cited her creative writing class as an example:

> We wrote poems in there. There was this kid who was so talented, like busting out with this poem . . . [using] these words I've never even heard. I'm like, "You're probably making them up." Then my poem is like, "Once upon a time . . . ," just basic words you hear all the time. That's what intimidates me too. My writing is not as good. I don't know all these words that they do.

When asked if White students actually put her down, Marisol said, "sometimes they laugh," but mostly it was the way she feels around White students. Gaby said much the same, pointing to "the looks that they give you," but also explaining that it was more her expectations based on things that have happened in the past. It is notable that these girls express such a sense of discomfort even though they are members of the varsity cheerleading squad and are well known on campus.

Because of their discomfort, some Mexican students will switch to "easier" classes to be with a larger number of Mexican students, even though they need the "tougher" classes to meet college admissions requirements. "You feel better among your own kind," students explained, and they noted, too, their unease when placed in classes "where you see just White people." When this happens, Mexican students generally sit in the rear of the classroom or to the side and rarely ask questions or contribute to discussion.

One Mexican student, an officer in the MSA club, described his behavior in classes with predominantly White students: "I am more quiet; I just talk about schoolwork. I don't talk about what I do in my free time. . . . I don't really talk that much." He and other students contrasted their behavior in these classes to their behavior in settings where they have the support of their friends. In AP Spanish classes, for example, where Mexican students not only are in the majority but generally are very comfortable using oral Spanish as the medium of exchange, they point out that they "help each other," "work better," and are "more active." Classroom observation supports this view. In these classes, interestingly, it is the White students who tend to be silent, reluctant to speak up, and cautious about drawing attention to themselves.

Clubs and Sports

Although students have little control over class placements, particularly those who wish to meet all requirements for college admission, they do have choices about which extracurricular school activities to participate in, if any. Again, most Mexican-descent students shy away from activities dominated by White peers. Careful analysis of sports and club rosters for the 4 years of our study reveal that far more White students participate in school-wide clubs and sports than do students of Mexican descent. In ninth grade, for example, only 11% of the Mexican-descent students were involved in a school-sponsored sport compared with 52% of their White classmates. For those who completed 4 years at HHS, sports participation rose to 30% for the Mexican-descent students and 72% for White students. Club membership follows a similar pattern. Only 6% of the Mexican-descent students joined a club their freshman year compared with 22% of the White students. Club participation increases each year for both groups, but Mexican students mainly join clubs such as MSA, where all or most of the members are Mexican. HHS sponsors five student clubs with 100% Mexican-descent membership and 12 with no Mexican-descent students (based on 1999–2000 club rosters and yearbook photos). In the rest, participation by students of Mexican descent is extremely low, and those who join tend to be third-generation students who speak only English and who fit comfortably into the middle-class mainstream of HHS. In sports it is much the same, with the exception of boys' soccer, rugby, and cheerleading.

As shown in the research literature, high school students who get involved in extracurricular school activities are more likely to remain in school (Davalos, Chavez, & Guardiola, 1999; Mahoney & Cairns, 1997), develop bonds with their teachers (Fletcher & Brown, 1998), identify with school (Marsh & Kleitman, 2002), and experience positive educational trajectories (Brown & Theobald, 1998; Eccles & Barber, 1999). In addition, participation in sports and clubs is correlated positively with greater leadership skills (Dobosz & Beaty, 1999); higher grades, aspirations, and levels of self-esteem; and improved race relations (Brown & Theobald, 1998; Holland & Andre, 1987; O'Brien & Rollefson, 1995). Research findings also indicate that students from wealthier families participate in extracurricular activities far more than their working-class peers (Eckert, 1989; McNeal, 1998; O'Brien & Rollefson, 1995), thereby "acquiring comparatively greater human and social capital" (Flores-González, 2002; Quiroz et al., 1996). However, when students from lower socioeconomic backgrounds do participate in extracurricular school activities, the benefits that accrue to them are significantly greater than those for wealthier students (Marsh & Kleitman, 2002). As Stanton-Salazar (2001) points out, extracurricular activities offer a site for the development of community and the acquisition of social capital, both much needed by working-class Mexican-descent students if they are to successfully navigate their way through high school and on to college.

Our findings are consistent with these studies, revealing that many

Mexican-descent students at HHS are involved in no sport or club, thus precluding them from access to the well-known advantages. There are many reasons for the low participation, including the cost, transportation problems, the time commitment, and inadequate opportunity to learn a sport at an early age, but added to these reasons is the fact that many Mexican-descent students believe they will not fit in. They explain: "Most sports and clubs are made up of White people, and if you join you probably feel out of place"; "we . . . feel embarrassed or afraid as to what other people might think"; and "you feel intimidated because you are thinking the White people are better than you."[6] The migrant student club is different, however, a setting where Mexican students know they will be welcome and supported.

THE MIGRANT STUDENT ASSOCIATION

MSA is a student-run club that functions in similar fashion to many student clubs on campus. Its members elect officers, hold weekly meetings, organize fund-raisers and community service events, and contribute to a range of school-wide activities held throughout the year. Much of the planning and socializing takes place in the office of the Migrant Education Program. MEP sponsors the club and the two MEP teachers, Mr. Rodriguez ("Mr. R.") and Mr. Guzman, serve as club advisors.[7] With 110 members in the 2001–02 school year, MSA is one of the two largest clubs on campus. Some students come to almost every meeting; others may only attend once a month or when there is an activity of particular interest. The club is open to all students, but almost all who participate are current or former migrant students.

The club mission, as stated in the *MEP Handbook,* is to "promote higher education, celebrate cultural differences, participate in school activities, and organize community service activities." MSA functions as both a social and an academic club—a hub of student life on campus for its members. Its activities reinforce a positive sense of identity for students as Mexicans and as academically oriented. In fact, it is the integration of these two aspects of students' identities that becomes a powerful catalyst for school engagement.

MSA is very inclusive. Its social and academic focus attracts and welcomes a wide array of students, freshmen to seniors, including recent arrivals from Mexico and those born in the United States, those in the top quartile of the class and those struggling academically, those who are at risk of gang affiliation and those with no gang association. Two thirds of the members are seniors, many of them attracted by the club's focus on higher education. One third of the senior members had a cumulative GPA of B- or better their senior year and had completed all the courses required for admission to a 4-year college. Other club members had lower GPAs, some much lower, and had completed only a few college preparatory classes. Three fourths of club members are female. (See Chapters 3, 4, 5, and 6, this volume, for more detailed attention to gender differences in school performance.)

We focus on several aspects of MSA, which together, we believe, help to contest the marginalization of Mexican-descent students at HHS and to support their school engagement: a strong sense of community; the development of norms and values that promote an integrated identity as Mexican and academically oriented; and the role of peers and adults as social resources.

Creating Community and Proacademic Identities

The drawing together of students' multiple worlds—home, school, peer, and community—is a hallmark of MSA and a major reason for the unusually high level of participation by club members. MSA is a community where students feel free to be themselves and where their Mexican identity is valued and supported. Sandra, a high-achieving student who is one of the club officers, and who also participates in other "mainstream" clubs, summed up her feelings about MSA: "It makes me very comfortable, it makes me feel safe, it makes me feel like I'm wanted, like I belong somewhere, like I'm important to someone." MSA is different from other clubs, she noted, because "everyone gets along" and because "I just feel like I'm more wanted." MSA members, she said, "see me as who I am and they respect me." Many other students made similar comments, describing how the club provides them with a sense of security and support in a school where they often feel neither supported nor accepted. Students consistently noted that everyone in MSA "treats us equally," it "makes us feel important," and it "allows people that are Mexican or migrant to have somewhere to go."[8] MSA helps to unite Mexican students on campus, gives them a voice and a presence in the larger school community, and helps them to make new friends. It also keeps some youth away from trouble, "like being out there and gang banging," as a couple of students observed. The sense of acceptance, trust, and fairness that MSA engenders is especially important to its members and provides the foundation and motivation necessary for academic engagement.

All MSA members are Spanish speakers, and the fact that they feel free to use either Spanish or English, or both, when interacting with one another and with MEP teachers about social and academic concerns, contributes directly to their comfort in MSA and related activities. "You feel you belong," one student explained, "because there are people that you know and that even speak the same language you do." In other school contexts students are more guarded in their speech, fearing they may be teased if their English is not "perfect" and worrying, too, that their use of Spanish may draw criticism from non–Spanish-speaking peers and teachers. MSA, thus, provides a much needed "safe space" for Mexican-descent students at Hillside High, where students feel free to express the range of their Mexican identities from styles of communicating to styles of appearance (see Fine, Weis, & Powell, 1997, for their discussion of the importance of "safe spaces"; see also Chapter 8, this volume).

In addition, MSA offers an environment where students feel secure in voicing opinions and taking initiative in ways they do not in other school settings among their White peers and teachers. One major club event that actively integrates students' home, peer, and school worlds is the end-of-year migrant-student awards ceremony and graduation banquet, held jointly with Appleton High. Each year, a student organizing committee is in charge of deciding most of the details: recruiting adult and student volunteers, seeking donations, choosing a venue, inviting speakers, and so forth. It is a time when all migrant students, parents, teachers, administrators, and community members come together to celebrate the academic achievements of graduating seniors who are part of the migrant program. Many are the first in their families to finish high school, and students use this occasion to formally thank their families and MEP for all their support. MEP teachers and staff also use this occasion to acknowledge and emphasize the importance of the various influences—family, community, church, and peers, as well as school—that support students' scholastic accomplishments. Organizing the banquet and ceremony is one of the many occasions where MSA students work together to help one another in the accomplishment of shared goals. It is an example of how MSA strengthens the bonds between students' academic, social, and cultural lives in order to form community at school.

Peers as Social Resources

MSA provides a training ground for students to develop leadership skills through running club meetings and through the organization of school and community activities. Club meetings typically include information about community and school events, volunteer opportunities, discussion and problem solving of issues relevant to students' lives, and information about college. In addition, MSA members help organize school-wide activities to celebrate Mexican holidays. Unfortunately, these celebrations are often contested by White peers and their parents and garner little support from school staff. In recent years the staff has chosen to remove these celebrations from the school calendar rather than to address the underlying issues causing the confrontations (for fuller discussion, see Hurd, 2003).

Fund-raising is another central activity, necessary to support the cost of college field trips, which, together with the end-of-year banquet, are a highlight of the club's work. Members also reach out to younger students in Appleton's elementary schools, helping them to see that they, too, can do well in school, and they offer assistance to families in need, through food and clothing drives. In such a fashion MSA supports both the norm and the value of sharing resources with one's community.

In similar fashion, students learn how to share academic resources with one another. We often observed students in the MEP office helping one another with schoolwork, and peer assistance extends to other sites outside of club activities and the migrant office. For example, members commented that they could reach out to "any student or advisor and talk to them really about anything." Students talk to one another about plans for college and look out for and assist one another when assigned to the same section of an advanced college prep class. They recognize that they "motivate each other," and they note explicitly that those going to college are "a good influence on the rest." Our interviews confirm that some students who initially had no plans to go to college find themselves considering the possibility. As one girl explained, "We motivate each other, the members. For example, Yadira and I, we talk about where we got accepted and we say 'Oh yeah! We are going to college.'" Another MSA member noted, "We first try to help each other, and then we talk to teachers."

The MSA T-shirt offers a visual symbol of the club's academic orientation. Designed by the students themselves each year, the shirt for the 2000–01 school year had a colorful Aztec calendar on the front along with the words *Migrant Student Association* and *Hillside High School*. On the back, bordered by more Aztec symbols, were the words *Only the educated are free, educate yourselves Raza!* Worn proudly, the shirt provided a constant reminder to club members of their proacademic Mexican student identity.

Although peer relations in the larger school leave many of the Mexican-descent students unwilling to engage fully in the schooling process, peer relations in MSA aid students in their academic endeavors. Students network with one another and with club advisors to share and acquire information about school activities, college admissions, and community work. With the leadership of the migrant teachers, students are socialized into a culture that values information sharing, networking, and peer support. In such a fashion, club members serve as resources for one another, consciously and actively helping each other achieve academic goals.

The Role of the MSA Advisors

The sense of belonging, trust, and mutual support that exists within the MSA does not just happen; it is created. Without the careful guidance of the

MEP teachers and the structure within which it operates, the MSA club might have a very different outcome. The teachers consciously and deliberately set out to build a space where students can bring their whole selves into the schooling process. "We need to provide an environment," Mr. R. notes, "where students feel they belong," and to do this, he explains, it is necessary to become friends with the students:

> I think in order for me to trust you, I need to feel that you're my friend. There's no way I'm going to share things with you or believe what you tell me, if I don't see you as a friend. It's something we really try to do with all our students.

Mr. R. also points to the importance of building relationships that extend beyond the formal classroom or school setting. Like many MEP teachers, Mr. R. lives in Appleton nearby many of his students, and he attends the same Catholic church many of them attend. He also plays soccer and basketball with the students on Saturday mornings. In such a fashion, Mr. R. takes an active role in students' lives outside of school, which in turn serves to promote stronger linkages between the students' home, school, community, and peer worlds.

Other MEP teachers exhibit similar qualities of care, involvement, and dedication to supporting the students personally and academically. They believe that by developing a close relationship with the students based upon trust and rapport, they can make it possible for students to put aside differences and to work together to create a proacademic community. MSA "becomes like a family," Mr. R. observed, once students "see that we really care and we want to help."

Many of the MEP teachers are themselves the children of migrant farmworkers, and they recognize that students view them as role models and even surrogate parents. "I really treat them like I was their father," Mr. R. explains. "If I see students doing some dumb things in the club, or saying some comments that they shouldn't be making, I'll act like the father. I'll call them aside and talk to them." He and other MEP teachers also continuously remind students that they need to stay in school, often driving home a point through the use of concrete examples or personal stories. At one MSA meeting, Mr. R. recounted how Juan, a club member, had recently told him that he didn't like to be bossed around. "I am the same way," Mr. R. explained, "but that's why I decided to go to school." He then reminded students that their parents work in the fields because they have no choice. "You," he said to the students, "have an option to get an education."

Mr. R. and the other MEP teachers also deliberately share personal stories with the students to create an environment within MSA where students feel safe to share what's going on in their lives. Advisors also talk to students about "*when* you get to college," and students who might never have envisioned higher education as a realistic goal come to see it as within their reach. In such a fashion, the MEP teachers help to mobilize an otherwise marginalized student population into an engaged, motivated, and resourceful peer group. It is a very deliberate and explicit process. The advisors and members collaborate to create and perpetuate a set of standards and beliefs based on school achievement. Their high expectations, their explicit support, and their availability draw students into a relationship with caring adults who are committed to their educational success. This adult-initiated caring relationship is a key to the migrant students' willingness to persist in school in spite of the many obstacles in their path (Bejínez, 1998).

Our study of the MSA, a school-sponsored and institutionally organized peer group, shows that it operates with demonstrable success in promoting and supporting school participation and achievement among its members, but it has little impact on the larger school. Because MSA is a supplemental school program, it is not within MEP's power, or that of the migrant-student club, to change the larger school. As noted by Stanton-Salazar (Chapter 2, this volume), pockets of peer and adult social capital within school settings may spur individual academic achievement and mobility, but they do little to alter the institutional structures that continue to marginalize working-class Mexican-descent students. In spite of the "we-ness" that students feel in MSA and in spite of the social and academic support they receive through MSA and MEP, a large percentage of these students continue to feel uncomfortable sitting in the central quad or interacting on an equal footing with non-Mexican peers. Even as seniors, many feel hesitant to participate actively in college preparatory classes where Mexican students are in the minority.

IMPLICATIONS FOR SCHOOL POLICY AND PRACTICE

HHS and other schools serving similar student populations need to actively and deliberately counter the alienating influences working-class Mexican-descent students frequently experience in school. Schools also need to contest prevailing notions that Mexicans are disinterested in education and therefore, to be successful in school, they must leave their "Mexicanness" at the schoolhouse door.

More specifically, we believe that our study highlights the importance of building community within schools. All high school students, and most especially those from marginalized minority backgrounds, participate more and do better academically in school settings where they are respected and accepted as equal members of the larger school community. Constructing an inclusive school community may be an essential factor in promoting academic success for working-class students of Mexican descent.

As a step toward building community and a sense of belonging within the larger school, it may be necessary at times to create and support social and cultural safe spaces that are ethnically segregated. The support of groups like the migrant student club can make the difference between staying in school and dropping out, or between taking basic classes and preparing for college. Moreover, as Fine and coauthors (1997) remind us, "a flight into sameness by a marginalized group may be essential for and not a distraction from integration" (p. 275).

[margin handwritten note: MSA for example]

Community building must be combined with other forms of institutional support and assistance. As noted throughout this chapter, and indeed this volume, students need entrée to the kinds of social relationships that can put them in touch with the resources they need to guide their academic progress. However, because these social relationships occur within a stratified school system where power and resources are unequally distributed, school personnel need to be proactive and purposeful about making sure all students, especially low-income minority students, have access to the particular kinds of information and support they need to be academically successful (Stanton-Salazar, 2001).

Peers play a pivotal role in helping students stay on track during high school. For students from working-class and immigrant families, whose parents in many cases do not possess the institutional knowledge or educational background to help their children succeed in high school, peers generally play an even more critical role than they do in the lives of youth from more advantaged circumstances. Moreover, school policies, programs, and practices directly influence the ways that peers interact, including the skills and knowledge they develop in working with one another. All too often school personnel overlook the power and responsibility they have for structuring peer relations in their classes, in extracurricular school activities, and in the everyday life of the school.

Extracurricular school activities, when well designed and supervised, can serve as an important force in creating community and fostering a sense of school membership. In addition, they can provide students access to the types of social relationships with adults and with their peers that foster and guide school success. They also have the potential to bring students into close caring relationships with adults who can serve as mentors, advocates, role models, and friends. Unfortunately, the low-income and minority students who stand to gain the most from these sorts of activities are often involved the least, a fact that has obvious implications for school policy. We return to these implications in Chapter 9, where more specific suggestions for school change are offered.

ACKNOWLEDGMENTS

The research discussed in this chapter was made possible through generous grants to the first author from the Spencer Foundation (MG #199900129) and the U.S. Department of Education/OERI (#R305T990174). We also wish to acknowledge all the students and staff from Hillside High School who have contributed to this work, and most especially we thank the students and teachers involved with MSA, whose many conversations with us have provided the basis for our understanding of this peer group.

NOTES

1. First- and second-generation students of Mexican descent typically refer to themselves as Mexican, irrespective of their country of birth. Some were born in Mexico; more were born in the United States, but in both cases most refer to themselves and are referred to by non-Mexican students at HHS as Mexicans. The term connotes ethnicity rather than nationality. However, not all Mexican-descent students identify themselves or are identified by others as "Mexican." Students whose parents are college educated, middle class, and assimilated into mainstream American culture are more likely to identify themselves as Mexican Americans. At HHS such students are few in number.

2. This estimate is based on the median family income for the Appleton census tracts with the highest concentrations of Mexican-descent families (U.S. Census, 2000b) and on data provided by the regional director of the Migrant Education Program regarding the average earnings of migrant workers (personal communication, July 23, 2002).

3. Following students' own usage, we refer to non-Hispanic White students as "Whites" or in some cases, when quoting students, as "Americans." We also recognize that these terms—*White* and *Americans*—are social constructions and that students of Mexican descent at HHS may themselves be both White and American, as well as Mexican.

4. To be eligible for MEP services, a child must have moved from one school district to another within the past 3 years in order to obtain temporary or seasonal work in agriculture or fishing, or to accompany family members seeking this kind of work. Each migratory move can initiate a new period of eligibility. Of the 160 migrant students in our sample, 146 received MEP services during high school; the other 14 received services prior to high school.

5. Coauthors Livier Bejínez (1998) and Cony Rolón collected much of the field data on the Migrant Education Program and the MSA club. Nicole Hidalgo, herself

a HHS graduate, assisted with field research on the larger school context, including classroom observations and student and teacher interviews. She also carried out research on Mexican students' participation in cheerleading (Hidalgo, 2001).

6. These comments come from an open-ended survey on club and sports participation completed by 170 HHS students in grades 9 through 12, including 72 students of Mexican descent.

7. MEP teachers are not part of the regular teaching staff at HHS but rather provide supplemental instruction and other forms of support to migrant students and their families (Bejínez, 1998; Gibson & Bejínez, 2002).

8. Student comments come from a survey given to 64 MSA members in March 2002 and from student interviews.

REFERENCES

Bejínez, L. F. (1998). *Caring, identity, and academic achievement: The role of the Migrant Education Program in a racially mixed high school.* Unpublished master's thesis, University of California, Santa Cruz.

Brown, B. B., & Theobald, W. (1998). Learning contexts beyond the classroom: Extracurricular activities, community organizations, and peer groups. In K. Borman & B. Schneider (Eds.), *The adolescent years: Social influences and educational challenges* (pp. 109–141). Chicago: The University of Chicago Press.

Davalos, D. B., Chavez, E. L., & Guardiola, R. J. (1999). The effects of extracurricular activity, ethnic identification, and perception of school on student dropout rates. *Hispanic Journal of Behavioral Sciences, 21*(1), 61–77.

Davidson, A. L. (1996). *Making and molding identity in schools: Student narratives on race, gender, and academic engagement.* Albany: State University of New York Press.

Delpit, L. (1995). *Other people's children: Cultural conflict in the classroom.* New York: New Press.

Dobosz, R. P., & Beaty, L. A. (1999). The relationship between athletic participation and high school students' leadership ability. *Adolescence, 34*(133), 215–220.

Donato, R. (1987). *In struggle: Mexican Americans in the Pajaro Valley schools, 1900–1979.* Unpublished doctoral dissertation, Stanford University, Stanford, CA.

Eccles, J. S., & Barber, B. L. (1999). Student council, volunteering, basketball, or marching band: What kind of extracurricular involvement matters? *Journal of Adolescent Research, 14*(1), 10–43.

Eckert, P. (1989). *Jocks and burnouts: Social categories and identity in the high school.* New York: Teachers College Press.

Fine, M., Weis, L., & Powell, L. C. (1997). Communities of difference: A critical look at desegregated spaces created for and by youth. *Harvard Educational Review, 67*(2), 247–284.

Fletcher, A. C., & Brown, B. B. (1998, February). *Adolescent versus peer participation in extracurricular activities as predictors of academic competence.* Paper presented at the Society for Research on Adolescence, San Diego, CA.

Flores-González, N. (2002). *School kids/street kids: Identity development in Latino students.* New York: Teachers College Press.

Gibson, M. A., & Bejínez, L. F. (2002). Dropout prevention: How migrant education supports Mexican youth. *Journal of Latinos and Education, 1*(3), 155–175.

Gonzalez, R., & Padilla, A. M. (1997). The academic resilience of Mexican American high school students. *Hispanic Journal of Behavioral Sciences, 19*(3), 301–317.

Goodenow, C., & Grady, K. E. (1993). The relationship of school belonging and friends' values to academic motivation among urban adolescent students. *Journal of Experimental Education, 62*(1), 60–71.

Hidalgo, N. D. (2001). *Cheerleading: Building bridges and promoting school success.* Unpublished bachelor's thesis, University of California, Santa Cruz.

Holland, A., & Andre, T. (1987). Participation in extracurricular activities in secondary school: What is known, what needs to be known? *Review of Educational Research, 57*(4), 437–466.

Hurd, C. A. (2003). *Belonging in school: The politics of race, class, and citizenship in the Pajaro Valley Unified School District.* Unpublished doctoral dissertation, University of California, Santa Cruz.

Mahoney, J. L., & Cairns, R. B. (1997). Do extracurricular activities protect against early school dropout? *Developmental Psychology, 33*(2), 241–253.

Marsh, H. W., & Kleitman, S. (2002). Extracurricular school activities: The good, the bad, and the nonlinear. *Harvard Educational Review, 72*(4), 464–511.

McNeal, R. B. (1998). High school extracurricular activities: Closed structures and stratifying patterns of participation. *Journal of Educational Research, 91*(3), 183–191.

Mehan, H., Villanueva, I., Hubbard, L., & Lintz, A. (1996). *Constructing school success: The consequences of untracking low-achieving students.* Cambridge and New York: Cambridge University Press.

O'Brien, E., & Rollefson, M. (1995). *Extracurricular participation and student engagement. Education policy issues: Statistical perspectives* (NCES-95-741). Washington, DC: Policy Studies Associates.

Osterman, K. F. (2000). Students' need for belonging in the school community. *Review of Educational Research, 70*(3), 323–367.

Osterman, K., & Freese, S. (2000). Nurturing the mind to improve learning: Teacher caring and student engagement. In S. T. Gregory (Ed.), *The academic achievement of minority students* (pp. 287–305). Lanham, MD: University Press of America.

Phelan, P., Davidson, A. L., & Yu, H. C. (1998). *Adolescents' worlds: Negotiating family, peers, and school.* New York: Teachers College Press.

Quiroz, P. A., Flores-González, N., & Frank, K. A. (1996). Carving a niche in the high school social structure: Formal and informal constraints on participation in the extracurriculum. *Research in Sociology of Education and Socialization, 11*, 93–120.

Solomon, D., Battistich, V., Kim, D., & Watson, M. (1997). Teacher practices associated with students' sense of the classroom as a community. *Social Psychology of Education, 1*, 235–267.

Stanton-Salazar, R. D. (1997). A social capital framework for understanding the socialization of racial minority children and youth. *Harvard Educational Review, 67*(1), 1–40.

Stanton-Salazar, R. D. (2001). *Manufacturing hope and despair: The school and kin support networks of U.S.-Mexican youth.* New York: Teachers College Press.

Stanton-Salazar, R. D., Vasquez, O. A., & Mehan, H. (2000). Engineering academic success through institutional support. In S. T. Gregory (Ed.), *The academic achievement of minority students* (pp. 213–305). Lanham, MD: University Press of America.

U.S. Census Bureau. (2002a). *Demographic profile (Table DP-3). Profile of selected economic characteristics, Hillside CDP, California: 2000.* [On-line.] Retrieved May 17, 2002. http://censtats.census.gov/cgi-bin/pct/pctProfile.pl

U.S. Census Bureau. (2002b). *Income and poverty in 1999: 2000 census tract (Table GCT-P14), Costal County, California* [On-line]. Available: http://factfinder. census.gov/bf/_lang=en_vt_name=DEC_2000_SF3_U_GCTP14_CO1_geo_id =05000US06087.html

U.S. Department of Education. (2002). *Migrant Education Program web pages* [On-line]. Available: http://www.ed.gov/admins/lead/account/secondarystudent.html

Valenzuela, A. (1999). *Subtractive schooling: U.S.-Mexican youth and the politics of caring.* Albany: State University of New York Press.

8

"Like Family, You Know?": School and the Achievement of Peer Relations

Jason Duque Raley

Selah: The one thing that sticks in my head that I love is like, even though it's bad, sometimes, if we have a paper to write, you know, we procrastinate or whatever. And then we all here late night, you know, Sunday night and the paper's due Monday. And we ordering pizza, and "Oh, help me with this quote." You know, that's like, I love that. You know? Even though sometimes I be ready to go, I do love being around you guys and just having that, you know? Just, like *family,* you know? *Family.* I don't know how to explain it.

Eddie: Yep. That's what it is. It's a *family.* That's all it is.

For Selah and Eddie, two seniors at Pacifica College Prep School, adequately characterizing their school experience is hard work. Pacifica has earned a robust reputation since its founding in 1996, its achievements trumpeted in the local headlines, the subject of a feature story in a national newspaper. It is a reputation built around a small set of verifiable facts. The school sets out to prepare students for admission to and success in college. The school day begins at eight o'clock and lasts until five—students often stay until late at night. Perhaps most notably, all students in the first three graduating classes (2000, 2001, and 2002) earned admission to 4-year colleges or universities. And this despite the odds: The school is located in a community best known for its per capita murder rate and barely-still-affordable housing, and it was founded by a teacher and basketball coach only 4 years from his undergraduate degree.

Three years of research (1998–2001) at Pacifica College Prep (all names of places and people are pseudonyms) sustains my sense that such facts do not capture the real texture of students' experience at the school. In particular, students proclaim the special value of their social relations, both among peers and between students and adults. These "trusting relations" turn out to be hard work, but their value is immense as they make possible "safe spaces" for students to work along the risky edges of learning and becoming. A full account of trusting social relations, "safe spaces," or risky learning would require a longer and more careful argument than the one I make here (see also Raley, 2003). In this chapter, I dig more deeply into the smaller piece of students' experience that is captured in Selah's and Eddie's comments: What does it mean for peer relations at a school to be like family? And how are such relations possible?

What follows is first an effort to find a conceptual way to examine peer relations, then an attempt to make sense of a few scraps of data, and finally a consideration of theoretical and other implications. Overall, this is an optimistic account. Although the report exposes live tensions students must face, it also records tensions overcome. Causal relationships among discrete phenomena (e.g., how peers influence school achievement) are somewhat outside the main thrust of this chapter. Likewise, any boundaries between the family and school, between peers and family, or among all the multiple social worlds of adolescents are not considered, though these interrelationships could well be explored. In particular, this chapter examines a certain kind of peer relations—peer-relations-like-family—as an achievement.

FINDING A CONCEPTUAL WAY

In Chapter 2, Stanton-Salazar makes a strong case for the importance of social capital in the academic achievement of working-class and Latino youth, as well as arguing that same-class and same-race peers can be sources of social capital. For Pacifica's students, peers may in fact be sources of socialization to proacademic norms or pathways to "social storehouses" of resources and support. Without diminishing the importance of social capital for access to learning and opportunity, or the importance of peers, this chapter does not deal directly with peer relations *as* social capital. This chapter is instead about the fabric of peer relations themselves, about the shape of peer relations within one school, and about the conditions and materials that make such relations possible.

The title of this chapter is a play on words that is significant both in terms of the findings reported here and for the theoretical frameworks that orient many of the chapters in this book. The concept that anchors the title is *peer relations*. What are peers? Peers are individuals with the same or similar status, where status is defined locally and with respect to a set of shared practices. In schools, where available statuses tend to be limited and highly defined, students constitute one set of peers, teachers another, and administrators a third. Depending on the school, a student's peers might be further delimited as other students at the same grade level (age, again) or a single group of classmates (this especially in schools that track students, where status in a school may be closely tied to perceived academic ability). It follows, then, that what counts at any moment as "peers" depends on defining the shared practices and available statuses in a given social setting.

Two basic ideas underlie the concept of *peer relations* as it is used here. First, this chapter examines peer relations as a kind of social relations, where social relations are "working agreements" or "consensuses" (Goffman, 1959, 1976; Kendon, 1990) that persons must agree upon and use together to make sense of each other (McDermott, 1977). Peer relations of whatever quality are seen, therefore, as a local and situated achievement, built in interaction from available cultural materials. In this way, and unlike *peer groups,* peer relations exist prior to analysis and are naturally observable and describable.

Second is the conviction that peer relations are an important context for learning (Erickson, 1982, 1987; McDermott, 1977; McDermott & Gospodinoff, 1979). Recent developments in theories of learning (cf. Brown, Collins, & Duguid, 1989; Cole, 1996; Lave & Wenger, 1991; Rogoff, 1990), especially those extending the work of Vygotsky (1934/1978), would likely take peer relations as a context for learning as a matter of fact. In any case, the way I mean it here is not at all the same as saying that peer relations *affect* learning; it is a claim that rests instead on the belief that contexts (including peer relations) and activity (including but not limited to *learning*) are mutually constituted (Erickson & Schultz, 1977; Mehan & Wood, 1975). Erickson (1987) offers an analogy that sets us in the right direction for thinking about the relation between peer relations and learning:

> To learn is to entertain risk, since learning involves moving just past the level of competence, what is already mastered, to the nearest region of incompetence, what has not yet been mastered. As learning takes place, the leading edge of the region of incompetence is continually moving. A useful analogy is that of riding a surfboard—in learning, one must lean forward into a constantly shifting relationship with the crest of the wave. (p. 344)

How does this implicate peer relations? In all its eloquence, the analogy suffers from the too-stark foregrounding of learning as an individual encounter with knowledge or skills. Erickson himself would surely say the same (cf. Erickson, 1982). Surfing involves a great deal more than paddling a board, standing up, and maneuvering up and down the face of a wave. It involves knowing where the surf spots are, getting to the spots, and reading the surf for the best way to enter the water. Once in the water, the surfer must figure out where the waves are likely to break, make his way into the cluster of other participants, position himself to catch the wave, and, finally, ride it. Meanwhile, others are watching. If, while surfing, he displays a lack of etiquette or skill, he can expect few opportunities to actually catch many more waves. Without any exchange of words among the other surfers, he could find himself forced just out of position for many future waves. So the risk in learning, as much as an individual risk, is also a social risk. In classrooms no less than at a local surf break, social relations are always already implicated in learning. For adolescents, who spend so much of their non-solitary time in and out of school with peers (Csikszentmihalyi, Larson, & Prescott, 1977), peer relations are perhaps the most important kind of social relations. What does this have to do with the relationship between peer relations and school achievement? Despite best efforts to design good assessment tools, learning and school achievement are not the same thing. But school achievement does involve a kind of learning, even if it is only learning how (and when and where) to perform (or not-perform) in a way others can recognize and understand.

We can now return to this chapter's guiding question, though with a more carefully chosen set of conceptual tools that better reflect the chapter's title: What does it mean for the peer relations at this school to be experienced *like family*? What conditions obtain, what materials are available, to make possible the achievement of peer-relations-like-family as a context for learning?

CONDUCTING THE RESEARCH

Wedged between a major commuter freeway and the San Francisco Bay, Bayview is a geographically bounded community of 25,000 (State of California, 1997); a significant majority of its residents are African American, Latino, Pacific Islander, and South Asian. The city's history is difficult, marked most prominently by its social and economic isolation from the much more vast public resources of neighboring Silicon Valley. Bayview's only public high school closed in 1976, ostensibly as a result of declining enrollment in the six high schools in the larger school district, but historically rooted in poorly conceived desegregation policies. From 1976 to 1997, Bayview families had three basic schooling options. Parents could bus their children to public high schools in distant, more affluent, and often less familiar communities where, as the school district's own statistics show, 65% of high school students from Bayview drop out. Besides the statistics, the consensus among parents and students regarding the poor quality of Bayview's K–8 public schools was remarkable. And, evidently, the stigma of being a Bayview student and resident is hard to shake. In at least some cases, students with nearly flawless academic records from Bayview's elementary and middle schools report being assigned to the lowest academic tracks with little in the way of explanation. As an alternative, parents could enroll their children in expensive private schools, where scholarships are awarded most commonly for athletic prowess and only rarely for academic promise.

Pacifica College Prep School was founded in 1995 as a third alternative, designed specifically for Bayview's college-aspiring students. Pacifica College Prep is a small, independent, nonprofit, college preparatory high school. *Independent* is a reference to Pacifica's "hoped-for distance from the sources of political, educational, and financial control that apply to public schools" (Peshkin, 2000, p. 10). Pacifica relies on donations and the income from a large endowment for its operating costs. The school's status as the central program of a *nonprofit* organization provides considerable tax advantages for both the organization and potential donors. Full scholarships for all students cover the yearly tuition of $7,000. Pacifica is also a *college preparatory* school, the label most central to the singular mission of getting Bayview students into college and a world of social, economic, and intellectual opportunity. The only available curriculum is college preparatory, and all students follow an academic plan based on University of California admissions requirements.

Finally, though not a part of its official designation, Pacifica's smallness is a vital part of everyone's experience. In the last year of the research reported here, Pacifica began a process of expansion to include middle school grades 8, 7, and 6. In the 1998–99 school year, there were 26 students in grades 9, 10, and 11 at the school. Three years later, there were over 70 students across all grades. Students and teachers never fail to mention Pacifica's small size as its most distinctive feature. Feelings about it are mixed: As a positive attribute, smallness permits individualized instruction and highly personalized relationships; as a negative attribute, it limits the range of available social contact and makes teachers' professional development a mostly individual affair.

In just over 8 years, Pacifica Prep evolved from an after-school tutoring and basketball program for middle schoolers into a school recognized regionally for preparing students for admission into and thriving in college. With few exceptions, and by the school's own standards, Pacifica's students do "make it." As mentioned earlier, all students in the school's first three graduating classes earned admission to a 4-year college or university, including highly ranked Ivy League universities, state colleges, private universities, and small liberal arts schools in all regions of the country. Despite this track record, higher education is hardly inevitable for incoming students. Though admissions criteria described in Pacifica's public documents include past school performance, admissions decisions are, in practice, almost entirely based on the perception of students' willingness to commit to the rigorous academic program, a perception based on interviews with students and families, teacher recommendations, and prior personal knowledge. Along with the high-achieving students, Pacifica admits students with documented learning disabilities, thick disciplinary folders, and widely varying skills in all school subject areas. Some students have college-educated parents, but most parents have not attended college, and many parents never graduated from high school. Some students' families have plentiful economic resources; other families are poor.

Pacifica's students are an ethnically and linguistically diverse group of African Americans, Latinos, Pacific Islanders, and Asian Americans who speak Spanish, Hindi, Arabic, Tongan, and Samoan. Most students are additionally fluent in more than one dialect of English. All but two of the Latino students were the children of immigrants from Mexico, reflecting a relatively recent immigration pattern that is rapidly changing the demographics of Bayview. In the end, and though all students are persons of color, the school is decidedly heterogeneous.

From fall 1998 until spring 2001, I spent nearly 3 years in field research at Pacifica College Prep. By the beginning of the second year of fieldwork, I had chosen to focus the research on the 13 students in the Class of 2002.[1] These students are the main group of "peers" for the study. Five of the 13 were Mexican American, though they also called themselves Hispanic, Latino, or Mexican depending on the exigencies of the immediate setting. The flexibility of students' self-identification is a point worth noting. Although it is certainly the case that students identified as members of one or another ethnic group, this identity was infrequently brought to the fore in students' lives inside the school. Students' ethnic identities were far more often a part of their lives in spaces outside the school, when security guards followed them as they strolled the local mall, cashiers gave them sidelong glances at the coffee shop, or their accents were the object of derision. In spite of the fact that ethnicity was not something students often used to identify themselves at school, and though ethnically homogenous groupings of students were rare, I will pay closest attention to data that come from or involve Pacifica's Mexican and Mexican American students. That said, there are no empirical data to suggest that peer relations for Mexican and Mexican American students at Pacifica are demonstrably different from the peer relations for the rest of students.

This work followed the predictably meandering path of long-term ethnographic research. Theoretical frameworks that oriented the first year of study gave way to the pressures of evolving findings (though not always willingly). As work progressed, shadowing, map-making, and audio-recording naturally occurring talk supplemented the early, basic methods of participant observation and interviewing. In the end, I interviewed nearly everyone at the school at least once and conducted from two to six interviews with each member of the Class of 2002. I spent considerable time with students in and out of school, driving them home, grabbing a bite to eat, attending church, watching television. I audiotaped hundreds of hours of both casual conversation and classroom activity. Informal analysis began with the first day of observation, though more formal methods of data coding and the analysis of social interaction characterized later stages of research.[2] One result of that effort was an understanding of "safe spaces" and the delicate work it takes to make them, findings already mentioned. But to understand "safe spaces" meant appreciating the indisputable importance of social relations—and of peer-relations-like-family in particular.

SOME FINDINGS

The two quotes that opened this chapter frame my understanding of peer relations at Pacifica College Prep. Such accounts are commonplace. From students:

> To me, it's like a big ol' family. It's like a second family. Because everybody get along.
>   We like brothers and sisters, to tell you the truth. We've fought with each other. We have argued with each other, we've cried with each other.

And from a teacher:

> It feels like the whole school really is a family. The students are like siblings, and it's just such a close environment, and we know each other on so many different levels, that it's not a traditional school experience.

But while labeling social relations as familylike may evoke a feeling of security and well-being, it does not get us far in understanding peer relations as local achievements. To appreciate the nature of peer-relations-like-family, I offer something of the "shape" of these relations at Pacifica. Following this, I offer a few observations about students' lives at Pacifica as mutually constituted conditions that make possible the achievement of peer-relations-like-family.

The Shape of Peer-Relations-Like-Family

Cliques and categories. Folk knowledge tells us that cliques are every-where, in schools and out, providing a powerful source of social and developmental pressure for adolescents. From the pioneering work of Coleman (1961), Gordon (1957), and Hollingshead (1949), through more contemporary studies in psychology (Adler & Adler, 1995), anthropology (Clement & Harding, 1978; Cusick, 1973; Palonsky, 1975), sociology (Fine, 1979; Peshkin, 1991), and sociolinguistics (Eckert, 1989), the ubiquity and force of adolescent cliques and social categories are taken as a matter of common sense. This makes Pacifica's shortage of cliques noteworthy. Here is Carlos, a senior:

> *Carlos:* Sometimes I hang out with Tony. He a freshman. He don't re-ally be out on the streets and stuff, but, I love sometimes to talk to him, "What's up, Tony?" He tell me stuff, you know, tell me who he have a crush on or something. Ask me advice or some-thing, and sometimes we just talk. Most of the time I hang out with Andre, we just kick it, laugh, Kevin, Andre. Sometimes I hang out with the freshman girls, and we just talk, make 'em laugh and everything. So it's like, not really a particular group. I kick it with everybody.
> *JR:* Why do you think that's the case?
> *Carlos:* I don't know, it's like, it's like one big family here.

Carlos's description of his own experience is mostly borne out in the long-term observations of students. Students do spend a significant portion of the day in class with the same group of peers, and shared assignments mean classmates also spend much noninstructional study time together. But in the available time—in art and photography class, extracurricular organizations, athletics, and the interstitial time between classes and at lunch—students travel more or less freely across age, interest, and gender groups.

It is not the case that students do not form social groupings. An exceptional example lasted through the second half of my second year of fieldwork. On a field trip to Yosemite, several male students in the Class of 2002 had the chance to spend extended, close time with each other and used at least part of it for the confessions and revelations typical among teenage boys. The result was a pact of secrecy (along with a pledge of fealty) and even a proper name for "our clique." "BBH" developed a logo and a set of e-mail aliases. Within days of the group's return to campus, "cliques" proliferated, each with its own set of distinctive symbols and some with equally enigmatic names, one even claiming a special way of walking. A few claimed shared elementary school history, others claimed neighborhood affiliation, still others claimed common preferences for styles of dress. All, interestingly, were gender-specific.

As an honorary member of BBH, I was held to secrecy. At the same time, I invoked my responsibility as a researcher and friend to all, and I enjoyed access to the many conversations that surrounded this multitude of new "cliques." I learned codes and special walks, and I participated in the evolving game, whose objective was to learn the secrets (mostly symbols) of other cliques without compromising one's own. If not encouraged, cliques were at least tolerated by school faculty and staff. The fun and unbridled laughter that surrounded these activities warrant their interpretation as "play." In the context of the "game," cliques were a way to engage playfully across the very boundaries constructed to distinguish one clique from another. In this case, cliques actually increased the frequency of peer relations across existing boundaries. This is in contrast to any expectation that cliques must isolate students.

The postscript to this story of cliques is interesting. The only group in existence by the conclusion of the research was the one that started it all: BBH. As college loomed for its members, the function seemed to have evolved into an emotional and academic support group. The game around cliques died off, but the function of one changed to meet students' emerging needs.

"Knowing each other." Time and time again, students explain curious things about Pacifica with a kind of stock phrase: "Because we know each other." When asked about the general absence of stable cliques, students explain that it is "because we know each other." When asked about their willingness to ask for help, and how they know whom to ask, students explain that "we just know each other." When asked about why one can always find at least a few students on campus, even very late at night or on weekends, students reply that it is "because we know each other."

In my fieldwork at Pacifica, I witnessed only one physical altercation among students. Two members of the basketball team who had been "jawing" with each other for a week met each other outside a classroom and spent a few seconds bumping chests and voicing challenges before another student stepped between them. Because of students' knowledge of other high schools—primarily through stories told to them by friends or siblings, but also through the personal experience of visiting high schools as younger students—students realize that the scarcity of open, often physical, conflict distinguishes Pacifica. I asked students to try to explain this scarcity; the following account from Veronica is representative of almost all others:

> You bond so close together that you don't want to see that person fight this person over something stupid. So you eventually try to say, "C'mon, guys," you know, "Why you wanna fight," you know? . . . They'll say something, they get a teacher or something. And at [the nearest public high school], nobody cares, you know, you don't really get time to bond with everybody so tight like that, they don't really care, you know? It's not *them* that's gonna be fighting, it's *you*. If anything, they want to see how you fight, they want to see *you* fight.

For Veronica, "bonding with everybody so tight" and "caring" depend on getting "time." Giving the students and teachers as many chances as possible to "know each other" is an explicit objective of Pacifica's directors and faculty. Extended, multiday field trips are not uncommon, and even those that go badly by any academic standards are considered a success if they have given students (and teachers) a chance to know each other better. One benefit of the school's freedom from the strict procedures of most public schools is that teachers commonly accompany students to lunch, organize short excursions, drive students home from school, and plan review sessions on nights or weekends, often followed by movies. With students spending so much sustained time together in and out of school, they come to know a lot about each other, even across any natural feelings of antipathy between individuals. Students (and teachers) also have ample opportunity to see each other in action across a range of roles and settings. A level of genuine, complex interpersonal knowledge is, in many ways, unavoidable for Pacifica students. Students not only know each other as something other than members of social groups or cliques, but they know each other across situations and over time.

Peers as social and academic resources. The quote that opened the chapter offers another valuable lead for understanding peer-relations-like-family. Specifically, there is something notable about getting help from each other that is part of the shape of peer relations at Pacifica. Pacifica's curriculum is demanding; when asked what they would tell prospective students about the school, students say, almost without exception, that it is "hard work." As hard as the work is, individual students do not carry the burden by themselves. Students ask each other for help all the time, either from the nearest student or, in moments of more serious need, from whichever student is known to be an "expert" in the problem area. Students cluster in small groups to work on math assignments. They read drafts of essays to each other, or sometimes only a single sentence or paragraph. They share resources for research projects, exchanging addresses for relevant, informative websites. One student leans over another's emerging painting and asks, "How'd you make that color?"

All students have at least one period during the day that is a designated "tutorial" period. Students not participating in extracurricular activities may even have two. Designated students may work with adult tutors two or more days each week. Otherwise, students use this period to work on unfinished assignments, do on-line research on one of the wireless laptop computers, or prepare for upcoming exams. Wandering the campus during this period, any observer would note how widespread are working groups of two or more students.

Conditions That Make Possible Peer-Relations-Like-Family

The organization of physical space. Among other things, the organization of physical space at Pacifica seems important for peer-relations-like-family, especially the relative rarity of stable cliques. In Eckert's (1989) study of social categories at Belten High School, lunchtime was so routinized that she could always count on finding students in the same places at the same times. By contrast, I often felt as if I was spending half of my day trying to track down individual students. Unless I was searching for a student during her normal class time, when I had a good chance of finding her in a specific classroom, she could be anywhere—drawing in the art studio, running on the lawn, shooting hoops (or just watching) in the gym, editing film in the computer lab, studying (or just talking) in an available nook. Students also have access to notebook computers with wireless connection to the school's network. Students are therefore almost always mobile, even when they are composing the final drafts of an essay.

If students are likely to be anywhere at Pacifica, spaces are likely to be used for anything. There are no signs posted to prohibit students from entering rooms or buildings. At Pacifica, students occupy nearly whatever space is available, and they do so individually and in groups. Over 3 years, I was unable to define any "territories" (Eckert, 1989; Scheflen, 1976) or other uses of space that could be easily categorized.

There are also few stable temporal boundaries on the use of space at Pacifica. Though Pacifica's school day begins at eight and lasts until five, I rarely visited campus, day or late night, when I wasn't able to find some student, somewhere, doing something. Selah's opening quote described a scene where students were working at the school on a Sunday night. Though the description provided the background for a claim Selah was making about peer relations being *like family,* the scene is also fairly remarkable in the broader context of U.S. public schooling. In how many schools could we find students at a school on a Sunday night? In how many places are students *welcome* at school during "nonschool" hours?

The relationship between the organization of space and the shape of peer relations at Pacifica depends on the understanding of peer relations that is the foundation for this chapter. Peer relations are an achievement; students and others must construct the local shape of peer relations, in their activities and with available cultural materials. At Pacifica, where so many spaces are always already multipurpose, where doors are not locked and even the office telephone is as likely to be used by a student as by an adult, students are less well-equipped to do the boundary work necessary to produce and maintain cliques. In other words, without spaces to "own," students will find that space is not readily available as a prop for the dramatic performance of cliques and categories (cf. Varenne, 1982). This makes it more likely that students will be able to construct peer-relations-like-family. One interesting consequence of the way space is organized at Pacifica is that students and teachers are visible to each other almost all of the time. This visibility is of another type than that offered by Foucault (drawing on Bentham) and his panopticon (1979), where structure gives one privileged person or class of persons the ability to see what is going on among all other persons all the time. At Pacifica, the fact that any one space could be inhabited at any moment by other persons means that visibility gets distributed among persons: I might not see you, but someone else whom I will see is likely to, and so on.

Academic supports and the fear of failure. Competition among individuals or groups is a central part of the culture of most schools in the United States (Goldman & McDermott, 1987; Smith, Gilmore, Goldman, & McDermott, 1993). By and large, competition is set up so some must fail in order for others to achieve. Even where winners and losers are not always clear (as they are in spelling bees and class rankings), the logic of the normal curve predominates. Failure means much more than the inadequate display of knowledge; it may also mean losing the game of school. It is against this backdrop that students' (and teachers') fear of failure makes sense. And where competition for the scarce resource of school success frames students' experience, differences in school achievement are readily available material for building a specific kind of noncooperative peer relations.

Pacifica operates under the dual assumptions that students and families do *not* know the intricacies of preparing for college and that the school bears primary responsibility for educating and assisting. The school employs a full-time college counselor, whose job includes organizing and distributing informational resources, designing college planning workshops for students' families, locating and facilitating students' summer internships, and helping seniors prepare college and scholarship applications. In practice, this means the college counselor meets individually with each senior student several times each week to review progress and make plans. He makes phone calls to colleges and foundations to advocate for students. He has developed college admissions essay-writing workshops and has invited college admissions officers from private and public universities to discuss the admissions process with Pacifica's students. In the end, the college counselor offers students the benefit of a teacher, a coach, a partner, an advocate, and, in some ways, a concerned and college-educated parent.

Pacifica's subject-matter curriculum is explicitly designed around University of California admissions requirements. This curriculum is college preparatory inasmuch as it seeks to educate students for admission to college. The college counselor is a principal figure in what amounts to a parallel curriculum, one organized for learning about admission to and success in college. Mostly hidden from public view, the about-college curriculum is embedded in the day-to-day life of the school and is mostly located in the regular flow of talk among teachers and students. A teacher reprimands a student with a comment that "that won't play in college." A teacher frames a classroom activity as "a debate, like a college-type discussion." Students and teachers joke about how a college professor might or might not act. The college counselor warns students that they "won't get this kind of help in college." Not only are students' future college careers positively assumed, but college is melted into the nooks and crannies of daily life.

There is a downside to this. Unsurprisingly, the generosity of support for students generates some adult suspicion that students take for granted their wide access to resources and opportunity. Students may come to expect review sessions on any Saturday afternoon, or one-on-one assistance with an essay, or structured time to work collaboratively on a project. Comments recorded in interviews and observational field notes attest to the frustration teachers can feel. It seems reasonable that being "like family" makes it more likely that students will expect certain things from teachers and from the school. In any case, student expectations and teacher frustration seem two sides of a relational coin. That said, support continues to be forthcoming.

With all of this support decreasing the likelihood of failure, what happens to students' fear of failure? Sitting in an SAT preparation class early in my research, I noted one student clearly searching the work of his classmates for answers—glancing from one desk to another, looking furtively at the teacher, and even meeting my gaze with a look of embarrassment (he continued cheating despite having been "caught"). In another case, two students were asked to leave the school after stealing the teacher's master copy of a science test and using it to fill in answers. Teachers talk about cheating with incomprehension. "Why," one teacher asked, "would they steal a test when we offer them so much help?" Rephrasing the teacher's question with our own purposes in mind: "With all this help, what were students afraid of?"

Without offering any conclusive answers, a basic understanding about the importance of "belonging" to the group may help us make sense of cheating. In the same interview that generated this chapter's opening quote, Selah said this:

> We all know that our education is important. We're not trying to front for anybody else. We're not trying to put on a show, show this next student that, "Oh, you know, I'm so serious about my grades." We *all* know that. That's why we *here*. So that's established, you know, in the fact that we're here from eight to five and working hard. We don't get something we ask the next person for help, showing that we're interested in our work. It says it for itself.

Selah's emphasis on "we," especially her expanded and emphasized "we *all*," suggests a shared academic identity, rooted in being *"here,"* in which "seriousness" and "interest" are markers of belonging. Correspondingly, it makes sense that failure—or even disinterest—will be a marker of not belonging. Less an issue of relative standing, academic success or failure may be consequential as a criterion for belonging. The fact that students have access to support that borders on prodigal means that school performance is framed as a personal choice. No longer comprehensible as a consequence of either intellectual deficit or lack of support, to fail would seem to indicate a lack of effort; school failure may then be read as a deficiency in character. The students I studied at Pacifica College Prep School fear failure, but their fear seems to be of a different type. They seem to fear being left out of the group, a fear different from the fear of being beaten by another person on a test. But fear of being left out can be just as debilitating in its own way. As a case in point, cheating—even on a practice SAT test that doesn't "count" for a grade—may make sense as an effort to preserve the symbols of belonging.

Peer relations, then, may be framed in terms of commitment to school achievement, while measurable differences in school achievement do not seem to lead to the formation of cliques. It becomes possible then for one student's strengths in math (or chemistry or English or art) to be a resource and not a threat. What Pacifica offers is an environment where success and failure are not part of a zero-sum game—the success of any student is folded into the "success narrative" of the school—and where social and academic resources are varied, extensive, and readily available.

Teachers and teacher–student relations. In schools, peer relations are never too distant from teacher–student relations. It is not just the case that student–teacher relations matter for peer relations. It is, rather, that they are interwoven pieces of the same cultural fabric, woven, in fact, from much of the same material thread. At Pacifica, peer-relations-like-family are part of a larger system of social relations that students and teachers also talk about as being "like family." Students describe teachers as being like aunts and uncles, older brothers and sisters, or parents. Teachers describe their own roles similarly, often to explain their terrific commitment of time and energy. Remarkable as the quantity of time and energy teachers spend with students may be, the quality of teacher–student relations (in the language of this chapter, their shape) is more noteworthy, and perhaps more relevant.

For teacher–student relations to be "like family" demands that adults be able to see kids through lenses other than aptitude tests, reading scores, or a student's last draft of an essay on Homer's *Odyssey*. Teachers at Pacifica do not talk about students as if such measures were closely coupled to a student's intellectual ability or personality. On the contrary, teachers frequently and openly discuss ways of working *with* but not *through* assessment tools. Of course, teachers lament the clarity of thinking in an expository essay, or students' last minute preparation for presentations they have had weeks to work on. What matters is that teachers work to know students independently of their academic performance. At the root of this lies a deep commitment among teachers to consider each student as an individual, to come to know his or her unique abilities and needs.

Teachers and administrators actively share responsibility for the social and academic well-being of students. When teachers can find the time and space to sit down together, they often compare notes and experiences, sometimes drawing new conclusions about where a student is heading and how such paths might be redrawn, other times concluding that a student is "just having a bad week." Though such time and space are chronically short, a sizable part of each staff meeting is devoted to discussing the situations of individual students, and teachers complain when staff meetings leave no time for such conversations. In some cases, conferences with a student's family members might be planned or changes proposed to a student's program.

Reinforcing such relations at school can strain the out-of-school lives of teachers. Elizabeth, a social studies teacher, echoes the voices of many of her colleagues:

> *Elizabeth:* I like them a lot. So I can't help but want to get to know
> them better, and, I don't know, I just can't imagine being that sur-
> face teacher who just sends them on their way.
> *JR:* Is there a down side to it?
> *Elizabeth:* Yeah (laughs). I have no social life (laughs). I'm not sure
> that I'll get one again. I've got my dog.

Spending evenings and weekends at school; making the time to drive students to lunch, to basketball games, or to home at the end of the day; committing to making sure that every student has access to whatever resources he might need to survive the demands of a college prep curriculum: Such things can exact a toll on teachers' lives. Pacifica's teachers are like teachers anywhere, but as participants in social relations that are "like family," the sense of responsibility can make it difficult to keep things in a healthy balance. Though the best of Pacifica's teachers make the time for keeping themselves healthy and involved in other, nonschool relationships, many acknowledge that they "feel bad for not being able to be [at Pacifica] all the time, to be there whenever students need me."

La Migra at School

Life is never as easy as I have made it seem so far, especially for adolescents, and especially for Mexican American students in U.S. public schools. The Mexican American students at Pacifica—along with the African American and Asian/Pacific Islander students—have to deal with, for example, the frustration in trying to figure out one's own identity and/or sense of self; interpersonal conflicts with other Pacifica students; the temptation to spend less energy for school and more energy earning money (within and outside of legal boundaries); the politics of ethnicity in Bayview and surrounding communities; the challenge of raising a child as a young, unmarried parent; and, as they prepare to leave for college, the trepidation students feel going into a new world they define as largely "White" (a gloss for a range of characteristics that make the "outside" world different from that with which they are most familiar). All the same, peer relations—and the larger system of social relations of which they are a part—remain fundamentally relevant as contexts for working out (or working through) these challenges.

At the same time that the knowledge that comes from sustained contact may enable certain kinds of peer relations to flourish, it does not always prevent conflict, and can even be used to exploit vulnerabilities. This comes from a teacher:

> We had a unit on immigration, and we were talking about current attitudes and Proposition 227, and sort of these anti-immigration, particularly towards Mexico, attitudes. And a lot of the African American students looked up and were like, "Well, but it *is* difficult when you go to a school, and they don't speak English." And just kind of making jokes about things like that. And the good thing is, I was sort of defending the Latino perspective, and then a couple of the students, Juan especially, finally spoke up and then some of them were like, "Oh, I get what you're saying. I see what you mean." And until [the Latino students] were able to share their experiences, the other [African American and Pacific Islander] students were closed off to learning about it.

Embedded in the teacher's story is an account of the way that some peers may be constructed as a set of "others." For at least one group of students, these others are "they" who "don't speak English." But if in the teacher's story the distinction among groups of peers seemed more or less neutral (and easy enough to handle by making it possible for students to share their experiences), it took on an electric charge outside the classroom.

Powerful tensions are already present in Bayview, particularly around the large influx of new immigrants competing for housing in a regional market where the only affordable housing is in Bayview, itself undergoing a crisis of gentrification. Leaning against the railing near the art studio one afternoon, Victorio described a group of students continuing to make jokes about his accent, even "joking" that *la migra* (officers from the INS, the Immigration and Naturalization Service) were coming to get him. This group of students included African Americans, Pacific Islanders, and even one second-generation Mexican American student. The distinction between students who speak English and those who do not (or who speak with an accent) took on a special meaning here, connected to the ongoing tensions roiling the community. And it hardly seems the "peer-relations-like-family" of interest to this study.

When confronted about it in the days that followed, the students who made fun of Victorio's accent and announced the arrival of *la migra* explained away the offense, labeling it "no big deal" because "we know each other." Rather than being the foundation for "peer-relations-like-family," "knowing each other" in this case may have made it *more* rather than *less* likely that already-planted seeds of conflict would grow, as students were able to claim their comments were keyed as "play" when, in fact, they cut deeply—in Bateson's (1955) terms, what students were calling a "nip" was really a "bite."

The school faculty did respond aggressively to the conflict, creating new sets of rules around "capping" (i.e., public insulting) and devoting several class sessions to "working out" the problem. By the end of my field-work, the conflict seemed to have dissipated; the same students who stood on opposite sides of the immigration issue were helping each other through a difficult essay the last time I visited campus, and the student who had suffered the brunt of the insults, returning to Pacifica after a short move out of town, reported to me that everything was "real cool now."

There is never a guarantee that *knowing each other* will be a positive resource for peer relations, but far more often than not, Pacifica students seem to manage to sit down together, to work and play together, to make up code names and figure out chemistry formulas and install public art projects together. They do so across differences in ethnicity, language, religion, academic achievement, socioeconomic status, and athletic ability.

IMPLICATIONS WORTH THINKING ABOUT

Most people begin their thinking about Pacifica with the fact that all of Pacifica's students go to college. Educational research, from research on the psychology of "at-risk students" to studies on the politics of school reform, tells us this is rare and remarkable. The same research pushes us to look for particular kinds of lessons, cast in familiar terms. Shouldn't we force every student through a college-prep curriculum? Shouldn't we tear down the walls of classrooms, opening up a school's spaces to students? Shouldn't we keep our classes small and keep kids together in every class period? Shouldn't we eliminate tracking of all kinds, or perhaps gather all college-aspiring students together so that they might benefit from a rigorous curriculum? The same search for lessons makes clear the questions not addressed in this chapter: What kind of leadership is there? What about a discipline program? How do parents get involved?

This chapter begins from a different idea, one notably less concerned with explaining the academic achievements of Pacifica's students than with understanding the shape and texture of their social relations. Even then, there exists a similar and equally justifiable demand for lessons and questions. How exactly do we get peer-relations-like-family? Even though this chapter was never about explanation, two features of Pacifica are worth considering as likely "causes" of the quality of peer relations there.

The first "cause" comes from Pacifica's admissions policies. "With all the students already wanting to go to college," one might say, "of course there aren't very many conflicts. Of course cliques aren't scary. Of course it's hard to find harmful competition." That all students have aspirations to attend college does mean that motivation is not an issue, at least not on the first day of school. But the fact that a group of individuals shares a hope for higher education is certainly no guarantee for a certain kind of peer relations. Some of the most fractured peer relations exist in our schools' honors and advanced placement classes, where students are constantly on the lookout for threats to individual glory (Goldman & McDermott, 1987; Pope, 2001). We also know that the shape of college aspirations is variable (Chapter 3, this volume), leaving no strong case for the enduring effect of all students' wanting to go to college. As a candidate explanation for the peer relations at Pacifica, this is uncompelling.

The second explanation is more compelling than the first, and may actually have been simmering in the background over the course of the chapter. Early on, I noted that for students and teachers, the *smallness* of Pacifica is one of its most distinctive features. A close coupling of Pacifica's small size with the quality of peer relations there is not difficult to imagine: Pacifica is small, so students spend a lot of time together, in various settings and for various purposes. Through this extensive contact, students get to know each other. Once they know each other, it becomes easier for students to interact across age, ethnicity, language, and academic-achievement lines. Interpersonal connections, inevitable in a small school, transcend such differences.

Not only do I think such a view is cynical, but to work too hard at drawing implications for policy, to identify *causes* of peer-relations-like-family, misses the more fundamental points of this chapter. Peer relations like those at Pacifica *are* more likely in a small school than at a large high school, insofar as students and teachers in smaller schools have more opportunities to know each other more deeply and across a wider variety of settings. Smaller schools will also have fewer resources with which students and teachers may construct borders and boundaries. Just as critical may be an environment where the failure inherent in interindividual competition is not available as a source of fear, as well as a division of space that permits freedom of movement and multiple use. Adults' commitment to "knowing" students provides a social relational foundation for peer-relations-like-family, and teacher's refusal to see students through the lens of SAT scores or grade-level reading ability keeps one set of materials commonly used to sort people into groups a little further out of reach. In the end, we ought to keep in mind that peer-relations-like-family are an achievement, a "working consensus" that purposeful design can only ever make *possible* (at best) or *impossible* (at worst). The important point is that social relations are built from available materials, and that we ought to carefully consider how what we do opens (or forecloses) possibilities of rich, meaningful relations among students.

Some will express a legitimate concern about the long-term fate of these young people. They will most assuredly gain admission into college, but will their experience at Pacifica prepare them for life in the "real world"? In a world lubricated by the currency of social capital (Coleman, 1988; Stanton-Salazar, 1997; Chapter 2, this volume), will these students have enough of it to participate? How will Pacifica's pervasive achievement ideology prepare students for the disappointments that they will surely face? What will happen when help is not so easy to get as at Pacifica?

Before any students get to the "real world," they will have to get through school. Those who already know how to "do school" (Pope, 2001) will use their knowledge, skills, attitudes, and relationships to open the door to the "social storehouses" of resources and support (Chapter 2, this volume). Those who do not already know how to "do school" require not only connections to people who can provide them access to such "social storehouses" but also a context of social relations that make real learning possible. How will Pacifica students do when they get to the real world? At the very least, they will not have been sorted out of the system. They will also have had the opportunity to learn who they are and what they love, how the world works for and against them, and the great benefit of adapting, seeking and sharing expertise, taking risks. They may even carry with them the skills and inclinations to help them build their own contexts of sustaining relations. In short, these students may have learned something about *learning.* This small piece of the holy grail of human becoming will, I wager, serve them well.

ACKNOWLEDGMENTS

This research would not have been possible without the good will and patience of Pacifica's directors, teachers, and, most of all, Pacifica's students. The research was supported through a Stanford University President's Fellowship and enjoyed the expert (and forgiving) guidance of the late Dr. Alan "Buddy" Peshkin.

NOTES

1. Over the course of the study, the number of students in the Class of 2002 ranged from 13 to 17 as families moved into and out of Bayview or new students were admitted.

2. These included the following: (a) constant comparative methods of coding

qualitative data (Glaser & Strauss, 1967); (b) theory and methods of analyzing social interaction (Birdwhistell, 1970; McDermott & Gospodinoff, 1979; Scheflen,
1966, 1976); and (c) an ethnomethodologically informed consideration of how these
two approaches might fit together (Garfinkel, 1967; Moerman, 1988).

REFERENCES

Adler, P. A., & Adler, P. (1995). Dynamics of inclusion and exclusion in preadoles-
cent cliques. *Social Psychology Quarterly, 58,* 145–162.

Bateson, G. (1955). The message "This is play." In B. Schaffner (Ed.), *Group processes.*
New York: Josiah Macy, Jr. Foundation.

Birdwhistell, R. (1970). *Kinesics and context.* Philadelphia: University of Pennsylvania Press.

Brown, J. S., Collins, A., & Duguid, P. (1989). Situated cognition and the culture of
learning. *Educational Researcher, 18*(1), 32–42.

Clement, D., & Harding, J. (1978). Social distinctions and emergent student groups
in a desegregated school. *Anthropology and Education Quarterly, 9*(4), 272–282.

Cole, M. (1996). *Cultural psychology.* Cambridge, MA, and London, England: The
Belknap Press of Harvard University Press.

Coleman, J. S. (1961). *The adolescent society.* New York: The Free Press.

Coleman, J. S. (1988). Social capital in the creation of human capital. *American Journal of Sociology, 94,* S95–S120.

Csikszentmihalyi, M., Larson, R., & Prescott, S. (1977). The ecology of adolescent
activity and experience. *Journal of Youth and Adolescence, 6*(3), 281–294.

Cusick, P. (1973). *Inside high school.* New York: Holt, Rinehart and Winston.

Eckert, P. (1989). *Jocks and burnouts: Social categories and identity in high school.* New
York: Teachers College Press.

Erickson, F. (1982). Taught cognitive learning in its immediate environments: A
neglected topic in the anthropology of education. *Anthropology and Education
Quarterly, 13*(2), 149–180.

Erickson, F. (1987). Transformation and school success: The politics and culture of
educational achievement. *Anthropology and Education Quarterly, 18*(4), 335–356.

Erickson, F., & Shultz, J. (1977). When is a context? Some issues of theory and
method in the analysis of social competence. *Quarterly Newsletter of the Institute for Comparative Human Development, 1*(1), 5–10.

Fine, G. A. (1979). Small groups and culture creation: The idioculture of Little
League baseball teams. *American Sociological Review, 44,* 733–745.

Foucault, M. (1979). *Discipline and punish: The birth of the prison.* New York: Vin-
tage Books.

Garfinkel, H. (1967). *Studies in ethnomethodology.* Englewood Cliffs, NJ: Prentice-Hall.

Glaser, B., & Strauss, A. (1967). *The discovery of grounded theory: Strategies for qualitative research.* Chicago: Aldine.

Goffman, E. (1959). *The presentation of self in everyday life.* New York: Anchor.

Goffman, E. (1976). Replies and responses. *Language in Society, 5,* 257–313.

Goldman, S., & McDermott, R. (1987). The culture of competition in American schools. In G. Spindler (Ed.), *Education and cultural process* (pp. 282–299). Prospect Heights, IL: Waveland Press.

Gordon, W. C. (1957). *The social system of the high school: A study in the sociology of adolescence.* Glencoe, IL: The Free Press.

Hollingshead, A. B. (1949). *Elmtown's youth.* New York: Wiley and Sons.

Kendon, A. (1990). *Conducting interaction: Patterns of behavior in focused encounters.* Cambridge, UK: Cambridge University Press.

Lave, J., & Wenger, E. (1991). *Situated learning: Legitimate peripheral participation.* New York: Cambridge University Press.

McDermott, R. P. (1977). Social relations as contexts for learning in school. *Harvard Educational Review, 47*(2), 198–213.

McDermott, R. P., & Gospodinoff, K. (1979). Social contexts for ethnic borders and school failure. In A. Wolfgang (Ed.), *Nonverbal behavior: Applications and cultural implications* (pp. 175–195). New York: Academic Press.

Mehan, H., & Wood, H. (1975). *The reality of ethnomethodology.* New York: Wiley Interscience.

Moerman, M. (1988). *Talking culture: Ethnography and conversation analysis.* Philadelphia: University of Pennsylvania Press.

Palonsky, S. B. (1975). Hempies and squeaks, truckers and cruisers: A participant observer study in a city high school. *Educational Administration Quarterly, 11*(2), 86–103.

Peshkin, A. (1991). *The color of strangers, the color of friends: The play of ethnicity in school and community.* Chicago: University of Chicago Press.

Peshkin, A. (2000). *Permissible advantage: The moral consequences of elite schooling.* Chicago: University of Chicago Press.

Pope, D. C. (2001). *"Doing school": How we are creating a generation of stressed-out, materialistic, and miseducated students.* New Haven, CT: Yale University Press.

Raley, J. (2003). *Safe spaces?: Risk, trust, and learning at the margins.* Unpublished doctoral dissertation, Stanford University.

Rogoff, B. (1990). *Apprenticeship in thinking: Cognitive development in social context.* New York: Oxford University Press.

Scheflen, A. (1966). Natural history method in psychotherapy. In L. Gottschalk & A. Auerback (Eds.), *Methods of research in psychotherapy.* New York: Appleton-Century-Crofts.

Scheflen, A. E. (1976). *Human territories: How we behave in space-time.* Englewood Cliffs, NJ: Prentice-Hall.

Smith, D., Gilmore, P., Goldman, S., & McDermott, R. (1993). Failure's failure. In E. Jacob & C. Jordan (Eds.), *Minority education: Anthropological perspectives* (pp. 209–231). Norwood, NJ: Ablex.

Stanton-Salazar, R. D. (1997). A social capital framework for understanding the socialization of racial minority children and youths. *Harvard Educational Review, 67*(1), 1–39.

State of California. (1997, May). *Population Estimates for Cities & Counties.* Sacramento: Department of Finance, Demographic Unit.

Varenne, H. (1982). Jocks and freaks: The symbolic structure of the expression of so-
cial interaction among American senior high school students. In G. Spindler
(Ed.), *Doing the ethnography of schooling* (pp. 210–235). Prospect Heights, IL:
Waveland Press.

Vygotsky, L. (1978). *Mind in society: The development of higher psychological processes*
(M. Cole, V. John-Steiner, S. Scribner, & E. Souberman, Eds.). Cambridge, MA:
Harvard University Press. (Original work published 1934)

9

Peers and School Performance: Implications for Research, Policy, and Practice

Patricia Gándara & Margaret A. Gibson

Schools are places where adolescents interact publicly with their peers across time and in a variety of settings. Although schools are not the only settings where such exchanges occur, they are clearly an important venue and key to studying the complex ways in which peer relations influence schooling outcomes. Contributors to this volume examine a multiplicity of peer relations from perspectives that make the institution of schooling central to the analysis. From their respective disciplines of anthropology, psychology, sociology, and educational policy studies, they highlight the types of interactions and influences that occur among Mexican-descent youth and between Mexican-descent youth and their non-Mexican peers. In this concluding chapter, we summarize major findings and locate prior analyses within recommendations for research, policy, and practice, specifically linking the ways in which findings may be applied to improving educational outcomes for Mexican-descent students.

PEER INFLUENCE AND SCHOOL ACHIEVEMENT

Developmental theorists have long viewed peers as influential in social and emotional development and peer acceptance as a critical feature of normal adolescent identity development (Erikson, 1968; Marcia, 1980). Research on adolescents has pointed as well to a link between peer influence and school success, although generally as a negative force distracting adolescents from academic engagement and achievement (Brown, Clasen, & Eicher, 1986; Coleman, 1961; Kandel, 1973; Pearl, Bryan, & Herzog, 1990; Snyder, Dishion, & Patterson, 1986). The studies presented in this volume also investigate ways in which peers undermine educational progress, and why they do. In addition, they explore the ways in which peers support one another's academic achievement and the roles that schools themselves play in shaping peer relations.

For example, several contributors investigate how peers pull Mexican-origin youth away from school engagement: through a desire to look "cool" by not admitting to spending much time studying (Chapter 3, this volume), through acting out in class to garner favor from friends (Chapter 4, this volume), and through overt rejection of classroom and schooling norms (Chapter 5, this volume). Others focus on peers as a positive influence on academic success. In Chapter 6, Heather Lewis-Charp and her colleagues demonstrate that when high schools are organized more inclusively, students have far greater opportunities to mix with and be supported by a wide variety of peers. Similarly, Margaret Gibson and coauthors in Chapter 7 describe how a school-sponsored student club provides critical academic and social support to its members. Further, in Chapter 8, Jason Raley shows us that when high schools are structured for support, students will challenge themselves and one another to learn, free from concerns about being negatively evaluated. Together, these chapters illustrate how peers influence school achievement in a variety of ways through multiple mechanisms. They illustrate as well the complexities involved for working-class students of Mexican descent in receiving academic support from peers.

As noted in Chapter 1, Mexican-descent youth frequently attend schools with inadequate resources and teachers who are either professionally underprepared or have little knowledge about their students' social, cultural, and linguistic backgrounds. The schooling of U.S. Mexican youth must also be understood in light of the socioeconomic and historical forces that have privileged some groups in this country over others. Barriers related to poverty, discrimination, and segregation, along with the ongoing pressures placed on many Mexican-descent students to abandon their Mexican culture, have had and continue to have an impact on students' educational progress even across generations. Although educational attainment improves from the first (or immigrant) generation to the second, progress stalls with the third generation (Grogger & Trejo, 2002).

Something happens, or doesn't happen, with Mexican-origin youth that precludes the vast majority from gaining access to college degrees.

Our data suggest that a lack of peer support and access to peer, as well as adult, social capital are important aspects of this underachievement. As detailed in Chapter 3, working-class Mexican-origin youth generally do not talk about future educational plans among themselves or with their parents (for similar findings, see Schneider & Stevenson, 1999; Csikszentmihalyi & Schneider, 2000). This is in part because adolescent youth tend to cluster with friends of the same ethnicity and social class, particularly in high school contexts of relative segregation and socioeconomic inequality. When working-class Mexican-descent youth are surrounded by coethnic peers who are struggling academically or who exhibit antischool attitudes and behaviors, as is too often the case, they end up having little opportunity to interact with students who model a proschool, proacademic identity and who plan to go to college.

Peer influence takes many forms, especially in the earlier years of adolescence. Young people may feel pressured by peers to engage in risky behaviors, as experimentation with taboo activities is a hallmark of many adolescents' initiation into adulthood (Csikszentmihalyi & Schmidt, 1998). Older teenagers have established a stronger sense of personal and ethnic identity and are usually less vulnerable than ninth graders to the impact of peer pressure. However, as Gándara and coauthors in Chapter 3 caution, not all youth experience *peer pressure* in the same way.

Adolescents also experience normative peer influence from "other kids" who attend their same school. Depending on the norms for behavior and achievement that are fostered by the whole school community, this influence may either promote or hinder learning. Students experience this *normative influence* not through direct pressure but through more indirect means. The fact that students tend to dress and behave like their friends is not necessarily because they are "pressured" to do so but probably more accurately reflects a process whereby they simply take on the norms of those individuals with whom they identify or wish to identify. In similar fashion, we find that students who attend classes with many high achievers tend to achieve at high levels; those surrounded by low achievers frequently internalize a norm of low achievement. Furthermore, when classmates are constantly disruptive, students are likely to adopt similar behavior patterns themselves, even as they express sympathy for the teacher who is struggling to maintain classroom order. Students who are not active participants in the disruption also find their academic learning seriously compromised (see Chapter 4, this volume).

Another form of influence is *peers as gatekeepers*, directing who belongs where within a school's social and academic hierarchy. Even schoolmates who are almost strangers can exert substantial, albeit indirect, influence on the behavior of their peers. This is especially common in situations where students from one ethnic or social class group hold unequal power and status within the school, as was the case with the White students at Hillside High, described by Gibson and colleagues in Chapter 7. In this case, a very large percentage of the Mexican-descent youth felt alienated and even intimidated by their more privileged White peers, and as a result they were frequently uncomfortable sharing classes or activities with them. On the other hand, peers can be like family members, that is, persons with whom one shares deep social and emotional bonds and who serve as a key source of support and acceptance. But "peer-relations-like-family" can lead students in startlingly different directions, toward school engagement and preparation for college (see Chapter 8, this volume), or away from school and into gangs (see Chapter 5, this volume).

GENDER ISSUES

Just as achievement is not distributed equally among ethnic groups, neither is it distributed equally by gender. Among working-class Mexican-origin students, the differences are substantial. Overall, males are leaving school earlier and doing less well academically (Gándara, 2001; Mortenson, 1999). Some of the processes that lead to these differences are highlighted across the chapters of this volume.

Not only do Mexican-origin females report less pressure from peers to engage in risky behavior than do males, but they also report a greater desire to be viewed as "good students" (see Chapter 3, this volume). In addition, females are more likely to become involved in the kinds of activities that can engage them with school, such as college-access programs and extracurricular activities (see Chapter 7, this volume; Gándara, 2001). Mexican-descent females may also find it easier to cross cultural borders within school settings than do their male counterparts (see Chapter 6, this volume).

Mexican-origin males, on the other hand, not only experience greater peer pressure to engage in risky behaviors but this pressure lasts late into their teens and long after this sort of peer pressure appears to have dissipated for females (see Chapter 3, this volume). Males are also more likely to engage in academically undermining acting-out performances in class (see Chapter 4, this volume) and to become involved in behaviors that pull them away from school altogether (see Chapter 5, this volume). Similar gender differences have been observed among a range of other working-class minority groups (Fordham, 1996; Gibson, 1982, 1997; Solomon, 1992; Waters, 1996).

CREATING SPACES OF BELONGING

As Raley reminds us in his discussion of Pacifica College Prep High School in Chapter 8, "social relations are always . . . implicated in learning," for learning is a socially situated process that occurs in participation with others (Brown, Collins, & Duguid, 1989; Cole, 1996; Lave & Wenger, 1991; Rogoff, 1990). Ricardo Stanton-Salazar in Chapter 2 makes a similar point, noting that "our paradigm for understanding success and failure in school has to be a relational one." We concur. High school students' ability to make choices about engaging in their studies and participating comfortably in their surroundings is situated within and negotiated through their relationships with peers on an ongoing basis.

A strong theme that runs throughout this volume is the importance of creating a sense of belonging in school, and this includes a level of comfort and positive connection with both one's peers and one's teachers. Yet working-class youth of Mexican origin often feel unconnected to their schools and to the academic values they espouse. High school students with limited proficiency in English are especially vulnerable to feelings of marginalization. These students are often ignored or even looked down on by other students and even by teachers (see Chapter 4, this volume; Gutiérrez, 2003). Fearful of being ridiculed by English-speaking peers for their less than perfect English, they stick to themselves, forming their own peer enclaves. Schools contribute to this isolation by placing English learners together in the same classes for much of the day and sometimes for years on end with little opportunity for mixing socially with native English speakers.

Even when language is not a divide, Mexican-origin students tend to come together in same-ethnicity peer groups in part because of a sense of marginalization in school (see Chapter 3, this volume). Many Mexican-descent students, females more often than males, report a general sense of not belonging in school. Males, too, feel marginalized, but they have different ways of expressing their discomfort. As Hurd in Chapter 4 and Vigil in Chapter 5 remind us, when appropriate and welcoming spaces in school are not available to students, they will construct alternative spaces of belonging. These spaces may involve the creation of a subculture within the school (the ELD peer group) or outside the school (the gang). In these contexts, peer support comes at the expense of schooling. The boys' failure to engage academically is not so much evidence of resistance to education as it is evidence of their sense that they have no real relationship to the school or the people in it. In the absence of strong connections with teachers or with other more academically oriented peers, some youth will misbehave and then drop out—or be pushed out—of school. Their classroom antics are reflective of their marginalized social positions and experiences both at school and in other aspects of their lives.

Ninth-grade students, particularly those with special learning needs, are at greatest risk of feeling disconnected (and disrespected) and thus, too, at greatest risk of psychological or physical withdrawal from school. Classroom (mis)behavior for these students becomes a way to sidestep failure and garner respect from friends facing similar difficulties. These younger students, as Gándara and coauthors point out in Chapter 3, are also those who feel the greatest pressure to conform to perceived expectations of their friends.

Yet spaces of belonging can be created that support school objectives and affirm the identity and backgrounds of working-class Mexican-origin youth. Lewis-Charp and her coauthors in Chapter 6 describe a high school where differences are both acknowledged and celebrated and where students routinely interact across social, cultural, and linguistic borders. Raley's study in Chapter 8 provides another example of a high school site where students routinely mix across social class and ethnic lines. In this school, peer relations are the fabric with which students construct "safe spaces" in which to engage learning, and each other. In this small school—it has only 70 students—students derive a sense of belonging, as in a family, from the constant contact with one another and from the school's noncompetitive structure. "Peer-relations-like-family" should never be taken for granted. Rather, as Raley makes clear, they are an achievement, and they can provide students, including those designated "at risk," the context for helping one another across class and ethnic lines so that they can all complete a rigorous college preparatory curriculum. Of course, small schools also face their own challenges and must trade size for the ability to offer a broader range of courses and more extensive extracurricular activities.

At schools where students are separated along class and ethnic lines, and where the teachers and administration seem unable or unwilling to change the status quo, such integrated safe spaces are far more difficult to achieve. Still, it is possible to create pockets of safety and belonging. In Chapter 7, Gibson and her colleagues examined the power of an institutionally organized peer group—the Migrant Student Association—to create a space on campus where students enjoyed a strong sense of community and both academic and social support from other Mexican-descent students. Not all club members were migrant, but all had parents who were immigrants from Mexico, and all were native Spanish speakers. Essential to the club's success are its attention to drawing together students' home, school, community, and peer worlds in mutually supportive ways; its constant reinforcement of the norms and values that support school success;

and the ongoing academic and social support provided to members both by peers and by the club's advisors.

The MSA case exposes an unresolved tension in the literature regarding the extent to which schools should promote structures and organizations that allow students to retreat into ethnically homogeneous safe spaces. The findings from this study suggest strongly that the support of a group like MSA can make the difference for otherwise marginalized students between their staying in school and dropping out, and between taking basic classes and preparing for college. Quoting Michelle Fine, Gibson and coauthors conclude that in some school settings "a flight into sameness by a marginalized group may be essential for and not a distraction from integration" (Fine, Weis, & Powell, 1997, p. 275). In the absence of major changes in the ways that many high schools are structured, segregated safe spaces may also be a necessary tool for promoting the academic success of Mexican-descent youth. However, this must always be tempered with the knowledge that clustering coethnic peers who may lack access to important information and social networks runs the risk of isolating these same students. Healthy schools must work hard to achieve a balance between creating safe spaces and integrating all students into the core of the schooling enterprise.

THE ROLE OF SOCIAL CAPITAL IN ACADEMIC ACHIEVEMENT

In Chapter 2, Stanton-Salazar laid out a social-capital framework for understanding how working-class minority students, including the large majority of U.S. Mexican youth, may acquire the kinds of social capital that can facilitate their academic progress and success. Given the types of academic support that many Mexican-origin youth need and given the sense of alienation they too often feel, it is not enough that they simply attend schools with middle-class peers and teachers who themselves embrace the norms and values that can lead to academic success. As Stanton-Salazar makes clear, for working-class minority youth to achieve success in school requires more than their simply being exposed to the academic values and identities of the "others." It requires that the social relations of working-class minority students be mobilized as social resources. In addition, schools must make available to these students the kinds of institutional support that can counter their marginalization, help them "master the academic curriculum," and teach them the rules that govern who gets ahead in the system and how. Once again this leads us to the importance of relationships with peers and with key adults who can function as a mediating link or pathway to needed resources.

Too often, Mexican-descent youth do not become engaged in the types of relationships that can put them on and keep them on a path to college. This is particularly true for students who find themselves marginalized in school because of tracking, school segregation, isolation in second-language-acquisition programs, and institutional racism (Flores-González, 2002; López & Stanton-Salazar, 2001; Valdés, 2001; Valenzuela, 1999; Vigil, 1999). As the studies by Gándara and coauthors, Hurd, and Vigil (see Chapters 3, 4, & 5, this volume) all illustrate, Mexican-descent youth, males in particular, may acquire a kind of capital from their peers that helps them gain status within their own peer groups, but they may lack the types of connections needed with teachers and college-bound schoolmates to help them succeed academically.

Yet schools can be structured in ways that bring Mexican-descent youth into close and supportive relationships with academically oriented peers. Peers, including those of similar working-class status, can also function as a link to the resources needed to prepare for college (see Chapters 2, 6, 7, & 8, this volume). Scholars may wish to debate whether this should be termed "peer social capital" or simply "peer social resources." In either case, what is clear is that both working-class and middle-class peers can play an essential role in helping Mexican-descent youth succeed in school and prepare for college.

LEARNING TO CROSS BORDERS

There is mounting evidence that the ability to move seamlessly among groups who are different with respect to social class, cultural background, and academic skill is linked to greater engagement in learning and long-term social, academic, and economic success (Gándara, 1995; Gibson, 1998; Phelan, Davidson, & Yu, 1998; Schofield, 2001). Researchers believe that having a clear sense of one's own identity is probably necessary to develop the self-confidence that allows a person to move in and out of multiple social circles (Gándara, 1995; Tatum, 1997). Although the research is largely correlational, the theory is that individuals need a reasonably strong sense of self in order to be able to "border cross." And, in turn, such students are the most capable of acquiring both social and cognitive skills through their interactions with diverse peers that support learning (Phelan, Davidson, & Yu, 1998).

Of course, it is entirely possible that more successful students are simply more adept in their social as well as their academic lives. However, as Lewis-Charp and colleagues argue in Chapter 6, the school context itself can either foster or inhibit border crossing for students and, properly structured, schools can be sites where students learn to appreciate their own cultural identities while also acquiring border-crossing skills. They hypothesize, too, that border-crossing behavior, such as that exhibited by Mariella in their case study, increases the accumulation of peer social capital. By constructing opportunities for diverse students to interact in meaningful and supportive ways, and in settings where working-class students are accorded equal status by their more privileged peers, schools can foster greater peer acceptance of all students, increase a sense of belonging among traditionally marginalized students, and enhance opportunities to increase academic achievement.

THE ROLE OF SCHOOLS

Just as peer influence is shaped by the kinds of relations that students have with one another, peer relations in turn are shaped by the context in which they are formed. There is considerable evidence, for example, that the particular school a student attends has a significant effect on learning outcomes (Coleman [and others], 1966; Goodlad, 1984; Kahlenberg, 2001). Schools are key sites for social-capital accumulation and distribution. However, schools are not organized in a fashion that ensures the distribution of human and social capital will be equal. Rather, they are structured in ways that promote greater accumulation of social capital by some student groups than by others. Middle-class and upper-income peers are likely to bring more than their book bags to school. They bring social capital in the form of family social networks that provide information and access to elites in the system. They also bring parents with the political clout to ensure that the school provides the resources necessary for their children's academic success.

On the other hand, immigrant students with limited proficiency in English, and in particular those whose parents lack these same kinds of connections, are often placed in classes with native-born students who have weak commitments to school and histories of poor achievement. They thus have little opportunity to mix with academically oriented peers who know what it takes to get to college. Moreover, the "acting out" performances of alienated ELD students often control classroom activity. Frequently unrecognized is the fact that students' disruptive behaviors often mask other issues. Similar to subjects in Steele's (1997) work on stereotype threat, some of those who have spent years on end in ELD classes adopt a stance of "not caring" as a shield against appearing "intellectually inferior."

The ELD classroom described by Hurd in Chapter 4 provides an excellent example of how schools moderate the distribution of human and social capital by essentially controlling which peers a student comes in contact with throughout the day. In almost all public high schools, classes are organized in such a way that students with learning advantages are placed in upper-level, college preparatory, advanced placement, and honors courses, while students with learning disadvantages (low parental education or limited proficiency in English, as well as true learning disabilities) are placed in low-level, remedial, and non-college-preparatory courses (Oakes, 1985). The result is that the advantaged and the disadvantaged are separated, rarely coming together in mutually beneficial activities. Because it is in the day-to-day contact with socially and economically advantaged students, in and out of class, that a major source of social capital is dispensed, the disadvantaged never have equal access. Even when they do attend the same classes, they frequently feel uncomfortable, as though they do not belong, and thus their interactions with more advantaged peers are circumscribed.

Such responses are not inevitable. In fact, most students do care about getting a good education, but they have been turned off to the process of schooling itself. In school settings such as Pacifica College Prep (PCP), where students do not fear evaluation by peers, where competition is not reinforced, and where they are provided ample assistance, students will engage one another in learning, and they will work very hard to succeed academically (see Chapter 8, this volume). As a condition of gaining admission to PCP, all students must commit themselves to preparing for college, but this in itself is no guarantee of success. PCP staff and students work hard to create and sustain an achievement ethos among students who are not usually expected to be college bound.

Not all schools are as successful as PCP in meeting the needs of working-class and minority youth, nor are they as well financed. But there is much that public high schools can do. In Chapter 6 Lewis-Charp and colleagues' comparative study of two high schools offers an especially striking example of the ways that the school context (i.e., school leadership, policies, programs, and practices) shapes peer relations. In schools like Woodrow High, where the staff devise proactive ways to bring youth together across racial, class, and cultural divides, opportunities for cultural expression and academic achievement are advanced. On the other hand, in schools like North Vernon High, where positive peer relations are not made a priority by teachers and administrators, it may be almost impossible for supportive intergroup relations to flourish.

Extracurricular school activities (clubs and sports) are another important site of social-capital accumulation. Research shows that high school students who participate in extracurricular activities have higher educational aspirations, report lower levels of drug use and delinquent activity, show evidence of enhanced self-esteem and self-confidence, and identify more with school (Brown & Theobald, 1998; Marsh & Kleitman, 2002). Gibson and coauthors (Chapter 7, this volume) also found an increased sense of efficacy among the students who were involved in the migrant student club. Participation in such activities can interrupt the normal processes whereby some students are excluded from access to social capital, by placing them in ongoing contact with college-bound peers and with teachers who themselves serve as role models. However, working-class and minority students are often excluded from such opportunities not only because of school tracking practices but also because they are not part of the "in crowd" that controls informal selection into high-status school activities. Further, when they do join, they often feel unwelcome, as though they do not fit in among their more advantaged peers. Scheduling is another issue, because many working-class youth cannot participate in activities held in the after-school hours owing to work or family responsibilities. And in schools with minimal resources, there may be simply an insufficient number of "slots" for all students to get involved in even one sport or club (Quiroz, Flores-González, & Frank, 1996). For all these reasons, Latinos are least likely of all major ethnic groups to participate in extracurricular activities (Brown & Theobald, 1998).

POLICIES AND PRACTICES THAT MAKE SENSE

One may draw numerous conclusions from the studies presented in this volume about the kinds of things that should be different in order to change the schooling conditions for U.S. Mexican youth. Certainly, we would begin by embedding these youth in peer contexts that are supportive of high academic achievement. Then we would distribute both adult and peer social capital more equitably. It is far more difficult, however, to design specific policy changes that would achieve these ends. It is not possible to move all low-achieving Mexican-origin students into high-achieving schools where the reference groups of students would all be college bound. Moreover, simply placing students into high-achieving schools is no guarantee that they will have access to the resources and the social capital that exist there. Social structures that are created and sustained both inside and outside of school are too firmly entrenched to allow for easy transformations. Nonetheless, there are actions that those who set policy at the school, the district, and the state levels can take to address the inequities in educational achievement that are so painfully evident among Mexican-origin students. Much is related to the organization of schools.

- All students need to feel a sense of membership in the school community, and they also need to belong to some kind of friendship group where they feel safe, respected, and accepted. Hence teachers and other school staff need to take leadership in creating the opportunities for students to become integrated into academically supportive peer groups through structured activities organized and sponsored by the school. Such institutionally organized peer groupings need to occur in classroom settings as well as in extracurricular activities (clubs and sports) and in the broader social life of the high school (e.g., community service activities, mural painting, school improvement projects). Institutionally organized groups should also provide abundant opportunities for informal interactions to occur. The relationships that students form through these activities, both with their peers and with adults, often prove central to success in school.

2)

- Because it is in the ninth grade that students feel most vulnerable to pressures to engage in risky (and academically undermining) behavior, it is critical that schools create mechanisms for Mexican-origin students to become connected to academically supportive peers in the first few months of high school. This would mean, among other things, organizing classes so that lower achieving students are in meaningful academic and social contact with higher achieving peers—not just sitting in the same classrooms but also participating in well-structured collaborative learning activities that emphasize equal status and equal contribution. We recommend that all ninth graders have at least some classes that are small (no more than 20 students); this is especially important for students who are English learners, as well as those who need extra academic support. And this can be achieved by allowing schools significant discretion in class sizes. We also recommend cross-age mentoring, with consciously structured opportunities for older and younger students to engage in school activities together. Research shows that academic achievement among working-class Latino youth improves when these youth are encouraged through school contexts to interact with college-bound peers, including older peers and peers from different ethnic and social-class backgrounds.

3)

- Large high schools need to find ways to organize themselves into smaller communities. Schools within schools, academies within schools, or "houses" where students and teachers work and learn together for a number of years are all important interventions. However, in the absence of an understanding of how students come to feel that they do or do not belong at school and knowledge of how to create a sense of belonging among students who presently feel marginalized, their value is limited. Thus one of the most important structural reforms to which we must commit is to bring the enterprise of schooling to a human scale, in which *every student is known* as a person and where teachers and students can form relationships based on trust, respect, and caring. Teachers must also have the training needed to adjust their teaching strategies to build supportive classroom communities.

• Because a school's structure and culture *do* make a difference for peer relations and, as a consequence, for academic outcomes, schools need to consciously organize themselves in ways that not only allow students to border-cross but actively promote this. Schools need to provide students with both the opportunities and the skills to move in and out of different racial, ethnic, socioeconomic, and skill groups as a regular feature of their daily school routine. Schools also need to educate students about the ways in which racial and cultural differences separate students, at times marginalizing and alienating them. Moreover, school staff members need to help students recognize how their own actions can contribute to such marginalization.

• Many Mexican-origin youth and their families lack basic information about post-high-school opportunities because they are not part of the social networks that have access to this information. Such information needs to be embedded in every class and taught as part of the routine of schooling. Schools also need to help build networks of Mexican-origin parents who can share information with each other and connect to counselors, teachers, and administrators. This requires cultural and linguistic sensitivity and competence on the part of school staff.

• Community building must be combined with other forms of institutional support and assistance. Teachers and administrators need an understanding of the role of social capital in the development of students' aspirations and in their willingness to commit to schooling. They need to know that students who have access to and feel comfortable in accessing important information and support networks in school are more likely to be academically successful, but that students without this social capital have far less opportunity to succeed. Without peers and teachers who can convey these messages on an ongoing basis, exhortations to "study hard because you will get a better job" ring hollow. And the idea that by doing well in high school, one gets more of the same, can in fact be a disincentive to study for students for whom high school was just a series of assaults on their self-esteem, and who never felt they belonged there.

• Mexican-descent students need contact with adults in school who understand their lives outside of school, who value their home language and culture, who hold high expectations for their success in school, and who can serve as mentors, role models, and advocates.

• Many students find meaning and success in school through extracurricular pursuits. This is a chief reason that schools offer drama clubs, sports teams, debate teams, and ethnic organizations. Yet the students most in need of these sorts of connections are also those least likely to become involved in these "voluntary" school activities. For a host of reasons, including feeling unaccepted and having competing demands on their after-school time, Mexican-origin students are less likely than others to engage in extracurricular school activities. To provide these important opportunities for more students, schools need to remove the "extra" from extracurricular activities by building these activities into the regular school day, requiring them of all students, and assigning teachers to supervise them as part of their regular teaching assignments. Such connections are especially important for students when they first enter high school. Reorganized time and slightly longer school days may be required in order to incorporate critically important features of extracurricular activities into the school day.

• Ethnic and socioeconomic divisions are part of the structure of our society, and they are reflected in our schools to the detriment of many Mexican-origin youth. When divisions exist, school personnel need proactively to devise strategies to overcome them. In racially divided schools it may also be necessary to create and support social and cultural safe spaces that are ethnically segregated and that provide students with the kinds of cultural and academic support they need to be successful in school. The creation of safe spaces does not happen by chance but rather requires specialized skills. We do not routinely teach these skills to our teachers or our administrators, but we should.

• Teachers and administrators will need additional professional training in order to implement these policies. First, they need to understand more about adolescent development, and they need to know that some features of development may vary by ethnicity, social class, and school context. They also need to understand the performative nature of the acting out that occurs in their classes and that intervening with *individual* students will not interrupt the essentially social nature of these performances. Moreover, they need to know that students will act out when they feel their identity or self-esteem is being assaulted. Too often schools in this country are staffed by teachers and administrators whose cultural knowledge does not match that of their students and their families. This needs to change.

• Because of the current crisis in providing sufficient numbers of qualified teachers and administrators to staff our schools (Ingersoll, 2001; Shields et al., 1999), some policy makers wish to lower the barriers to entry in these professions. This is clearly the wrong approach (Darling-Hammond, 2001). Instead it is imperative that we increase the preparation and ongoing support that teachers and administrators receive, so that these educators will remain in the schools that serve these youth and continue to make a difference in the way they are served.

- Finally, we acknowledge that the recommendations we make are not cost free. Most of what we have called for here cannot be implemented without increased resources to schools—in the form of time for planning and coordination, time for thoughtful interaction with students, increased training of school personnel, and quite possibly compensation that reflects the increased demands placed on those who are responsible for our students' education. Policy makers will have to believe that the investment will merit the return. We hope that we have made that case in this volume.

FUTURE RESEARCH

At the same time that we offer recommendations to the field of education for strengthening the bonds of connection among Mexican-origin students, their teachers, and the peers who could help them to achieve greater academic success, we are acutely aware that research in this area falls short of offering a blueprint for how exactly to do this. Our research to date points to the importance of creating a sense of belonging among students, understanding the role of peers in shaping both academic behavior and aspirations, and developing the kinds of programs and interventions that can help to achieve these goals. Some researchers have experimented with creating fundamental social change within schools but usually in single sites or programs (see, e.g., Darling-Hammond, Ancess, & Ort, 2002; Fine et al., 1997; Henze [et al.], 2002; Mehan, Villanueva, Hubbard, & Lintz, 1996; Meier, 1995, 2002; Oakes, Quartz, Ryan, & Lipton, 2000; Olsen & Jaramillo, 2000; Weis & Fine, 2000). Creating large-scale change, on the other hand, represents a challenge of a different order. Large public schools are notoriously resistant to change (Cuban, 1990; Sarason, 1991), and it could be argued that change at the level of social relations—because they reflect broader social realities—is among the greatest challenges.

The chapters of this volume have attempted to map, and contribute to, our current understanding of the role of social processes, especially among peers, in the achievement of U.S. Mexican youth. We have learned a great deal through the work of our contributors and others. One lesson that we derive from this body of work is that there are real differences in the ways that many Mexican-origin students experience school when their experiences are compared with those of their non-Latino peers. The differences are the result of both the marginalization they experience in their schools and their resourceful attempts to create their own forms of social capital that combat this marginalization. We find the evidence compelling that these differences must be taken into consideration in any efforts to improve achievement outcomes. At the same time, we are heartened by the evidence that schools, under certain conditions, can make a difference. Yet there is still important research to be done. We need better skills for intervening in the social structures of adolescents' worlds, and we need to figure out how to prepare school personnel to do this effectively. We need to create a stronger sense of belonging in school for all students, not just for those for whom "school" comes easily. We need to learn how to design schools that counter the inequities in the broader society and that allow opportunities for students to engage meaningfully with each other across class, ethnic, and gender lines. We need to learn how to prepare students to become competent "border crossers" in school and in life. In highlighting successes, as well as ongoing challenges, we have sought to illuminate a pathway to a research agenda that will not simply document problems but add to the knowledge base of how to improve the social integration and academic achievement of Mexican-origin youth in U.S. schools.

REFERENCES

Brown, B. B., Clasen, D. R., & Eicher, S. E. (1986). Perceptions of peer pressure, peer conformity dispositions, and self-reported behavior among adolescents. *Journal of Personality and Social Psychology 22*, 521–530.

Brown, B. B., & Theobald, W. (1998). Learning contexts beyond the classroom: Extracurricular activities, community organizations, and peer groups. In K. Borman & B. Schneider (Eds.), *The adolescent years: Social influences and educational challenges* (pp. 109–141). Chicago: The University of Chicago Press.

Brown, J. S., Collins, A., & Duguid, P. (1989). Situated cognition and the culture of learning. *Educational Researcher, 18* (1), 32–42.

Cole, M. (1996). *Cultural psychology.* Cambridge, MA: The Belknap Press of Harvard University Press.

Coleman, J. S. (1961). *The adolescent society.* New York: The Free Press.

Coleman, J. S., [and others]. (1966). *Equality of educational opportunity.* Washington, DC: U.S. Government Printing Office.

Csikzentmihalyi, M., & Schmidt, J. (1998). Stress and resilience in adolescence: An evolutionary perspective. In K. Borman & B. Schneider (Eds.), *The adolescent years: Social influences and educational challenges* (pp. 1–17). Ninety-seventh yearbook of the National Society for the Study of Education. Part I. Chicago: University of Chicago Press.

Csikszentmihalyi, M., & Schneider, B. (2000). *Becoming adults: How teenagers prepare for the world of work.* New York: Basic Books.

Cuban, L. (1990). Reforming again, again, and again. *Educational Researcher, 19,* 3–13.

Darling-Hammond, L. (2001). The challenge of staffing our schools. *Educational Leadership, 58,* 12–17.

Darling-Hammond, L., Ancess, J., & Ort, S. W. (2002). Reinventing high school: Outcomes of the coalition campus schools project. *American Educational Research Journal, 39*(3), 639–673.

Erikson, E. (1968). *Identity, youth and crisis.* New York: Norton.

Fine, M., Weis, L., & Powell, L. C. (1997). Communities of difference: A critical look at desegregated spaces created for and by youth. *Harvard Educational Review, 67*(2), 247–284.

Flores-González, N. (2002). *School kids/street kids: Identity development in Latino students.* New York: Teachers College Press.

Fordham, S. (1996). *Blacked out: Dilemmas of race, identity, and success at Capital High.* Chicago: University of Chicago Press.

Gándara, P. (1995). *Over the ivy walls: The educational mobility of low income Chicanos.* Albany: State University of New York Press.

Gándara, P. (with Bial, D.). (2001). *Paving the way to postsecondary education: K–12 intervention programs for underrepresented youth.* Washington, DC: National Postsecondary Education Cooperative, National Center for Education Statistics.

Gibson, M. A. (1982). Reputation and respectability: How competing cultural systems affect students' performance in school. *Anthropology and Education Quarterly, 13*(1), 3–27.

Gibson, M. A. (1997). Complicating the immigrant/involuntary minority typology. In M. A. Gibson (Ed.), Ethnicity and school performance: Complicating the immigrant/involuntary typology [Theme issue]. *Anthropology and Education Quarterly, 28*(3), 431–454.

Gibson, M. A. (1998). Promoting academic success among minority students: Is acculturation the issue? *Educational Policy, 12*(6), 615–633.

Goodlad, J. (1984). *A place called school.* New York: McGraw-Hill.

Grogger, J., & Trejo, S. (2002). *Falling behind or moving up? The intergenerational progress of Mexican Americans.* San Francisco: The Public Policy Institute of California.

Gutiérrez, D. (2003). *The social organization of immigrant students in one rural high school.* Unpublished doctoral dissertation, University of California, Davis.

Henze, R. C., [et al.]. (2002). *Leading for diversity: How school leaders promote positive interethnic relations.* Thousand Oaks, CA: Corwin Press.

Ingersoll, R. (2001). *Teacher turnover, teacher shortages, and the organization of schools.* Seattle: University of Washington, Center for the Study of Teaching and Policy.

Kandel, D. B. (1973). Adolescent marihuana use: Role of parents and peers. *Science, 181,* 1067–1069.

Kahlenberg, R. (2001). *All together now, creating middle-class schools through public school choice.* Washington, DC: Brookings Institution Press.

Lave, J., & Wenger, E. (1991). *Situated learning: Legitimate peripheral participation.* New York: Cambridge University Press.

López, D., & Stanton-Salazar, R. D. (2001). Mexican-Americans: A second generation at risk. In R. Rumbaut & A. Portes (Eds.), *Ethnicities: Children of immigrants in America* (pp. 57–90). Berkeley: University of California Press.

Marcia, J. (1980). Ego identity development. In J. Adelson (Ed.), *The handbook of adolescent psychology* (pp. 159–187). New York: Wiley.

Marsh, H. W., & Kleitman, S. (2002). Extracurricular school activities: The good, the bad, and the nonlinear. *Harvard Educational Review, 72*(4), 464–511.

Mehan, H., Villanueva, I., Hubbard, L., & Lintz, A. (1996). *Constructing school success: The consequences of untracking low-achieving students.* New York: Cambridge University Press.

Meier, D. (1995). *The power of their ideas: Lessons for America from a small school in Harlem.* Boston: Beacon Press.

Meier, D. (2002). *In schools we trust: Creating communities of learning in an era of testing and standardization.* Boston: Beacon Press.

Mortenson, T. (1999). Where are the boys? The growing gender gap in higher education. *College Board Review, 188,* 8–17.

Oakes, J. (1985). *Keeping track.* New Haven, CT: Yale University Press.

Oakes, J., Quartz, K. H., Ryan, S., & Lipton, M. (2000). *Becoming good American schools: The struggle for civic virtue in education reform.* San Francisco: Jossey Bass.

Olsen, L., & Jaramillo, A. (2000). When time is on our side: Redesigning schools to meet the needs of immigrant students. In P. Gándara (Ed.), *The dimensions of time and the challenge of school reform* (pp. 225–250). Albany: State University of New York Press.

Pearl, R., Bryan, T., & Herzog, A. (1990). Resisting or acquiescing to peer pressure to engage in misconduct: Adolescents' expectations of probable consequences. *Journal of Youth and Adolescence, 19*(1), 43–55.

Phelan, P., Davidson, A., & Yu, H. C. (1998). *Adolescents' worlds: Negotiating family, peers, and schools.* New York: Teachers College Press.

Quiroz, P. A., Flores-González, N., & Frank, K. A. (1996). Carving a niche in the high school social structure: Formal and informal constraints on participation in the extracurriculum. *Research in Sociology of Education and Socialization, 11,* 93–120.

Rogoff, B. (1990). *Apprenticeship in thinking: Cognitive development in social context.* New York: Oxford University Press.

Sarason, S. (1991). *The predicable failure of educational reform.* San Francisco: Jossey-Bass.

Schneider, B., & Stevenson, D. (1999). *The ambitious generation: America's teenagers, motivated but directionless.* New Haven, CT: Yale University Press.

Schofield, J. W. (2001). Maximizing the benefits of student diversity: Lessons from school desegregation research. In G. Orfield (with M. Kurlaender), (Ed.), *Diversity challenged: Evidence on the impact of affirmative action* (pp. 99–110). Cambridge, MA: The Civil Rights Project at Harvard University.

Shields, P., Esch, C., Humphrey, D., Young, V., Gaston, M., & Hunt, H. (1999). *The status of the teaching profession: Research findings and policy recommendations.* Santa Cruz, CA: The Center for the Future of Teaching and Learning.

Snyder, J., Dishion, T. J., & Patterson, G. R. (1986). Determinants and consequences of associating with deviant peers during preadolescence and adolescence. *Journal of Early Adolescence, 6,* 23.

Solomon, P. (1992). *Black resistance in a high school: Forging a separatist culture*. Albany: State University of New York Press.

Steele, C. (1997). A threat in the air: How stereotypes shape intellectual identity and performance. *American Psychologist, 52,* 613–629.

Tatum, B. (1997). *Why are all the Black kids sitting together in the cafeteria?* New York: Basic Books.

Valdés, G. (2001). *Learning and not learning English: Latino students in American schools*. New York: Teachers College Press.

Valenzuela, A. (1999). *Subtractive schooling: U.S.-Mexican youth and the politics of caring*. Albany: State University of New York Press.

Vigil, J. D. (1999). Streets and schools: How educators can help Chicano marginalized gang youth. *Harvard Educational Review, 69*(3), 270–288.

Waters, M. (1996). The intersections of gender, race and ethnicity in identity development of Caribbean American teens. In B. Leadbeater & N. Way (Eds.), *Urban girls: Resisting stereotypes, creating identities* (pp. 65–81). New York: New York University.

Weis, L., & Fine, M. (Eds.). (2000). *Construction sites: Excavating race, class, and gender among urban youth*. New York: Teachers College Press.

About the Editors and
the Contributors

Patricia Gándara is professor of education at the University of California at Davis, associate director for the University of California Linguistic Minority Research Institute, and codirector for Policy Analysis in California Education (PACE), a policy research consortium. Professor Gándara's research interests include equity and access in education and the education of linguistic and ethnic minority groups. She is author of *Over the Ivy Walls, the Educational Mobility of Low Income Chicanos* (1995, SUNY Press); *Paving the Way to Postsecondary Education* (2001, U.S. Department of Education), and "A Study of High School Puente: What We Have Learned About Preparing Latino Youth for Postsecondary Education" (2002, *Journal of Educational Policy*).

Margaret A. (Greta) Gibson is professor of education and anthropology at the University of California, Santa Cruz. She received her PhD in educational anthropology from the University of Pittsburgh in 1976. Her research focuses on the school performance of immigrant and minority youth with particular attention to home–school–community relationships and to how school context and peer relations influence student participation and achievement in high school settings. Major publications include *Accommodation Without Assimilation: Sikh Immigrants in an American High School* (1988, Cornell), *Minority Status and Schooling* (coedited with John Ogbu, 1991, Garland), and *Ethnicity and School Performance: Complicating the Immigrant/Involuntary Minority Typology* (Theme issue, 1997), *Anthropology and Education Quarterly*.

Jill Peterson Koyama is a doctoral student in anthropology and education at Teachers College, Columbia University. Ms. Koyama received her MEd from the University of Washington in 1999. Her research focuses on language policy appropriation across multiple educational contexts, particularly in American high school settings in which linguistic minorities are designated as "English language learners." She has recently presented work at the annual meetings of the American Anthropological Association and the American Educational Research Association, as well as the 2003 conference, Teaching Across the Americas.

Livier F. Bejínez is director of the Summer Bridge Program at the University of California, Berkeley. She received her BA in classical studies from the University of California, San Diego, and her bilingual teaching credential and MA in education from the University of California, Santa Cruz. Her research focuses on migrant education, student–teacher relations, and issues of college access for underrepresented students. Her published work appears in the *Anthropology and Education Quarterly* and the *Journal of Latinos and Education.*

Diane Friedlaender is a social scientist at Social Policy Research Associates in Oakland, California. Dr. Friedlaender received her BA in anthropology from the University of California, San Diego, in 1991 and her doctorate in education policy from the University of California, Los Angeles, in 1998. Dr. Friedlaender's research interests include social justice and racial equity in education, school/community relations, and school reform. In addition to writing numerous papers and reports, including one published in the *Research in Middle Level Education Quarterly,* Dr. Friedlaender teaches multicultural foundations to teacher- and administrative-credential candidates.

Nicole Hidalgo obtained a BA in anthropology with highest honors from the University of California, Santa Cruz, in 2001, and she is currently a doctoral student in education there, specializing in the social context of education. She has also worked as a research associate at the University of California, San Diego, analyzing district-wide school reform efforts, and as a postgraduate researcher at the University of California, Santa Cruz, engaging in ethnographic research on Mexican-descent high school students' peer relations and academic achievement. Ms. Hidalgo's research interests include indigenous education, language, peer relations, and underrepresented students.

Dianna Gutiérrez-Becha is a doctoral candidate in education at the University of California, Davis. She is currently the evaluation coordinator for the Migrant/Optimal Learning Environment Project. Ms. Gutiérrez-Becha's research interests include the development of social capital among migrant/immigrant high school youth, culturally and linguistically responsive strategies for teachers, and migrant education. She has presented at the annual conferences of the American Educational Research Association, the California Association for Bilingual Educators, and the National Association of State Directors of Migrant Education.

Clayton A. Hurd is currently a postdoctoral fellow in the department of education at the University of California, Santa Cruz. He received his BA with honors in development studies from Trinity College (Connecticut) in 1992 and earned his doctoral degree in cultural anthropology from the University of California, Santa Cruz, in 2003. Dr. Hurd has done ethnographic research on schooling in both the United States and Latin America (including Ecuador, Guatemala, and Mexico). His scholarly interests include learning as a social phenomenon, critical race theory, schooling in historical perspective, space/place issues, linguistic anthropology, cultural citizenship, transnational theory, and social history.

Heather Lewis-Charp is a social scientist at Social Policy Research Associates in Oakland, California. Ms. Lewis-Charp received her BS from the University of California, Berkeley, and her MA in education from the University of California, Santa Cruz. Her research interests include intergroup relations, adolescent development, racial and ethnic identity development, and civic engagement. She has written numerous papers and project reports, including work published by the Poverty, Race, and Research Action Council and an upcoming article in *Phi Delta Kappan*.

Susan O'Hara is assistant professor of teacher education at California State University, Sacramento. Professor O'Hara received her BA in mathematics and mathematical physics from University College, Dublin, Ireland. She received her MA in applied mathematics from the University of Southern California in 1995 and her PhD in education from the University of California, Davis, in 2000. Her research focuses on improving science and math instruction for linguistically and culturally diverse populations and using technology as a tool to positively impact the math and literacy skills of all students. Professor O'Hara has coauthored articles for numerous journals, including the *Journal for the Education of Students Placed at Risk* and *Science and Children*.

Jason Duque Raley is assistant professor in the Gevirtz Graduate School of Education, University of California, Santa Barbara. He received his PhD from Stanford University after several years as a classroom teacher and administrator. With training in anthropology and linguistics, Professor Raley focuses on social relations as a context for teaching and learning, especially in ethnically and linguistically diverse settings. He has additional interests in teacher learning and teacher knowledge, school–community relations, and research methodology. Professor Raley is currently at work on a book that combines long-term ethnography and microinteractional analysis to understand *trust* and its relationship to *democratic practices.*

Cony Rolón obtained a BA in mathematics with a minor in education from the University of California, Santa Cruz, in 2000. She is currently a post-graduate researcher with the PEERs Research Project there. Her research interests include Mexican-descent migrant students, out-of-school youth, and interethnic peer relations.

Ricardo D. Stanton-Salazar is associate professor of education and sociology at the University of Southern California. Professor Stanton-Salazar received his PhD in sociology from Stanford University in 1990. His research interests center on the social networks and social support strategies of urban youth and, in particular, the impact of these networks and strategies on school achievement. Major publications include *Manufacturing Hope and Despair: The School and Kin Support Networks of U.S.-Mexican Youth* (2001, Teachers College Press), "A Social Capital Framework for Understanding the Socialization of Racial Minority Children and Youths" *(Harvard Educational Review),* and "Informal Mentors and Role Models in the Lives of Urban Mexican-Origin Adolescents" *(Anthropology & Education Quarterly).*

James Diego Vigil is professor of social ecology at the University of California, Irvine. He received his PhD in anthropology from the University of California, Los Angeles, and has held various teaching and administrative positions. As an urban anthropologist focusing on Mexican Americans, he has conducted research on ethnohistory, education, culture change and acculturation, and adolescent and youth issues, especially street gangs. This work has resulted in several books and articles in various journals such as *Harvard Educational Review* and *Ethos.* His new book, *A Rainbow of Gangs: Street Cultures in the Mega-City* (2002, University of Texas Press), addresses cross-cultural themes among the street gangs of Los Angeles.

Hanh Cao Yu is a senior social scientist at Social Policy Research Associates in Oakland, California. Dr. Yu received her BS in business administration from the University of Southern California in 1989 and her doctorate in administration and policy analysis from Stanford University School of Education in 1995. Her research interests include intergroup relations, multicultural education, supports for vulnerable youth populations, and the relationship between civic engagement and youth activism. She has coauthored *Adolescent Worlds: Negotiating Family, Peers, and School* (1998, Teachers College Press) and numerous articles that appear in such journals as *Phi Delta Kappan, American Educational Research Journal,* and *Anthropology and Education Quarterly.*

Index